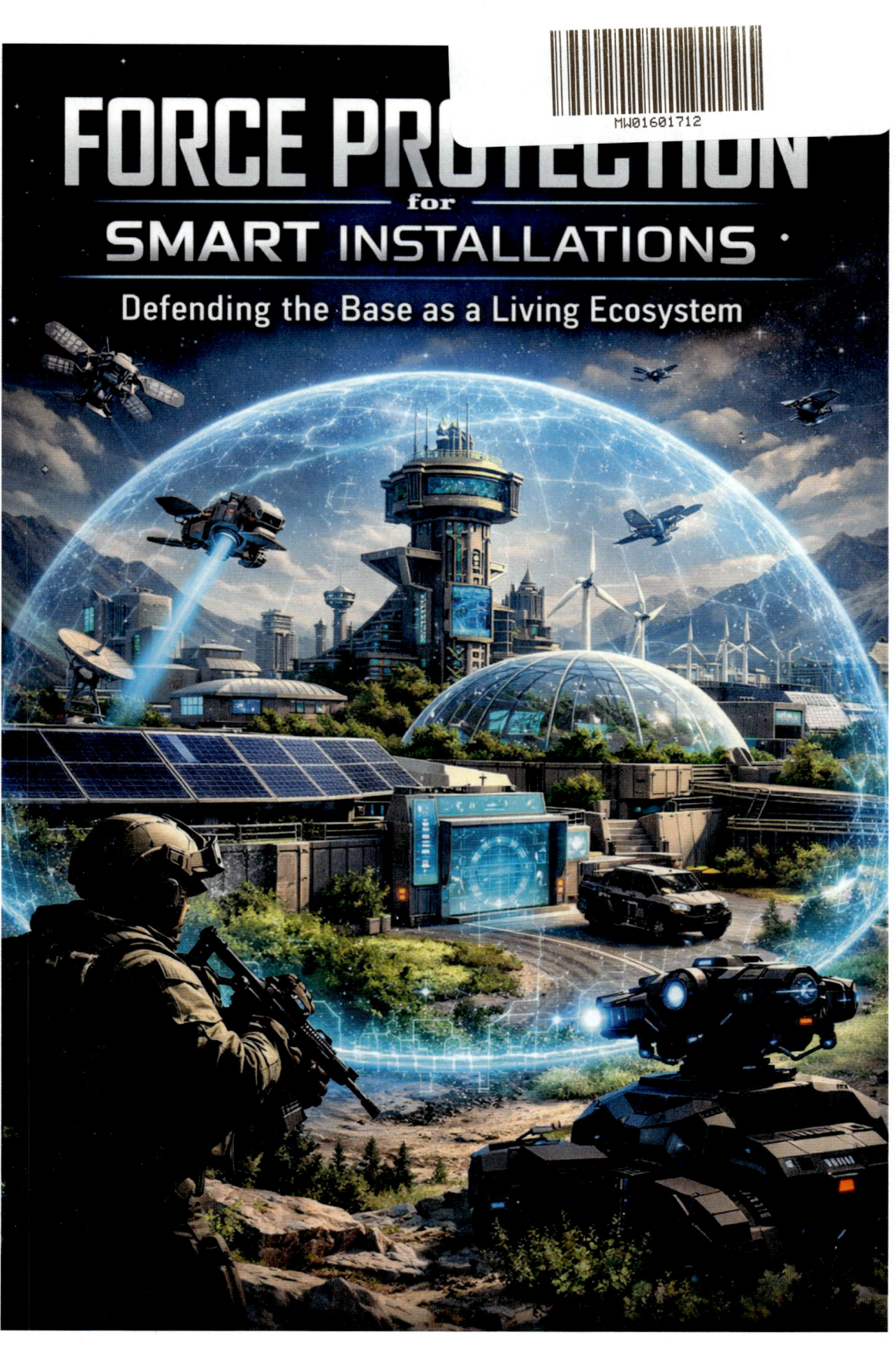

FORCE PROTECTION for
SMART INSTALLATIONS ·

Defending the Base as a Living Ecosystem

Force Protection for SMART Installations:

Defending the Base as a Living Ecosystem

By
Dr. Sean Carr

Dedication

This book is dedicated to the brave men and women of the armed forces, intelligence communities, and force protection agencies who tirelessly work to protect our nations from the ever-evolving threats of terrorism and asymmetric warfare. Their unwavering commitment, courage, and sacrifice in the face of danger are the bedrock of our national security. They operate in the shadows, often unseen and unacknowledged, yet their contributions are indispensable. This work is a testament to their dedication and a tool to enhance their capabilities in an increasingly complex and challenging world.

It is also dedicated to the victims of terrorism, whose lives have been tragically cut short or irrevocably altered by acts of violence. Their suffering serves as a constant reminder of the gravity of the threats we face and the urgent need for effective force protection strategies. Their resilience and strength in the face of adversity inspire us to strive for a safer and more peaceful world. We remember their loss and honor their memory by committing ourselves to the relentless pursuit of solutions and improvements in security protocols and intelligence gathering.

This dedication extends to the families of those who serve and those who have fallen. Their unwavering support and sacrifices often go unmentioned, yet their resilience is a cornerstone of the strength of our defense systems. The dedication and perseverance of these families provide the moral compass, reminding us of the human cost of conflict and reinforcing the necessity of effective strategies to mitigate those costs in the future. This book aims to contribute to that goal, offering practical tools and a strategic framework that can help protect those who protect us, spare innocent lives, and minimize the impact of violence on families and communities. Their silent strength and quiet dignity are what make our efforts meaningful. This is for them.

Table Of Contents

Chapter 1: The Evolving Battlefield: Redefining Installation Security

The global security landscape is undergoing a seismic transformation, an evolution so profound that it demands a fundamental re-evaluation of how we secure our most vital military installations. The predictable certainties of traditional, state-on-state warfare, characterized by clearly defined battlefields, identifiable adversaries, and conventional weaponry, are rapidly receding into history. In their place, a far more complex and insidious environment has emerged, one where the lines between conflict and peace, between state and non-state actors, and between physical and virtual domains have become increasingly blurred. This new reality, often described as hybrid or asymmetric warfare, presents a multifaceted challenge that static, perimeter-centric security models, the historical bedrock of installation protection, are ill-equipped to handle. The rapid proliferation of advanced technologies among a widening array of potential adversaries, from peer competitors to sophisticated non-state groups, necessitates an urgent paradigm shift in our approach to safeguarding U.S. military bases. Failure to adapt will render these critical assets increasingly vulnerable, potentially compromising national security and operational readiness.

For decades, military installations were conceived of as fortresses, designed to withstand conventional assaults and project power. Their security was largely predicated on physical barriers, robust patrols, and clearly markable perimeters. These models, honed over generations of warfare, relied on a predictable threat spectrum and a relatively stable technological environment. However, the twenty-first century has witnessed an unprecedented acceleration in technological advancement, democratizing access to sophisticated capabilities that were once the sole preserve of major state militaries. Consider the ubiquitous presence of unmanned aircraft systems (UAS). Once novelties, drones have evolved into sophisticated tools capable of persistent surveillance, precise reconnaissance, and even the delivery of explosive payloads. Adversaries are no longer limited to frontal assaults; they can now employ UAS to probe defenses, gather intelligence, or conduct harassment operations from beyond the immediate physical confines of a base, often at minimal cost and with deniability.

Documented incidents, such as the persistent incursions of unidentified drones over sensitive military facilities, underscore the inadequacy of traditional methods that were never designed to counter swarms of low-flying, agile aerial platforms. These events highlight a critical vulnerability: our established security protocols often lack the agility and technological sophistication to detect and neutralize these pervasive aerial threats before they can achieve their objectives. The challenge is not merely in detecting a drone, but in distinguishing between a harmless hobbyist and a weaponized intelligence-gathering platform, a task that strains traditional human-led observation and detection systems.

Beyond the aerial domain, the cyber realm has emerged as a critical new battlefield, one that directly impacts the functioning of every modern military installation. The very infrastructure that enables efficient operations, communication, and logistical support, networked systems, command and control (C2) platforms, energy grids, and even personnel management systems, is now intrinsically linked to the digital world. This interconnectedness, while offering immense operational advantages, also creates a vast attack surface for adversaries. Cyber threats are no longer theoretical; they are a daily reality. We have witnessed the disruptive power of ransomware attacks on critical infrastructure, such as the Colonial Pipeline incident, which brought a vital energy supply chain to a standstill. Applied to a military installation, a successful cyber-attack could have far more catastrophic consequences. Imagine the degradation or denial of essential command and control systems, the compromise of intelligence data, the disruption of vital utilities like power and water, or the manipulation of sensitive personnel records. Such attacks require no physical intrusion, no visible breach of perimeter fences, yet they can cripple an installation's ability to function, conduct operations, and even house its personnel safely. The sophistication of these cyber tools, coupled with the increasing skill of state and non-state actors in wielding them, means that traditional firewalls and antivirus software are no longer sufficient. A proactive, deeply integrated cyber defense strategy is not an optional add-on; it is an essential component of modern installation security.

The concept of the adversary has broadened considerably. The traditional dichotomy between state and non-state actors often fails to capture the complexity of contemporary threats. We now face a spectrum of adversaries, ranging from well-resourced nation-states employing highly sophisticated, multi-domain capabilities to decentralized terrorist networks and even criminal organizations leveraging advanced technologies for their own purposes. This diversity means that threat actors can be unpredictable, employing tactics and technologies that defy conventional categorization. They are adept at exploiting the seams between different domains of warfare, physical, cyber, space, and electromagnetic, and between different security disciplines, intelligence, law enforcement, and military operations. This leads to the emergence of what can be termed the systems-of-systems' adversary. Such an adversary does not rely on a single capability but orchestrates a symphony of diverse tools and tactics to achieve their objectives. For instance, a reconnaissance mission using drones might be coupled with cyber probes to identify network vulnerabilities, potentially followed by a social engineering campaign to gain insider access or disrupt communications. This integrated approach amplifies the impact of each individual action and poses a significantly more complex challenge for defense. Responding to a single threat vector is no longer sufficient; security must be designed to counter coordinated, multi-vector assaults that can unfold simultaneously or in rapid succession across multiple domains.

The human element, long recognized as both the strongest and weakest link in security, takes on an even more critical dimension in this evolving landscape. While technology advances at an unprecedented pace, adversaries continue to exploit the most fundamental vulnerabilities: human psychology and trust. Social engineering, the art of manipulating individuals into divulging confidential information or performing actions that compromise security, remains a highly effective tactic.

Phishing emails, tailored to exploit a sense of urgency or authority, can trick personnel into revealing login credentials. Vishing (voice phishing) or smishing (SMS phishing) can achieve similar results. Beyond these external manipulations, the potential for insider threats, whether malicious, negligent, or coerced, presents a persistent challenge. Individuals with authorized access, if compromised or motivated by disgruntlement, can inflict significant damage. The psychological operations (psyops) employed by adversaries can further destabilize environments, sow discord, and undermine morale, indirectly impacting security readiness. Consequently, maintaining installation security requires not only technological sophistication and robust physical defenses but also a profound understanding of human behavior, rigorous personnel vetting, continuous security awareness training, and the cultivation of a security-conscious culture that inoculates personnel against manipulation and strengthens the human firewall.

This complex tapestry of evolving threats, hybrid and asymmetric tactics, the proliferation of advanced technologies among diverse actors, the interconnectedness of physical and cyber domains, and the enduring vulnerability of the human element, collectively paints a picture of a battlefield that is in constant flux. The traditional, static, and perimeter-focused approach to installation security is no longer a viable strategy for ensuring the protection and operational readiness of U.S. military bases. It is an approach that is increasingly outmatched by the speed, agility, and sophistication of modern adversaries. The inherent limitations of legacy systems, designed for a bygone era of warfare, are becoming glaringly apparent. These systems often operate in silos, with limited interoperability and a reactive posture that is insufficient to counter the proactive, multi-domain strategies employed by today's threats. The sheer volume and velocity of information generated by modern sensor networks, coupled with the speed at which threats can materialize, necessitate a radical departure from traditional security paradigms. We must move beyond merely defending a perimeter to actively sensing, understanding, and responding to threats across the entire operational environment, in real-time, and in a coordinated manner.

The urgent need for this paradigm shift stems from the fundamental recognition that the nature of conflict has changed. Warfare is no longer confined to clearly delineated geographical battlefronts. It is increasingly waged across multiple domains simultaneously, land, sea, air, space, and cyberspace. Further, the distinction between combatants and non-combatants, between military and civilian infrastructure, and between peacetime and wartime has become increasingly ambiguous. Hybrid threats leverage a combination of conventional military power, irregular warfare tactics, economic coercion, disinformation campaigns, and cyber operations to achieve strategic objectives below the threshold of overt, large-scale armed conflict. This amorphous and persistent form of aggression blurs the lines of accountability and makes attribution challenging, further complicating defensive responses. For installations, this means that threats can originate from anywhere, at any time, and manifest in myriad forms. A cyber-attack might cripple an installation's logistical capabilities, a drone swarm could disrupt flight operations, or a sophisticated disinformation campaign could undermine personnel morale and public trust. Each of these threats requires a different set of countermeasures, but in the context of hybrid warfare, they are often employed in concert, creating a cascading effect that overwhelms traditional, siloed security responses.

The rapid advancement and widespread availability of technologies such as artificial intelligence (AI), advanced sensors, autonomous systems, and sophisticated cyber tools have empowered a broader range of actors to field capabilities previously exclusive to major military powers. Adversaries can now acquire or develop technologies that enable enhanced surveillance, precision targeting, electronic warfare, and cyber intrusion with relative ease and at a fraction of the cost of traditional military hardware. This technological parity or even superiority in specific niches presents a significant challenge. For instance, the commercial drone market has exploded, leading to low-cost, highly capable platforms that can be weaponized or used for intelligence gathering with minimal technical expertise. Similarly, advancements in cyber warfare tools are readily available on the dark web, offering potent capabilities to individuals or groups with malicious intent. This democratization of advanced technology means that even smaller, less sophisticated adversaries can pose a significant threat to well-defended installations, exploiting unforeseen vulnerabilities and employing novel tactics that challenge established defensive doctrines. The static, heavily fortified installations of the past, while still providing a baseline level of security, are increasingly vulnerable to these agile, technologically adept, and often asymmetric threats.

Therefore, the foundational premise for rethinking installation security must be an acknowledgment of this drastically altered global security environment. The static, perimeter-centric model, which prioritizes the physical integrity of a base's boundary, is a necessary but insufficient component of modern defense. It is akin to building ever-higher walls while ignoring the possibility of tunneling beneath them, flying over them, or simply disabling the internal systems that make the fortress habitable and functional. The contemporary battlefield is multi-domain, fluid, and increasingly contested by a diverse array of actors employing sophisticated technologies. This necessitates a shift towards an integrated, adaptive, and intelligent security framework that can provide pervasive awareness, rapid threat detection, and synchronized response across all dimensions of the installation's operational environment. The urgent need for this paradigm shift is not a matter of incremental improvement; it is a fundamental requirement for maintaining the security, readiness, and operational effectiveness of U.S. military installations in the face of twenty-first-century threats. This chapter serves to establish this imperative, laying the groundwork for a deeper exploration of how such a transformative approach can be conceptualized and implemented.

Beyond the imposing concrete barriers and the ever-present gaze of sentinels, traditional security measures, the bedrock of installation protection for generations, are increasingly revealing their inherent limitations. For decades, the primary strategy for safeguarding military installations revolved around establishing a robust physical perimeter, reinforced by diligent patrols and manned observation posts. The implicit assumption was that a formidable physical barrier, coupled with vigilant human oversight, could effectively deter or repel any threat. However, the evolving nature of conflict and the rapid proliferation of disruptive technologies have systematically undermined the efficacy of this static, perimeter-centric approach.

Adversaries, no longer bound by the constraints of conventional warfare, are adept at identifying and exploiting the chinks in this seemingly impenetrable armor. One of the most striking examples of these evolving threats is the ubiquitous and increasingly sophisticated unmanned aircraft systems (UAS), commonly known as drones. These aerial platforms, once the purview of hobbyists, have transformed into potent tools capable of circumventing traditional physical defenses with unnerving ease. A drone, by its very nature, operates in three dimensions, effectively rendering a physical fence or wall irrelevant once it ascends into the air. A determined adversary can launch a drone from miles away, well beyond the immediate vicinity of the installation's guarded perimeter, initiating reconnaissance missions or even delivering payloads without ever physically breaching the ground-level defenses. The sheer number and variety of drones available today, from small, commercially produced quadcopters that can carry miniature cameras or explosives, to larger, military-grade platforms capable of sustained flight and advanced sensor payloads, present a formidable challenge. Traditional radar systems, often designed to detect larger, faster-moving aircraft, can struggle to track or even identify smaller, slower drones, especially in cluttered environments or against ground clutter.

The human eye, even with the aid of binoculars, is a limited sensor, easily overwhelmed by the vastness of the sky or the speed at which a drone can traverse it. Incidents involving unidentified drones loitering near sensitive military sites, conducting surveillance, or even attempting to drop contraband over fences are no longer isolated anomalies but symptomatic of a systemic vulnerability. These incursions demonstrate that a focus solely on the physical boundary fails to address threats that can operate with impunity from above. The challenge is compounded by the potential for drone swarms, where multiple unmanned systems, coordinated by a single operator, can overwhelm layered defenses, saturate surveillance capabilities, and present a complex deconfliction problem for defensive counter-UAS (C-UAS) systems. Even if a physical perimeter is physically breached by ground forces, the ability of drones to provide real-time intelligence to those forces, or to deliver precision strikes, dramatically amplifies the threat posed by even a minor incursion.

The digital realm presents another critical vulnerability that legacy physical security measures are ill-equipped to address. While advanced electronic surveillance systems, such as motion sensors, thermal cameras, and intrusion detection systems, are integral to modern installation security, they too can be subverted or neutralized by cyber-enabled adversaries. A robust network of sensors, designed to alert security personnel to a physical breach, is rendered useless if the network itself is compromised. Sophisticated cyber-attacks can be employed to blind these sensors, feeding them false data, disabling them entirely, or manipulating their output to create a false sense of security. Imagine a scenario where a perimeter alarm is triggered, but the associated video feed displays an empty field due to a cyber-attack rerouting or corrupting the camera's data stream. This effectively allows an adversary to bypass the physical detection systems and proceed with their objectives undetected. The reliance on interconnected digital systems for everything from gate control to communication networks makes installations prime targets for cyber intrusion.

The very technologies intended to enhance security can, if compromised, become the weakest link. For instance, the electronic systems that manage access control at gates or internal checkpoints could be manipulated to grant unauthorized entry, or the communication channels used by security patrols could be jammed or intercepted, preventing them from responding to an incident. The speed and stealth with which cyber-attacks can be executed mean that by the time a physical breach is detected, the damage may already be done, or the adversary may have already exfiltrated critical data or caused irreparable disruption. This highlights a fundamental disconnect: traditional security primarily focuses on the physical intrusion, but increasingly, the most significant threats can materialize and execute their objectives entirely within the digital domain, leaving the physical perimeter largely irrelevant.

Perhaps the most insidious and enduring weakness within traditional security frameworks lies in its reliance on human vigilance and the susceptibility of individuals to manipulation. While guards and patrols are the visible embodiment of physical security, the human element is also a prime target for adversaries employing social engineering tactics. These methods exploit psychological principles and human tendencies, trust, curiosity, helpfulness, or fear, to trick individuals into compromising security. Phishing emails, spear-phishing campaigns, vishing (voice phishing), and pretexting are all common techniques. An adversary might pose as a trusted IT technician needing immediate access to a restricted area to "fix a critical system," or as a senior officer requiring urgent information, or even as a delivery person with a package for a specific individual, thereby circumventing access control protocols. The sheer volume of daily interactions and the constant flow of information within a busy installation can make it incredibly challenging for personnel to remain perpetually skeptical and vigilant.

Security awareness training, while crucial, cannot entirely inoculate individuals against highly personalized and sophisticated social engineering attacks. The potential for insider threats, whether malicious, negligent, or coerced, further underscores the limitations of purely external security measures. An individual with legitimate access, if compromised through blackmail, coercion, or ideological alignment, can willingly or unwillingly facilitate breaches that would be impossible through purely physical means. They can disable sensors from the inside, provide access codes, download sensitive data, or even plant malicious hardware. The traditional security model, with its emphasis on external threats, often underestimates the profound impact of internal vulnerabilities, especially when these vulnerabilities are actively exploited through psychological manipulation rather than brute force. This human dimension means that even the most fortified physical installation can be undermined from within, rendering the strength of its fences and the alertness of its patrols secondary to the susceptibility of its people.

The limitations of traditional security are further amplified by the adaptable and often asymmetric nature of modern adversaries. These actors are not bound by conventional military doctrines and are adept at exploiting the seams and blind spots inherent in rigid, predictable security systems. They understand that overwhelming a fortified perimeter with direct assault is often a losing proposition and therefore seek out less defended vectors. This can manifest in a variety of ways. For example, instead of attempting to breach a heavily guarded gate, an adversary might seek to disrupt the installation's essential utilities, such as power or water, through targeted attacks. While not a direct breach of the physical perimeter, such an action can cripple the installation's functionality, degrade its operational readiness, and create chaos that can then be exploited for further ingress. Similarly, adversaries may focus on disrupting logistics and supply chains that are critical to an installation's sustained operations. A successful attack on a transport hub or a key supplier, even if located far from the installation itself, can have a cascading effect that compromises security and operational capability.

The use of reconnaissance by unconventional means, such as bribing local civilians for information about patrol routes or security schedules, or utilizing open-source intelligence available online, can provide adversaries with the knowledge needed to bypass even well-established physical defenses. The increasing convergence of physical and cyber domains means that an attack can be multi-modal, with distinct actions occurring simultaneously or in rapid succession across different fronts. A drone might be used to distract security personnel at one location, while a cyber-attack targets communication systems in another, and a social engineering attempt is made on an unsuspecting individual at a third. Traditional security protocols, often designed to address singular threat types in isolation, struggle to cope with this synchronized, multi-domain assault. The reactive nature of many legacy systems means they are often responding to events that have already transpired, rather than proactively anticipating and mitigating potential threats across the entire spectrum of adversary capabilities. The notion of "bypassing" physical barriers extends beyond aerial and cyber intrusions to encompass the exploitation of operational blind spots. Patrols, by their very nature, follow predictable routes and cover defined areas. Adversaries can conduct extensive surveillance to identify gaps in coverage, blind spots in sensor networks, or times when patrol presence is known to be minimal. This intelligence allows them to plan ingress and egress routes that minimize the risk of detection.

The sheer scale of many military installations, particularly those in remote or expansive locations, makes comprehensive surveillance and patrol coverage an immense logistical challenge. It is simply not feasible to maintain constant, vigilant observation over every square meter of a vast perimeter. This inherent limitation creates opportunities for adversaries to employ techniques such as tunneling, scaling difficult terrain, or using covert insertion methods that are difficult to detect with standard patrols. Even the most diligent guard force can only be in one place at a time, and their ability to respond to an incident is constrained by factors such as distance, terrain, and traffic flow within the installation. The effectiveness of patrols can also be degraded by environmental factors such as weather, poor visibility, or simply the monotony of routine, which can lead to complacency. When combined with the possibility of electronic countermeasures that could temporarily blind or disrupt surveillance equipment, the physical barrier and patrol-based approach reveals itself to be more of a deterrent against unsophisticated threats than a guarantee of absolute security against a determined and technologically adept adversary.

The reliance on electronic surveillance as a secondary layer of defense, often integrated with physical barriers, also presents its own set of vulnerabilities. While cameras, motion detectors, and infrared sensors provide valuable situational awareness, they are not infallible. Adversaries can employ a range of techniques to defeat these systems. Thermal imaging cameras, for instance, can be tricked by using specialized thermal cloaking materials or by exploiting the natural thermal signatures of the environment. Motion detectors can be spoofed by emitting specific frequencies or by introducing decoys. Even sophisticated radar systems designed for perimeter detection can be subject to jamming or spoofing. The data generated by these sensors needs to be monitored, analyzed, and acted upon. This human-in-the-loop process introduces further potential points of failure. A surge in false alarms, a lapse in concentration, or a failure to interpret complex sensor data correctly can all lead to missed threats.

The sheer volume of data generated by a comprehensive sensor network can also be overwhelming, making it difficult for human operators to discern genuine threats from background noise. The connectivity of these electronic systems to broader networks creates vulnerabilities for cyber-attacks, as previously discussed. A system designed to detect physical intrusion can be subverted if its digital control systems are compromised, rendering the physical barrier and its electronic augmentation effectively useless. This complexity underscores the fact that while layered security is essential, each layer must be robust and resilient against a wide array of threats, not just the most obvious physical ones.

In essence, the persistent focus on physical fortifications and traditional patrolling represents a strategy designed for a bygone era of warfare. It assumes a threat that operates within predictable parameters and utilizes discernible physical means of attack. The contemporary threat landscape is characterized by its fluidity, its multi-domain nature, and the sophistication of its actors. Adversaries are no longer limited to frontal assaults; they can probe defenses from the air, exploit digital vulnerabilities, manipulate human psychology, and leverage the interconnectedness of global systems to achieve their objectives. The limitations of fences and patrols are not merely theoretical; they are demonstrated daily by the persistent challenges posed by drones, cyber-intrusions, and social engineering tactics. Consequently, a fundamental re-evaluation of installation security is not merely desirable; it is an imperative. The antiquated approach of solely relying on robust perimeters is insufficient to counter the pervasive and adaptable threats of the 21st century. A new paradigm is required, one that is not merely reactive and perimeter-focused, but proactive, pervasive, and intelligence-driven, capable of defending against threats that do not necessarily adhere to the physical boundaries we have so painstakingly erected.

The battlefield of the 21st century is no longer defined by distinct, isolated threats. Instead, we are witnessing the emergence of a far more formidable and intricate adversary: the "systems-of-systems" threat actor. This is not a single entity with a singular weapon, but a dynamic, interconnected nexus of capabilities that operate in concert, amplifying their individual impacts and presenting a challenge that transcends traditional, siloed defense paradigms. Imagine a scenario where an installation is not merely facing a drone attack, or a cyber intrusion, or a physical infiltration attempt, but a carefully orchestrated sequence of events where these seemingly disparate threats are interwoven and synchronized to achieve a common objective. This integrated approach is the hallmark of the modern, sophisticated adversary, one that leverages the full spectrum of available tools and techniques to probe, disrupt, and ultimately overcome defensive measures. This concept of a systems-of-systems adversary implies a level of coordination and integration that was once the exclusive domain of highly resourced state actors.

The democratization of advanced technologies has lowered the barrier to entry, allowing a wider array of malicious actors, from state-sponsored groups to sophisticated non-state organizations, to assemble and deploy complex, multi-faceted attack vectors. These actors are no longer limited to the blunt instruments of conventional warfare; they can seamlessly blend kinetic effects with digital disruption, psychological manipulation, and novel technological capabilities. For instance, a reconnaissance drone might not simply gather intelligence for a later physical assault. Instead, it could be part of a broader operation that simultaneously maps vulnerabilities in an installation's network infrastructure, identifies key personnel for social engineering attempts, and even tests the reaction times and protocols of existing defensive systems. The data gathered by the drone might then be fed into a sophisticated algorithm designed to pinpoint the optimal moment for a cyber-attack that incapacitates critical security systems, paving the way for a ground assault or the deployment of other offensive capabilities. This is not a series of independent events; it is a holistic strategy where each component is designed to complement and enhance the others.

The proliferation of unmanned aerial systems (UAS) is a prime example of how individual technologies are being integrated into a larger threat framework. While we have previously discussed the challenge posed by standalone drone incursions, the true threat emerges when UAS capabilities are fused with other domains. A swarm of drones, for instance, can be employed not just for surveillance or kinetic impact, but also as a component of a larger deception operation. Some drones might be directed to probe defenses at a high-threat entry point, drawing attention and resources, while others, perhaps smaller and more covert, exploit vulnerabilities created by this diversion to conduct intelligence gathering or deliver payloads in less guarded areas. Furthermore, drones can be used to deliver not only explosives but also electronic warfare payloads, designed to jam communications or disrupt sensor networks, creating critical windows of opportunity for follow-on attacks. The ability to launch and control these systems from remote locations, often beyond the immediate reach of traditional physical defenses, further amplifies their threat potential when integrated into a broader strategy.

Cyber warfare, too, is no longer a solitary endeavor but a critical enabler for other offensive actions. A sophisticated cyber-attack can cripple an installation's operational capacity without a single shot being fired. Imagine a scenario where an adversary gains access to an installation's command and control network. This access could be used to manipulate sensor data, creating false positives that distract security personnel, or to selectively disable critical defensive systems like active protection systems or early warning radar. The ultimate goal might not be to steal data, but to create the conditions for a physical breach by degrading the installation's ability to detect, track, and respond to an incoming threat. This is where the systems-of-systems concept truly comes into play. The cyber-attack might be timed to coincide with the launch of a drone swarm, or with the initiation of a physical infiltration attempt. The adversary has orchestrated a multi-domain assault, where the digital disruption directly supports and enhances the kinetic or physical aspects of the attack, making the overall operation far more dangerous than any single element would be in isolation.

Beyond the more tangible threats of drones and cyber intrusion, the systems-of-systems adversary also increasingly incorporates the domain of information and influence operations. Adversaries can leverage social media, disinformation campaigns, and psychological operations to sow discord, erode morale, or create confusion within an installation or its supporting community. These operations, while seemingly intangible, can have profound effects on operational readiness and security. Imagine an influence operation designed to undermine trust in security protocols or leadership, making personnel more susceptible to social engineering tactics or less likely to report suspicious activity. This psychological softening can precede or accompany more overt attacks, creating an environment where defenses are already compromised by internal doubt and distrust. When combined with the constant pressure of drone surveillance and the threat of cyber disruption, these influence operations add another layer of complexity, further blurring the lines between physical, digital, and psychological warfare.

The integration of directed energy weapons (DEW) represents another frontier in the evolution of the systems-of-systems adversary. While still emerging, the potential for DEWs, such as lasers or high-powered microwaves, to disrupt or disable electronic systems, sensors, or even personnel, offers a new vector of attack. A directed energy weapon could be used, for example, to temporarily blind surveillance cameras or to disable the communication systems of responding security forces, creating a critical window for another offensive action. This weapon system, when employed in conjunction with other capabilities, becomes another node in the adversary's integrated network of attack. The threat is not merely the existence of DEWs, but their deliberate and coordinated deployment as part of a larger, synergistic offensive strategy.

Defending against such a complex, integrated adversary requires a corresponding shift in defensive strategy. The traditional model of layered security, while still fundamentally important, must evolve to address the interconnected nature of these threats. Instead of treating each domain, physical, cyber, air, and information, as a separate entity to be defended, security must become an integrated, intelligent, and adaptive system that can recognize and respond to patterns of activity across all domains simultaneously. This necessitates the development of robust command and control architectures that can fuse data from disparate sensors, analyze complex threat patterns, and orchestrate a coordinated response that leverages all available defensive assets.

The goal is not simply to detect an incoming drone, or a network intrusion, or a physical breach, but to identify the confluence of indicators that signal a coordinated systems-of-systems attack and to mount a defense that addresses the entire threat, not just its individual components. This integrated defense must be predictive and proactive, anticipating potential synergistic attacks based on emerging threat intelligence and the adversary's observed capabilities, rather than merely reacting to events as they unfold. The rise of the systems-of-systems adversary demands an equally sophisticated, networked, and integrated defense, one that can stand against a threat that operates not just at the perimeter, but across the entire spectrum of conflict.

The modern battlefield, as we have established, is an intricate tapestry woven from diverse domains of conflict. While the kinetic and physical aspects of security often command immediate attention, a pervasive and equally devastating threat operates in the unseen realms of cyberspace and the electromagnetic spectrum. These are the domains of cyber and electronic warfare (EW), potent tools that adversaries can wield to cripple an installation's operational capacity, degrade its situational awareness, and sow chaos, all without firing a single projectile. The very interconnectedness that defines modern military installations, their reliance on digital networks for command and control, logistics, personnel management, and even the operation of physical security systems, paradoxically renders them profoundly vulnerable to these intangible assaults.

Cyber warfare, in its essence, is the exploitation of vulnerabilities within computer systems and networks to achieve strategic objectives. For a military installation, this translates into a direct assault on its operational nervous system.

Adversaries can seek to gain unauthorized access to sensitive networks through a myriad of methods, including spear-phishing campaigns targeting personnel, exploiting zero-day vulnerabilities in software, or even leveraging compromised insider credentials. Once inside, the potential for damage is immense. Data itself becomes a target; critical intelligence could be exfiltrated, operational plans stolen, or, more insidiously, data could be subtly manipulated. Imagine, for instance, a scenario where an adversary tampers with logistics databases, rerouting critical supplies or fabricating records of equipment malfunction, leading to operational delays and significant resource misallocation. This kind of data manipulation, while not immediately apparent, can have cascading effects that undermine an installation's readiness and effectiveness.

Beyond data exfiltration or manipulation, cyber intrusions can be designed to directly disrupt or disable essential base functions. The command and control (C2) systems, the very brain of an installation's operational capacity, are prime targets. A successful cyber-attack could sever communication lines, rendering different sections of the base unable to communicate with each other or with higher echelons of command. This would paralyze response efforts during a crisis, turning a localized incident into a potential catastrophe. Further, sophisticated adversaries could seek to degrade or disable the sensors and early warning systems that form the bedrock of installation security. This could involve feeding false sensor data to confuse or overwhelm security personnel, such as creating phantom targets to divert patrols, or outright disabling radar, surveillance cameras, and intrusion detection systems, thereby creating blind spots and opportunities for physical breaches. The integration of C2 systems with physical security infrastructure, such as automated gate controls, access card readers, and even the operation of defensive weapon systems, means that a cyber-attack can have direct, tangible consequences on the physical perimeter and internal security posture of an installation.

The threat is amplified by the concept of the "systems-of-systems" adversary. A cyber-attack is rarely a standalone event in the modern threat landscape. Instead, it is often meticulously synchronized with other forms of attack. A cyber intrusion designed to disable communication networks might be initiated precisely when an unmanned aerial system (UAS) swarm is detected approaching the installation, creating a window of opportunity for the drones to penetrate defenses while response forces are effectively deafened and blinded. Conversely, a successful cyber operation that incapacitates key defensive systems could pave the way for a physical infiltration, providing an adversary with the freedom to move undetected. The ability to orchestrate these multi-domain attacks underscores the criticality of understanding cyber threats not in isolation, but as integral components of a larger, synergistic assault strategy.

Electronic Warfare (EW) complements cyber warfare by targeting the electromagnetic spectrum, the invisible pathways through which much of our modern military communication, navigation, and sensing occurs. EW encompasses a range of capabilities, including electronic attack (jamming and deception), electronic protection (measures to counter jamming), and electronic support (detecting and identifying electromagnetic emissions). For military installations, the implications of EW are profound. Communication systems, from tactical radios to satellite links, are vulnerable to jamming. An adversary employing EW capabilities can effectively silence an installation, preventing the transmission of critical orders, intelligence updates, or distress calls. This jamming can be indiscriminate, affecting all users of a particular frequency band, or it can be highly targeted, focusing on specific communication nodes or even individual devices.

Beyond communications, sensor systems are also highly susceptible to EW. Radar systems, essential for air defense, surveillance, and tracking, can be spoofed or jammed, rendering them ineffective. Spoofing involves feeding false signals to the radar, causing it to misidentify targets, track phantom objects, or provide inaccurate positional data. Jamming, on the other hand, overwhelms the radar with noise, making it impossible to detect genuine targets. This degradation of radar capabilities can create a veil of invisibility for incoming threats, whether they are aircraft, missiles, or even smaller, less conventional aerial vehicles. Similarly, GPS and other satellite navigation systems, critical for everything from precise targeting to navigation of ground vehicles and aircraft, can be disrupted through jamming or spoofing. A compromised GPS signal could lead to navigation errors, mission failures, or even friendly fire incidents if guidance systems are misled.

The integration of cyber and EW capabilities presents a particularly insidious threat. An adversary might use EW to blind an installation's radar while simultaneously using a cyber-attack to disable its optical surveillance systems. This creates a synergistic effect where the loss of one sensing modality is compounded by the loss of another, leaving the installation effectively vulnerable to attack from multiple directions. The signals intelligence (SIGINT) capabilities inherent in EW are crucial for informing cyber operations. By monitoring electromagnetic emissions, adversaries can gain insights into network traffic, identify vulnerabilities, and map the installation's digital infrastructure, thereby enabling more precise and effective cyber intrusions. The constant, pervasive nature of these threats means that an installation is never truly "offline" from potential cyber and EW assault. Even during periods of relative calm, adversaries may be probing for weaknesses, collecting intelligence, or preparing for future attacks.

The widespread adoption of commercial off-the-shelf (COTS) technology within military installations, while offering cost and flexibility benefits, also introduces significant cyber vulnerabilities. These systems, often designed with open architectures and less stringent security protocols than their military-grade predecessors, can be attractive entry points for adversaries. The increasing reliance on the internet of things (IoT) for everything from environmental controls to automated machinery within an installation creates an expanded attack surface. Each connected device represents a potential gateway for intrusion. The sheer volume and diversity of these networked systems make comprehensive security monitoring and management an enormous challenge.

The consequences of a successful cyber or EW attack extend beyond immediate operational disruption. The loss of sensitive personnel data can have profound implications for individual privacy and national security, potentially exposing individuals to blackmail or targeted recruitment by adversaries. The erosion of trust in command and control systems, brought about by repeated or successful cyber intrusions, can have a debilitating effect on morale and unit cohesion. Moreover, the psychological impact of being under constant threat of unseen attack, where the enemy could be anywhere in the digital ether, can be significant, leading to heightened stress and reduced operational effectiveness.

Therefore, robust cyber defense and EW protection must be recognized not as ancillary security measures, but as fundamental pillars of installation security in the 21st century. This requires a proactive and multi-layered approach. It necessitates continuous monitoring of networks and the electromagnetic spectrum, the implementation of strong authentication and access control mechanisms, regular vulnerability assessments and patching, and comprehensive cybersecurity training for all personnel. It also demands investment in advanced threat detection systems, intrusion prevention technologies, and sophisticated EW countermeasures and resilience strategies.

The concept of "cyber hygiene" becomes paramount. Just as maintaining physical security protocols is essential, so too is adherence to strict digital security practices. This includes secure password management, vigilance against phishing attempts, secure use of mobile devices, and responsible handling of classified or sensitive information in digital formats. Training must evolve to address the nuanced and constantly changing tactics, techniques, and procedures employed by cyber and EW adversaries. Personnel need to understand not only how to operate systems securely but also how to recognize and report suspicious activity, whether it manifests as an unusual network alert or an unexplained anomaly in radio communications.

The integration of cyber and EW defense strategies is critical. These are not separate disciplines to be managed in silos. Offensive cyber operations often rely on SIGINT gathered through EW, and EW capabilities can be degraded or overwhelmed by sophisticated cyber intrusions. Therefore, defense strategies must similarly integrate. This means developing architectures that can correlate events across both domains, enabling a more holistic understanding of the threat landscape. For example, a sudden increase in radio jamming might be an isolated EW event, or it could be the precursor to a coordinated cyber-attack designed to exploit the resulting communication chaos. An integrated defense system would be able to identify such correlations and trigger appropriate responses across both cyber and EW defense teams.

The development of resilient and redundant systems is another key component of defense. Instead of relying on single points of failure, critical functions should be distributed and have backup systems that can take over in the event of an attack. This might involve having alternative communication pathways, redundant power sources, or distributed computing architectures. For EW, this means developing systems that are inherently resistant to jamming and spoofing, or that can quickly adapt to changing electromagnetic environments. This could include employing spread-spectrum technologies, adaptive antenna systems, or frequency-hopping radios.

The reliance on commercial off-the-shelf (COTS) technologies necessitates a rigorous vetting process and the implementation of robust security controls. This might involve using trusted vendors, implementing network segmentation to isolate vulnerable systems, and deploying robust endpoint detection and response (EDR) solutions. The proliferation of IoT devices requires a similar approach, with dedicated security strategies for these often overlooked components of an installation's digital infrastructure.

Ultimately, defending against the unseen assault of cyber and electronic warfare requires a paradigm shift in how we conceptualize and implement installation security. It demands a recognition that the physical perimeter is only one layer of defense, and that the digital and electromagnetic domains are equally vital battlegrounds. By fostering a culture of cybersecurity awareness, investing in advanced technologies, and integrating cyber and EW defense strategies, military installations can build the resilience necessary to withstand the complex and evolving threats of the 21st century. The ability to maintain operational integrity and situational awareness in the face of these invisible adversaries is no longer an option, but a fundamental requirement for survival and success on the modern battlefield.

The intricate web of cyber and electronic warfare defenses, as previously discussed, represents a significant evolution in installation security. Even the most sophisticated technological solutions are ultimately operated, managed, and sometimes exploited by individuals. This human element, often overlooked in favor of discussing firewalls and frequency jammers, remains one of the most critical and persistently vulnerable aspects of modern security. Adversaries understand this inherently. They recognize that while breaching a network's digital defenses can be challenging, manipulating the human mind to bypass those defenses is often a more straightforward and effective strategy. This is the domain of social engineering, insider threats, and psychological operations. tools that can be wielded to undermine the integrity of even the most hardened installation, not by attacking its systems directly, but by attacking its people.

Social engineering, in its essence, is the art of psychological manipulation to trick people into divulging confidential information or performing actions that compromise security. It preys on fundamental human traits: trust, helpfulness, curiosity, and a desire to avoid trouble. For a military installation, this can manifest in myriad ways. Phishing emails, perhaps the most common form, are designed to impersonate legitimate entities, urging recipients to click on malicious links or download infected attachments. These can range from seemingly innocuous requests for password updates to urgent alerts about security breaches, designed to elicit an immediate, panicked response that bypasses rational security protocols. Imagine a technician receiving an email that appears to be from IT support, requesting them to "verify their login credentials" by clicking a link. In the rush of a busy day, or under the stress of a simulated exercise, the instinct to comply can override caution, granting the adversary access to critical systems. The sophistication of these attacks is continually increasing, with attackers meticulously researching their targets to craft personalized messages that are far more convincing than generic spam.

Beyond email, social engineering can take place through phone calls (vishing), online social media platforms, dating applications, adult-content sites, and even in-person interactions. Adversaries increasingly use platforms such as Instagram, Only Fans, Facebook/Meta, LinkedIn, dating sites, and pornography websites to identify, target, and cultivate relationships with personnel over time. An adversary may impersonate a senior officer needing urgent information, a contractor requiring access, or a helpdesk technician troubleshooting a non-existent problem, often exploiting authority, urgency, or a desire to be helpful to bypass established security procedures.

For example, someone posing as a logistics officer could call a security checkpoint claiming to have misplaced their access credentials and requesting immediate entry for a time-sensitive delivery. Under operational pressure, personnel may feel compelled to expedite the request and circumvent verification protocols, inadvertently enabling unauthorized access. Similarly, social media interactions that appear casual or personal can be used to extract sensitive information. A service member engaging with an individual on a dating application may unknowingly reveal duty schedules, base locations, or travel timelines during routine conversation.

In more coercive cases, adversaries may employ blackmail or sextortion tactics through social media or adult-content platforms. For instance, an individual may be drawn into private conversations on Instagram or a dating application and encouraged to share explicit images or engage in video interactions. Once personal identity and professional affiliation are established, the adversary threatens to release the material to family members, command leadership, or the public unless the individual provides sensitive information, access credentials, or facilitates physical or digital entry. These tactics are particularly effective due to fear of personal, professional, and reputational damage, and they can rapidly escalate from online interaction to operational compromise. A threat many Force Protection professions are not prepared for or can advise leadership properly.

In physical environments, a seemingly harmless conversation with a new "contractor" on-site may involve subtle probing questions designed to gather intelligence on security routines, shift changes, response times, or the location of critical infrastructure. These tactics exploit natural human behaviors, trust, friendliness, curiosity, and social engagement. When combined across digital and physical domains, social engineering creates a persistent and low-cost intelligence-gathering method capable of defeating technical safeguards by targeting the human element, which remains the most vulnerable component of any security system.

The insider threat represents another profound vulnerability, one that often carries more weight due to the level of trust and access inherent to personnel within a secure facility. Insiders, whether malicious or unwitting, have the advantage of inherent familiarity with the installation's layout, procedures, and systems. A malicious insider might be motivated by ideology, financial gain, revenge, or coercion. They may already possess the necessary credentials and knowledge to bypass many technical security measures. For example, a disgruntled IT administrator could deliberately create backdoors, disable security software, or exfiltrate sensitive data over an extended period, making their actions difficult to detect. The sheer damage that a single compromised individual with privileged access can inflict is often far greater than what an external attacker could achieve through brute-force methods.

The "unwitting" insider, however, is often more prevalent and can be just as dangerous. This category includes individuals who, through negligence, lack of awareness, or simply making a mistake, create security vulnerabilities. This could involve leaving sensitive documents unattended, sharing passwords, falling victim to social engineering schemes, or improperly disposing of classified information. The sheer volume of information handled by personnel in a military installation means that the potential for accidental disclosure or compromise is ever-present. The reliance on shared access to systems, the ease with which digital information can be copied, and the sheer busyness of daily operations can all contribute to lapses in security. A common scenario might involve an individual downloading sensitive data to a personal USB drive for convenience, unaware of the potential for that drive to be lost, stolen, or infected with malware.

Psychological operations (PSYOPS) and influence operations also play a critical role in targeting the human element. While often associated with information warfare aimed at populations or enemy forces, these tactics can be subtly applied to personnel within an installation. Adversaries may seek to sow discord, erode morale, or create a sense of paranoia and distrust among personnel. This can be achieved through the dissemination of disinformation, the amplification of grievances, or the exploitation of existing tensions. A well-placed rumor, an inflammatory social media post from a seemingly credible source, or even targeted propaganda aimed at specific groups within the installation can have a corrosive effect on unit cohesion and individual focus. When personnel are constantly worried about internal divisions or external manipulation, their vigilance towards more direct security threats can diminish. The psychological stress of operating in an environment where trust is undermined can lead to errors, reduced effectiveness, and a greater susceptibility to other forms of manipulation.

The importance of personnel awareness and comprehensive training cannot be overstated in mitigating these human-centric vulnerabilities. A security-aware workforce is the first and often most effective line of defense. This goes beyond simply teaching individuals not to click on suspicious links. It involves fostering a security-minded culture where every individual understands their role in maintaining installation integrity. Training must be ongoing, dynamic, and tailored to the evolving threat landscape. This includes regular simulations of social engineering attacks, so personnel can practice identifying and reporting them. It involves educating individuals about the motivations and methods of adversaries, helping them to recognize the signs of a potential insider threat or influence operation. Understanding *why* a particular security measure is in place can significantly increase compliance and vigilance.

Vetting processes for personnel are also a critical component of managing insider threats. Thorough background checks, regular security reviews, and continuous monitoring of personnel behavior can help identify potential risks before they materialize. However, vetting is not a static process; it must be ongoing and adapt to changing circumstances. It also requires a nuanced approach that balances security needs with respect for individual privacy and avoids creating an overly oppressive environment that could itself lead to resentment and disaffection. The goal is to identify and mitigate risk, not to create a climate of suspicion that damages morale.

The psychological resilience of the force is a vital, though often intangible, aspect of security. Personnel who are well-rested, psychologically healthy, and have strong coping mechanisms are less likely to be susceptible to stress, coercion, or manipulation. This involves providing adequate support systems, promoting mental well-being, and ensuring that personnel are not overburdened. A fatigued or stressed individual is more prone to making mistakes, overlooking security protocols, and becoming a target for social engineering. Investing in the overall well-being of personnel is, therefore, an investment in installation security.

The integration of human security with technological defenses is paramount. While advanced intrusion detection systems can flag suspicious network activity, a well-trained individual is often the one who notices the subtle anomalies that technology might miss. Conversely, technology can augment human capabilities. For instance, behavioral analytics software can help identify patterns of activity that deviate from an individual's norm, potentially signaling an insider threat. Access control systems, when properly configured and monitored, can limit the damage an individual can inflict. The key is to create a symbiotic relationship where technology enhances human vigilance, and human insight provides context and critical judgment for technological alerts.

Consider the scenario of a simulated phishing exercise. If only a small percentage of personnel identify the email as malicious, it signals a significant training gap. If the exercise is followed by immediate, constructive feedback and targeted training modules, the effectiveness of the workforce in identifying future threats increases dramatically. This iterative process of training, assessment, and reinforcement is crucial. Similarly, in managing insider threats, developing clear reporting mechanisms for suspicious behavior, coupled with a promise of non-retaliation for good-faith reports, encourages personnel to come forward. This creates a distributed intelligence network where everyone is a potential sensor for security risks.

The challenge with the human element is its inherent unpredictability. Unlike a software vulnerability that can be patched, or an electronic signal that can be jammed, human behavior is complex and influenced by a multitude of factors. Adversaries will continue to probe for the weakest links, exploiting the very human traits that enable cooperation and trust. This makes the defense of the human layer an ongoing, dynamic, and fundamentally critical endeavor. It requires continuous adaptation, a deep understanding of human psychology, and an unwavering commitment to fostering a culture of security consciousness at every level of an installation's operations.

Without addressing the vulnerabilities inherent in people, the most advanced technological fortifications will ultimately prove insufficient to secure a modern military installation. The human mind, therefore, must be considered not merely as a user of security systems, but as a critical component that requires constant vigilance, training, and protection in its own right.

Chapter 2: The SMART Installation Framework: An Integrated Vision

The concept of a 'SMART Installation' transcends mere technological upgrades; it embodies a fundamental paradigm shift in how we conceptualize and implement security for critical defense infrastructure. It represents a deliberate evolution from fragmented, often reactive, security measures to a seamlessly integrated, adaptive, and inherently resilient defense ecosystem. This is not simply about deploying more sensors or enhancing network encryption, though these are vital components.

Instead, it is about fusing disparate security domains, physical, cyber, electronic warfare, and the human element, into a unified, intelligent entity capable of not only detecting and responding to threats but also anticipating and deterring them. The acronym 'SMART' itself is a distillation of this strategic intent: to create an environment that is continuously *Situationally* Aware, *Mechanically* integrated, *Adaptively* capable, *Resilient* in its operations, and *Technologically* advanced. This integrated vision is the bedrock upon which the entire SMART Installation framework is built, moving security from a state of constant reaction to one of proactive, predictive defense.

At its core, a SMART Installation is defined by its integrated nature. Traditional security models often operate in silos. Physical security teams manage perimeter patrols, access control, and CCTV surveillance. Cybersecurity professionals defend networks and digital assets. Electronic warfare units focus on spectrum dominance and counter-radar capabilities. While these functions are critical, their disconnection can create blind spots and inefficiencies. A cyber intrusion might go unnoticed by physical security, or an electronic jamming event might not be correlated with unusual physical activity. The SMART Installation breaks down these barriers. It envisages a unified operational picture where data from all security domains is collected, analyzed, and correlated in near real-time. Imagine a scenario where a perimeter breach detected by a motion sensor is immediately cross-referenced with network traffic anomalies and unusual radio frequency emissions. This correlation allows for a more rapid and accurate assessment of the threat, enabling a coordinated response that leverages the capabilities of all security disciplines.

This integration requires sophisticated data fusion architectures and common operating platforms that can ingest and interpret diverse data streams, transforming raw information into actionable intelligence. The objective is to move beyond merely monitoring individual components of security to understanding the holistic posture of the installation, recognizing that threats often manifest across multiple domains simultaneously. This unified approach ensures that no critical piece of information is lost in the transition between different security disciplines, thereby enhancing the overall effectiveness and efficiency of the defense.

The 'Situationally Aware' aspect of SMART signifies a profound increase in the installation's understanding of its operating environment, both internally and externally. This goes beyond basic surveillance. It involves the continuous collection and analysis of data from a vast array of sources, including advanced sensor networks (radar, lidar, acoustic, thermal), intelligent video analytics, cyber threat intelligence feeds, open-source intelligence (OSINT), weather data, and even social media monitoring. The goal is to build a dynamic, 360-degree view of the surrounding area, potential threats, and the installation's own vulnerabilities. This awareness allows for the proactive identification of anomalous activities, potential precursor events to an attack, or deviations from normal operational patterns. For instance, subtle changes in ambient noise levels might indicate the approach of unauthorized personnel, or a sudden surge in dark web chatter discussing the installation's specific systems could foreshadow a cyber-attack. This constant flow of data, processed by intelligent algorithms and overseen by human analysts, creates a living map of the security landscape, enabling commanders to make informed decisions before a situation escalates. It means understanding not just *what* is happening, but *why* it might be happening and *what* is likely to happen next. This predictive capability is a cornerstone of moving towards a proactive security posture.

Mechanically Integrated' refers to the underlying infrastructure and systems that enable the seamless operation of a SMART Installation. This involves not only the interoperability of diverse hardware and software components but also the robust, resilient network architecture that underpins them. It means ensuring that sensors can communicate with command and control systems, that automated response mechanisms can be triggered without human delay when necessary, and that data can flow freely and securely across all security domains. This mechanical integration also extends to the physical and digital hardening of these systems. Networks are designed with redundancy and failover capabilities to withstand cyber-attacks or physical disruption. Power systems are protected with robust backup solutions.

Access control systems are layered and audited continuously. The focus is on building a reliable, robust backbone that can support the complex demands of integrated security operations, ensuring that the system functions as a cohesive whole, rather than a collection of disparate parts. This requires a holistic approach to systems engineering, where security considerations are embedded from the initial design phase, rather than being an afterthought. The objective is to create an environment where technological components work in concert, amplifying their individual capabilities through synergistic interaction.

The 'Adaptively Capable' dimension of a SMART Installation is its ability to dynamically adjust its security posture in response to evolving threats and changing operational contexts. The threat landscape is not static; it is in constant flux. Adversaries develop new tactics, techniques, and procedures (TTPs) with alarming speed. A SMART Installation is designed to learn and adapt. This can manifest in several ways. For example, if the system detects a new type of cyber-attack vector, it can automatically update its intrusion detection signatures, reconfigure firewalls, or even deploy virtual countermeasures. If intelligence suggests an increased threat of aerial surveillance, the installation might dynamically adjust its counter-UAS (unmanned aircraft system) posture, reallocating sensor assets or activating jamming capabilities in specific zones. This adaptability also extends to human factors. Training protocols can be dynamically updated based on identified vulnerabilities or emerging social engineering tactics, ensuring that personnel remain at the forefront of defense. This continuous learning loop, driven by threat intelligence and system performance, allows the installation to maintain its security effectiveness against an unpredictable adversary, avoiding the obsolescence that can plague static defense systems.

'Resilient in its Operations' is a critical characteristic of any SMART Installation, emphasizing its ability to maintain essential security functions even in the face of significant disruption or attack. Resilience is not just about preventing failure; it is about the capacity to absorb damage, recover quickly, and continue operating. This involves building redundancy into critical systems, implementing robust backup and recovery plans, and designing defense strategies that can degrade gracefully rather than collapse entirely. For instance, if a primary communication network is compromised, the installation must have alternative, secure communication channels available. If a key sensor array is disabled, other overlapping sensors must be able to compensate. This resilience extends to the physical infrastructure, ensuring that critical facilities can withstand direct attacks or environmental hazards.

Resilience encompasses the human dimension, ensuring that personnel are trained to operate effectively under duress and that command and control structures can adapt to disruptions. The aim is to create an installation that can withstand a significant blow and continue to fulfill its mission, rather than being rendered inoperable by a single point of failure. This is particularly vital in the context of modern warfare, where adversaries increasingly target critical infrastructure with the intent of degrading an adversary's ability to project power.

The 'Technologically Advanced' aspect highlights the foundational role of cutting-edge technologies in enabling the other components of the SMART Installation. This includes AI and machine learning for predictive analytics and automated threat detection; advanced sensor fusion to create a unified operational picture; secure, high-bandwidth communication networks; sophisticated cyber defense tools; and potentially directed energy weapons or advanced electronic warfare capabilities. However, it is crucial to emphasize that technology is an enabler, not an end in itself. The true value of these advancements lies in how they are integrated and utilized to achieve the overarching goals of awareness, adaptability, and resilience. The deployment of advanced technology must be guided by a clear strategic vision and a deep understanding of operational requirements. It is about leveraging technology to augment human capabilities, automate routine tasks, and provide commanders with the most accurate and timely information possible. The goal is not simply to have the latest gadgets, but to deploy them intelligently as part of a coherent, integrated security strategy.

The transition to a SMART Installation is not merely a technical upgrade; it is a strategic imperative. It requires a holistic approach that recognizes the interconnectedness of physical, cyber, electronic, and human security domains. By embracing the principles of Situational Awareness, Mechanical Integration, Adaptive Capability, Resilience, and Technological Advancement, installations can transform from static targets into dynamic, intelligent defense ecosystems. This integrated vision moves beyond traditional, siloed security measures to create a proactive, predictive, and ultimately more robust defense against the complex and evolving threats of the modern era. The objective is to establish an environment where the installation itself becomes an active participant in its own security, constantly learning, adapting, and defending itself with a unified, intelligent force. This conceptual framework provides the essential foundation for designing and implementing advanced security architectures that can meet the challenges of the future.

The evolution of defense strategy necessitates a fundamental re-evaluation of how security domains are managed. For decades, military and intelligence installations have operated under a model of distinct, often compartmentalized, security disciplines. Physical security, focused on the tangible aspects of perimeter defense, access control, and surveillance of physical space, has traditionally been managed separately from cybersecurity, which guards the integrity and confidentiality of digital networks and information systems. Similarly, electronic warfare (EW), dealing with the control of the electromagnetic spectrum, and the crucial human element, personnel security, insider threat mitigation, and operational psychology, have often been treated as independent considerations. This siloed approach, while effective in simpler times, is increasingly insufficient in the face of modern, multifaceted threats that exploit the interfaces between these domains. A SMART Installation framework fundamentally challenges this paradigm by advocating for the deliberate and systematic fusion of these security domains. This is not merely about co-locating different security teams or sharing basic information; it is about creating a deeply integrated ecosystem where the detection of an anomaly or threat in one domain automatically informs and triggers actions or heightened vigilance in others.

Consider a scenario where an advanced persistent threat (APT) group launches a sophisticated cyber-attack targeting the installation's command and control network. In a traditional, siloed environment, the cybersecurity team might detect unusual network traffic, attempt to isolate affected systems, and engage in forensic analysis. Meanwhile, the physical security team might remain unaware of the cyber intrusion, continuing their patrols and surveillance as usual. The EW unit might be monitoring for hostile jamming or signals intelligence but might not correlate specific RF emissions with the cyber activity. The human element, potentially susceptible to social engineering as a precursor to the cyber-attack, might not be on high alert. In a SMART Installation, however, this cyber intrusion would not be an isolated event. The detection of anomalous network behavior would be instantly cross-referenced with other sensor data. For instance, if the cyber-attack coincides with unusual radio frequency activity in the vicinity of critical network infrastructure, or with the detection of an unauthorized unmanned aerial system (UAS) attempting to approach the installation, these disparate pieces of information would be fused by the system's intelligence core.

This fusion of data creates a richer, more accurate threat picture. The cyber intrusion is no longer just a network event; it becomes part of a potential multi-domain attack. The cybersecurity team would receive alerts not only about the network compromise but also about concurrent physical and electronic anomalies. This integrated awareness allows for a significantly more effective and rapid response. Instead of solely focusing on digital forensics, cybersecurity personnel can coordinate with physical security to reinforce critical network nodes, potentially apprehending individuals attempting to gain physical access to compromised systems. Simultaneously, the EW team can be directed to actively monitor and counter any electronic signals associated with the cyber-attack or the accompanying UAS activity, potentially disrupting the adversary's ability to exfiltrate data or coordinate their attack. The human element also becomes a more active participant; personnel aware of a multi-domain threat are better positioned to recognize and report suspicious behavior, acting as distributed sensors and reinforcing the installation's overall security posture.

The synergistic effects of this domain fusion are profound. By correlating events across physical, cyber, and electronic domains, the SMART Installation can achieve a level of situational awareness that is orders of magnitude greater than the sum of its individual parts. For example, a detected physical intrusion attempt, perhaps a breach of a perimeter fence or the unauthorized entry into a restricted area, can be automatically analyzed in conjunction with network traffic and communication patterns. If the physical breach occurs simultaneously with a surge in encrypted network communications originating from within the installation, or with the activation of unauthorized radio frequencies, it strongly suggests a coordinated insider threat or an externally supported infiltration. This correlation elevates the perceived threat level, prompting a more immediate and robust response, potentially involving tactical teams, cyber defense units, and EW countermeasures. The system can prioritize resources based on this fused intelligence, allocating security forces to the most critical areas and initiating pre-defined response protocols tailored to the specific nature of the multi-domain threat.

The fusion of security domains enhances the ability to detect and deter threats that might otherwise go unnoticed. Many advanced adversaries no longer rely on a single vector of attack. They understand the interconnectedness of modern defense infrastructure and seek to exploit the weakest link, often leveraging multiple domains simultaneously to overwhelm defenses. A purely physical defense might be bypassed by a sophisticated cyber-attack, while a purely cyber defense might be vulnerable to an insider threat facilitated by a physical security lapse. The SMART Installation's integrated approach acts as a deterrent by presenting a unified, formidable defense that is far more difficult to penetrate. The knowledge that any attempt to compromise one domain will be instantly flagged and correlated with activities in others compels adversaries to consider the comprehensive defensive capabilities of the installation, making it a less attractive target.

The human element, often cited as both the strongest and weakest link in security, is particularly amplified through domain fusion. By providing personnel with a more comprehensive understanding of the evolving threat landscape, beyond just their immediate area of responsibility, their awareness and proactive engagement are significantly enhanced. For instance, physical security personnel might be alerted to potential insider threats based on cyber behavior analysis, such as unusual login patterns or access to sensitive data outside their job scope, even if no physical breach has occurred. Conversely, cybersecurity analysts might be alerted to physical anomalies that could indicate compromised access points to network infrastructure, such as unusual maintenance activity or unauthorized presence near server rooms. This shared awareness fosters a more cohesive security culture, where every member of the installation understands their role in the broader security ecosystem. Training can also be tailored more effectively, focusing on realistic, multi-domain threat scenarios that personnel are likely to encounter, thereby improving their preparedness and response capabilities.

The implementation of domain fusion requires sophisticated technological enablers. Advanced data fusion algorithms, powered by artificial intelligence (AI) and machine learning (ML), are essential for processing the vast and diverse streams of data generated by sensors, networks, and human reports. These algorithms must be capable of identifying patterns, anomalies, and correlations in real-time, distinguishing between benign events and genuine threats. Secure, high-bandwidth communication networks are also critical to ensure that data can be shared instantaneously and reliably across different security agencies and systems within the installation. Common operating platforms and standardized data formats are necessary to facilitate interoperability between disparate systems, allowing for seamless integration of information from physical security cameras, cyber intrusion detection systems, EW sensors, and human intelligence. The development of these technologies and infrastructure is a significant undertaking, but it is a necessary investment to achieve the level of integrated defense that the SMART Installation framework demands.

Consider the application of fusion in countering unmanned aerial systems (UAS). A traditional response might involve dedicated counter-UAS sensors and response mechanisms. However, a SMART Installation would integrate this capability with other domains. If a UAS is detected, the system would not only alert the counter-UAS team but also analyze potential entry points into the installation that the UAS might be targeting. This analysis would draw on physical security data, such as the status of perimeter sensors and CCTV coverage in the suspected landing or approach zone.

Simultaneously, network traffic would be monitored for any communications associated with the UAS or its operators, and EW assets could be tasked with identifying the UAS's communication frequencies and potentially jamming them. Furthermore, human intelligence might be leveraged, with personnel in the vicinity of the detected UAS being prompted to report any suspicious ground-based activity or individuals observed operating the drone. This multi-layered, fused response is far more likely to neutralize the threat and gather actionable intelligence on the adversary's methods and intent compared to a single-domain approach.

The integration of electronic warfare into this fusion model is particularly potent. EW capabilities, such as signals intelligence (SIGINT), electronic support measures (ESM), and electronic jamming, can provide critical context for events in other domains. For example, if a physical security alert is triggered by unauthorized movement near a sensitive facility, ESM systems could identify any clandestine communication devices being used by the individuals involved. This intelligence can be immediately passed to cybersecurity teams, who can then monitor for related network activity, and to physical security commanders, who can use this information to refine their tactical approach. Conversely, if a cyber-attack is detected, EW assets can be directed to scan for the specific radio frequencies or communication protocols being used by the attacking entities, potentially locating their origin or disrupting their command and control. This dynamic interplay ensures that all available spectrum and signal intelligence is leveraged to provide a comprehensive understanding of the threat.

The fusion of security domains is not a static configuration; it is a continuously learning and evolving process. As the system collects data on threats and responses, AI and ML algorithms can identify new patterns and correlations, refining the integration process and improving the accuracy of threat assessments over time. This adaptive capability ensures that the SMART Installation remains effective against emerging threats and evolving adversary tactics. The feedback loop from operational deployment, what worked, what didn't, and what was learned, is integrated back into the system, driving continuous improvement. This iterative process of data collection, analysis, integration, and adaptation is at the heart of a truly SMART defense posture, moving beyond static defenses to a dynamic, intelligent, and perpetually improving security architecture. The ability to learn from past events, both successful and unsuccessful engagements, and to proactively adjust security protocols based on this learning is a defining characteristic of advanced defense.

The practical implementation of domain fusion within a SMART Installation requires a strong emphasis on interoperability standards and data sharing protocols. Without common language and frameworks for data exchange, the "fusion" remains superficial. This means that different security systems, whether they are commercial off-the-shelf (COTS) or custom-developed, must be able to communicate and integrate their data effectively. This often necessitates the development of middleware, standardized APIs, and common data models that can translate information from diverse sources into a format that can be understood and processed by the central intelligence fusion engine. The challenge is not just technological; it also involves overcoming organizational barriers and fostering a culture of collaboration between previously separate security disciplines. Training programs must be designed to emphasize cross-domain awareness and cooperation, encouraging personnel to think beyond their immediate responsibilities and to understand how their actions impact and are impacted by other security functions.

Another critical aspect of domain fusion is the concept of "defense in depth" applied across all security domains. Instead of relying on a single layer of defense within each domain, a SMART Installation employs multiple, overlapping layers that are interconnected. For instance, physical security might have layered perimeters, intelligent surveillance, and robust access control systems. Cyber security would involve network segmentation, intrusion detection and prevention systems, endpoint security, and data loss prevention. EW would have capabilities for spectrum monitoring, jamming, and deception. The fusion of these layered defenses means that a failure in one layer of one domain can be compensated for by the intact layers in other domains. If an adversary breaches the outer physical perimeter, the automated alerts trigger enhanced cyber monitoring and potentially EW countermeasures, while also reinforcing internal physical security checkpoints.

This interconnected layering creates a far more robust and resilient defense architecture, significantly increasing the difficulty for adversaries to achieve their objectives.

The effectiveness of domain fusion is also dependent on the quality and timeliness of the intelligence fed into the system. This includes not only sensor data but also human intelligence (HUMINT), signals intelligence (SIGINT), open-source intelligence (OSINT), and intelligence derived from cyber threat feeds. The fusion engine must be capable of ingesting, validating, and correlating these diverse intelligence sources to build a comprehensive and accurate picture of the threat landscape. This requires advanced analytical capabilities, including AI-powered tools for anomaly detection, predictive analysis, and pattern recognition. The system must be able to identify subtle indicators of compromise or precursor activities that might be missed by human analysts working in isolation. By integrating all available intelligence, the SMART Installation can move from a reactive posture to a proactive and even predictive one, anticipating threats before they materialize and taking pre-emptive action to neutralize them.

In essence, the fusion of security domains transforms an installation from a collection of disparate security measures into a singular, intelligent entity. It recognizes that in the modern operational environment, threats do not respect the artificial boundaries between physical, cyber, electronic, and human domains. An attack is rarely confined to a single area; it often ripples across multiple domains, exploiting interdependencies. The SMART Installation framework provides the architectural vision and operational philosophy to counter such integrated threats effectively. By breaking down traditional silos and fostering a unified approach, it enhances situational awareness, optimizes response times, amplifies defensive capabilities, and ultimately creates a more secure and resilient defense posture capable of meeting the complex challenges of contemporary security threats. This integration is not merely an enhancement; it is a fundamental requirement for survival and operational effectiveness in the evolving landscape of national security.

The efficacy of a SMART Installation hinges critically on its ability to perceive its environment with unprecedented clarity and to interpret that perception with superior intelligence. This is achieved through the strategic deployment and integration of advanced sensing technologies, coupled with the application of sophisticated analytical capabilities. These two pillars, pervasive sensing and intelligent analytics, form the technological bedrock upon which comprehensive situational awareness is built, enabling the transition from reactive defense to proactive threat mitigation.

The concept of advanced sensing within a SMART Installation moves far beyond traditional, domain-specific sensor suites. Instead, it envisions a heterogeneous, interconnected network of sensors that collectively provide a 360-degree, multi-dimensional view of the installation's operational environment. This includes, but is not limited to, a vast array of technologies designed to monitor physical space, electromagnetic spectrum, and digital networks. Consider the physical domain: this can encompass high-resolution radar systems capable of detecting movement at extended ranges, including low-flying unmanned aerial systems (UAS) and ground vehicles, even in adverse weather conditions. Coupled with this would be sophisticated acoustic sensors that can identify the type of vehicle or even potentially the direction and number of individuals by their footsteps. Optical sensors, ranging from standard CCTV to advanced infrared (IR) and thermal imaging cameras, provide visual confirmation and detailed tracking of activities, able to penetrate darkness and detect heat signatures indicative of human presence or operational equipment. Beyond these, lidar systems can generate detailed 3D maps of the environment, useful for detecting subtle changes or unauthorized intrusions into normally unoccupied spaces. Advanced biometric sensors at access points, integrated with video analytics, ensure only authorized personnel enter restricted areas. Even passive sensors, such as seismic detectors buried along perimeters, can alert to attempts at breaching the boundary through digging or tunneling.

In parallel, the electromagnetic spectrum is no longer a blind spot but a richly informative domain. Electronic warfare (EW) sensors, including Electronic Support Measures (ESM) receivers, are vital for detecting, identifying, and locating radiating emitters. This can range from the detection of unauthorized Wi-Fi hotspots and rogue radio transmissions to the identification of sophisticated military-grade communication signals. Directional finding (DF) capabilities are crucial for triangulating the source of these emissions, providing vital intelligence on the location of adversaries or their equipment. Spectrum analyzers can map the entire RF environment, identifying unusual or unexpected signal activity that might indicate jamming, spoofing, or clandestine communications.

Passive radar systems can leverage ambient signals to detect objects without revealing their own presence, offering a stealthy surveillance option. Cyber sensors, inherently different but equally crucial, are embedded within the network infrastructure. These include Intrusion Detection Systems (IDS) and Intrusion Prevention Systems (IPS) that monitor network traffic for malicious patterns, behavioral analytics tools that identify anomalous user or system activity, and endpoint detection and response (EDR) solutions that provide deep visibility into individual devices. Network flow analysis tools can map data movement, identifying exfiltration attempts or unauthorized access.

The true power of these advanced sensing capabilities is unlocked when they are not treated as isolated systems but as interconnected nodes within a larger network. The data streams from radar, acoustic sensors, thermal cameras, ESM receivers, and network monitoring tools converge into a unified platform. This integration allows for unprecedented correlation of events. For instance, if a radar system detects an object approaching the perimeter, an acoustic sensor identifies it as a drone, and an optical camera provides visual confirmation, the system can instantly classify this as a potential threat. If, simultaneously, network sensors detect an attempt to probe the installation's Wi-Fi network or unusual RF activity associated with drone control frequencies, the threat assessment is immediately elevated. This interconnectedness means that an anomaly detected in one domain automatically triggers enhanced scrutiny and data collection from other domains. A physical breach attempt might be correlated with suspicious network login attempts from a nearby device, or unusual radio transmissions detected by EW sensors. This cross-domain correlation provides a far richer and more accurate picture of the threat than any single sensor could offer.

The sheer volume of data generated by such a pervasive sensing network is immense. Raw sensor readings, network logs, video feeds, and signal intelligence reports would quickly overwhelm human analysts. This is where advanced analytics, powered by artificial intelligence (AI) and machine learning (ML), becomes indispensable. These algorithms are designed to process, sift through, and interpret this data deluge, transforming it into actionable intelligence. At its core, AI/ML excels at anomaly detection. By establishing baselines of normal activity, what constitutes typical network traffic, usual RF spectrum usage, or expected physical movement patterns, these algorithms can identify deviations that might indicate malicious intent. For example, an ML model trained on historical network traffic can flag a sudden spike in outbound data from a server that rarely communicates externally, or unusual port access attempts that deviate from established protocols. Similarly, in the physical domain, AI can analyze video feeds to detect loitering, unusual patterns of movement, or the presence of unauthorized objects in sensitive areas. In the EW domain, AI can rapidly analyze complex signal patterns to identify novel or disguised threats that might evade traditional signature-based detection.

Beyond simple anomaly detection, advanced analytics enable predictive capabilities. By analyzing historical threat data, adversary tactics, techniques, and procedures (TTPs), and current sensor inputs, AI models can forecast potential future actions. For instance, if multiple indicators suggest an impending cyber-attack, such as increased phishing attempts, probing of network defenses, and unusual network reconnaissance activity, predictive algorithms could assess the probability of an attack targeting specific systems and forecast the likely timeframe. This predictive power allows for pre-emptive defensive measures. If the system anticipates an attempt to compromise a particular server, security teams can proactively harden its defenses, increase monitoring, or even disconnect it from the network before an actual breach occurs. In the physical realm, predictive analytics could anticipate likely ingress points based on observed reconnaissance activities or identify patterns of suspicious behavior that often precede a physical intrusion.

AI and ML are crucial for threat identification and classification. Rather than just flagging an anomaly, these systems can learn to categorize it based on its characteristics. For instance, an EW sensor might detect a new radio frequency emission. Instead of just reporting "unknown signal," an AI classifier, trained on vast datasets of known signals, could identify it as a specific type of encrypted communication, a known jamming technique, or a signal consistent with a particular class of adversary equipment. This rapid and accurate classification significantly speeds up the response process by providing immediate context to the detected event. Similarly, network traffic anomalies can be classified as malware activity, brute-force attacks, or data exfiltration attempts.

The ultimate goal of these advanced sensing and analytics capabilities is to enable rapid, informed decision-making. The fusion of sensor data with AI-driven analysis creates a dynamic, real-time operational picture that is far more comprehensive and insightful than previously possible. When a multi-domain threat emerges, for example, a coordinated physical intrusion attempt coinciding with a sophisticated cyber-attack, the SMART Installation's integrated system can process all relevant data streams simultaneously. The physical breach is identified, its location pinpointed, and the number of intruders estimated. Simultaneously, network sensors detect the cyber activity, identifying affected systems and potential access vectors. EW sensors might detect communications associated with the intruders. AI algorithms correlate these disparate pieces of information, assessing the overall threat level, identifying the most probable objectives of the adversary, and suggesting optimal response strategies.

This intelligence is then presented to decision-makers through intuitive interfaces, often in the form of dashboards that highlight critical events, threat assessments, and recommended actions. This reduces the cognitive load on human operators, allowing them to focus on strategic decision-making rather than sifting through raw data. For example, a commander might be presented with a visual representation of the installation showing the location of the physical intrusion, the compromised network segments, and the estimated adversary positions, along with a recommended deployment of security forces and cyber defense units. The system can even automate certain responses, such as locking down specific network segments or activating localized electronic countermeasures, based on pre-defined rules and the assessed threat level.

The implementation of such advanced sensing and analytics requires significant investment in infrastructure, technology, and skilled personnel. High-bandwidth, secure communication networks are essential to transmit the massive amounts of data generated by sensors in near real-time. Robust data storage and processing capabilities are needed to handle the volume and complexity of the data. The development and continuous training of AI/ML models require access to large, diverse, and representative datasets. Personnel must be trained to operate and interpret the outputs of these advanced systems, understanding their capabilities and limitations. This includes not only technical specialists but also operational commanders who need to trust and effectively leverage the intelligence provided by the AI.

Examples of these technologies in action illustrate their transformative potential. Consider the use of distributed acoustic sensing (DAS) along perimeter fences. These fiber optic cables can detect vibrations caused by footsteps, vehicles, or digging, providing an early warning of physical intrusion attempts with a high degree of accuracy and spatial resolution. When combined with thermal imaging cameras and AI video analytics, the system can not only detect a person but also track their movement, identify their potential destination, and distinguish between authorized personnel and intruders. In the cyber domain, advanced User and Entity Behavior Analytics (UEBA) tools can detect insider threats by identifying deviations from normal user activity, such as accessing files outside of an employee's typical duties or attempting to log in from an unusual location, even if no explicit malicious command has been issued.

In the realm of electronic warfare, AI-powered signal intelligence platforms can sift through terabytes of intercepted signals to identify patterns, anomalies, and even potential future communication schedules of adversaries. This allows for more targeted and effective jamming or exploitation operations. The integration of drone detection radar with counter-UAS systems, further enhanced by AI that can analyze drone flight paths and correlate them with potential ground targets, allows for a rapid, multi-faceted response to aerial threats. The system can not only detect the drone but also predict its intended target, enabling the positioning of defensive assets and the initiation of electronic countermeasures before the drone reaches its objective.

The continuous learning aspect of AI/ML is also critical. As new threats emerge and adversary tactics evolve, the analytical models must adapt. This requires a feedback loop where the outcomes of defensive actions and the analysis of successful and unsuccessful threat mitigations are used to retrain and refine the AI algorithms. This ensures that the SMART Installation's sensing and analytical capabilities remain effective over time, constantly improving its ability to detect and respond to the ever-changing threat landscape. This adaptive intelligence is a hallmark of a truly "smart" defense posture, moving beyond static, rule-based systems to a dynamic, evolving, and highly resilient security framework. The success of the SMART Installation paradigm is therefore inextricably linked to its ability to see, understand, and predict, leveraging the full spectrum of advanced sensing and intelligent analytics to achieve unparalleled situational awareness and decisive operational advantage.

The preceding discussion has illuminated the foundational pillars of a SMART Installation: pervasive sensing and intelligent analytics, which together forge an unparalleled level of situational awareness. This advanced perception and understanding are not ends in themselves. Their true value is realized when they catalyze swift, decisive, and appropriate action. This is where the concept of integrated response mechanisms comes to the fore, transforming the SMART Installation from a passive observer into an active defender, capable of executing coordinated and automated actions that minimize the window of opportunity for adversaries. The objective is to establish a seamless transition from threat identification to actionable countermeasures, ensuring that the installation can react with speed, precision, and adaptability in the face of evolving threats.

At the heart of integrated response is the principle of automation, particularly in the initial stages of threat engagement. The sheer velocity and complexity of modern threats, especially in the cyber and electronic warfare domains, often outpace the capacity for direct human intervention without significant delay. Therefore, a critical function of the SMART Installation framework is the development and deployment of automated response protocols. When the integrated sensing and analytics platform identifies a specific type of threat with a high degree of confidence, pre-defined automated actions can be initiated instantaneously. For example, a sophisticated cyber intrusion attempt, characterized by specific malware signatures and network traffic patterns identified by AI algorithms, can trigger an immediate, automated response. This might involve isolating the affected network segment to prevent lateral movement, deploying virtual patching to block the exploit vector, or automatically provisioning updated security software to all endpoints. These actions, executed within milliseconds of detection, are crucial for containing threats before they can cause significant damage or compromise sensitive data.

Beyond the digital realm, automated responses extend to the physical and electronic domains. Consider the detection of an unauthorized unmanned aerial system (UAS) nearing a critical asset. Once the sensing suite, correlating radar, electro-optical/infrared (EO/IR) sensors, and acoustic data, confirms the threat and classifies it as hostile, automated countermeasures can be initiated. This could involve the directional activation of electronic jamming systems specifically tuned to disrupt the UAS's command and control (C2) link or GPS navigation. Simultaneously, the system might alert the relevant physical security units, providing them with the precise location, trajectory, and estimated altitude of the drone, along with the status of any active countermeasures. This level of automated, cross-domain coordination ensures that a single detected threat is addressed through multiple, synergistic means, significantly enhancing the probability of neutralization.

The physical security aspects of automated response are equally vital. In the event of a confirmed physical breach or an immediate, credible threat to a specific zone within the installation, the SMART Installation can initiate lockdown procedures. This might involve the automated deployment of physical barriers, such as retractable bollards or reinforced gates, to restrict movement. Access control systems can be instantaneously reprogrammed to deny entry to all but essential personnel in designated safe zones. Lighting systems can be reconfigured to guide personnel towards secure areas or to illuminate ingress/egress points for responding security forces. The synchronization of these physical actions, driven by the central intelligence platform, creates a dynamic and responsive security posture that can adapt to the unfolding threat scenario in real-time.

The emphasis on automation is not intended to diminish the role of human decision-makers. Instead, it is designed to augment their capabilities and optimize their workflow. The initial response phases are engineered for speed and efficiency through automation, freeing human operators from repetitive, time-sensitive tasks. This allows them to focus on higher-level cognitive functions, such as strategic assessment, complex problem-solving, and nuanced decision-making. When a threat is detected and automated responses are initiated, this information is presented to human commanders through intuitive, consolidated interfaces. These interfaces provide a clear overview of the situation, detailing the detected threat, the automated actions already underway, and potential next steps or escalating responses that may require human approval. For instance, if an automated cyber defense protocol successfully contains an intrusion, the system might present a summary report to the cyber commander, along with an option to approve a more thorough forensic analysis of the compromised systems. If the automated physical lockdown is initiated, the security commander receives real-time updates on the status of barriers and access points, along with the deployment status of security personnel.

The architecture of these integrated response mechanisms must be designed with robust escalation paths. While automation handles immediate threats, more complex or ambiguous situations, or those that surpass the pre-defined parameters of automated protocols, must seamlessly transition to human command and control. This requires clear communication channels, defined authority levels, and decision-support tools that present all relevant intelligence in an easily digestible format. For example, if an automated EW system detects an unfamiliar or highly sophisticated signal that it cannot classify, it can flag this as an anomaly requiring expert human analysis. The system would then route the raw signal data, along with any contextual information gathered from other sensors, to a human signals intelligence analyst for in-depth investigation. Similarly, if a physical intrusion attempt is met with automated defensive measures, but the adversary demonstrates unexpected capabilities or persistence, the situation would be escalated to a higher command echelon for strategic redirection of resources and personnel.

The effectiveness of these integrated response mechanisms is critically dependent on the quality and integrity of the data feeding the system. The adage "garbage in, garbage out" is acutely relevant. The sophisticated analytics and automated responses rely on accurate, reliable, and timely information from the sensing layer. Any degradation in sensor performance, communication link interruptions, or errors in data processing can lead to misclassification of threats and inappropriate or ineffective automated responses. Therefore, continuous monitoring of the sensing and communication infrastructure, along with robust error-checking and validation protocols for data streams, is paramount. The SMART Installation framework must incorporate self-diagnostic capabilities to ensure the health and accuracy of its entire operational ecosystem, from the most basic sensor to the most complex AI algorithm.

The development and refinement of these automated response protocols are an ongoing process. Adversaries continuously evolve their tactics, techniques, and procedures (TTPs), and a static set of automated responses will inevitably become obsolete. Therefore, the SMART Installation must incorporate a feedback loop, where the outcomes of both automated and human-led responses are analyzed. This analysis informs the continuous training and updating of AI models and the refinement of automated protocols. For instance, if an automated counter-drone response proves ineffective against a new type of drone jamming technology, this failure provides valuable data for developing new algorithms or adjusting jamming parameters. Likewise, if a particular sequence of automated cyber defenses successfully mitigates a novel attack vector, this success can be incorporated into the training data for future threat detection and response. This adaptive learning capability is essential for maintaining the relevance and efficacy of the integrated response mechanisms over time.

The implementation of such integrated response mechanisms necessitates a significant paradigm shift in how security operations are conceptualized and executed. It moves away from siloed, reactive approaches towards a holistic, proactive, and integrated model. This requires not only technological integration but also organizational integration. Security teams, cyber defense units, electronic warfare specialists, and physical security personnel must operate within a unified framework, sharing data, coordinating actions, and understanding their roles within the broader automated and human-led response ecosystem. Training programs must evolve to prepare personnel for this collaborative environment, emphasizing cross-domain awareness and the effective utilization of the intelligence and automation provided by the SMART Installation.

Examples of these integrated response mechanisms in action can be observed in sophisticated military and critical infrastructure protection scenarios. Imagine a scenario where a coordinated hybrid attack is launched against an installation. A physical intrusion attempt is initiated at the perimeter, simultaneously accompanied by a sophisticated cyber-attack targeting the command and control network. The SMART Installation's sensing layer detects the physical breach through perimeter sensors and identifies the cyber probes through network intrusion detection systems. The integrated analytics platform correlates these events, assessing the coordinated nature of the threat and its potential objectives. Automated response protocols are immediately activated. Physical lockdown procedures are initiated in the vicinity of the breach, and barriers are deployed. In the cyber domain, network segmentation isolates the affected systems, and automated security patches are pushed to critical servers.

Simultaneously, electronic warfare sensors might detect unusual RF activity associated with the physical intrusion, potentially indicating communication or remote operation of devices. This automated initial response buys precious time, containing the immediate effects of the attack, while simultaneously providing human commanders with a comprehensive, correlated picture of the evolving threat. They can then make informed decisions on deploying specialized response teams, allocating additional cyber defense resources, or initiating electronic countermeasures based on the aggregated intelligence. Another example could involve the defense against a high-value target assault. If intelligence suggests an impending attack by a well-equipped adversary group, the SMART Installation can pre-emptively adjust its defense posture. Predictive analytics might identify likely ingress routes based on past patterns or observed reconnaissance activities.

Automated systems can then be configured to enhance surveillance and sensor sensitivity in these predicted areas. For instance, thermal cameras might be tasked with increased coverage, and acoustic sensors fine-tuned to detect specific enemy movement patterns. In the cyber domain, increased network monitoring might be initiated for systems deemed most likely to be targeted. If an attack commences, the pre-configured automated responses are ready to be triggered instantly, from locking down critical network segments to engaging directed energy systems against incoming aerial threats. This proactive stance, enabled by integrated response mechanisms, shifts the defense from a reactive posture to one of calculated anticipation and immediate, precise execution.

The integration of AI-driven decision support tools further enhances the effectiveness of human command and control within the response framework. Instead of merely presenting raw data or a list of automated actions, these tools can offer prioritized recommendations based on the assessed threat, available resources, and desired outcomes. For instance, following the detection of a complex multi-domain threat, an AI assistant could analyze the situation and propose several optimal response strategies, outlining the predicted effectiveness, resource requirements, and potential risks of each. This decision support capability allows human commanders to rapidly evaluate options and make informed strategic choices, even under intense pressure. The ability to simulate the potential impact of different response actions before they are executed provides an additional layer of assurance and optimizes the allocation of limited resources.

The capacity of a SMART Installation to execute integrated and automated response mechanisms is as critical as its ability to perceive and understand its environment. By seamlessly translating threat identification into swift, appropriate, and often automated actions, these mechanisms ensure that the installation can effectively counter the dynamic and rapidly evolving threat landscape. The judicious application of automation, coupled with robust human oversight and clear escalation paths, creates a resilient defense posture that minimizes the adversary's window of opportunity. This intelligent, adaptive, and integrated approach to response is a defining characteristic of the SMART Installation, transforming it from a static target into a dynamic and formidable defender.

The inherent strength of the SMART Installation framework lies not just in its immediate capabilities but in its fundamental design for perpetual evolution. A security architecture built solely on current threat intelligence and existing technologies is a fragile edifice, destined to crumble under the relentless march of adversarial innovation and the accelerating pace of technological advancement. Therefore, scalability and adaptability are not ancillary features; they are core tenets woven into the very fabric of the SMART Installation, ensuring its enduring relevance and efficacy against the spectrum of future threats. This necessitates a deliberate architectural approach that anticipates change, embraces modularity, and fosters a dynamic learning environment.

At the heart of this forward-looking design is a commitment to modularity. The SMART Installation is envisioned as an ecosystem of interconnected, yet independently upgradeable, subsystems. This contrasts sharply with monolithic, bespoke security systems that become obsolete as single components age or as new paradigms emerge. For instance, the pervasive sensing layer, while currently incorporating advanced radar, lidar, EO/IR, acoustic, and cyber sensors, is designed to seamlessly integrate next-generation sensing modalities as they mature. Consider the burgeoning field of quantum sensing, which promises unprecedented precision and stealth detection capabilities. A modular framework allows for the straightforward incorporation of quantum-enhanced sensors without requiring a wholesale redesign of the entire installation's security infrastructure. Similarly, advancements in materials science could lead to new forms of passive, energy-harvesting sensors that require minimal maintenance and offer novel detection methods. These can be plugged into the existing network, extending the installation's observational reach.

This modularity extends critically to the intelligent analytics and response mechanisms. As artificial intelligence and machine learning algorithms advance, becoming more sophisticated in pattern recognition, anomaly detection, and predictive modeling, these new iterations can be deployed to augment or replace existing analytical modules. The framework is designed to accommodate these upgrades through standardized interfaces and data protocols, ensuring interoperability. Imagine the development of AI models capable of detecting novel forms of directed energy weapons or identifying sophisticated, multi-vector cyber-attacks that blend elements of known techniques in entirely new ways. The modular architecture ensures that these advanced analytical capabilities can be integrated and deployed efficiently, allowing the installation to stay ahead of emerging threats.

Crucially, the SMART Installation's adaptability is powered by its ability to learn and evolve its response protocols. Adversaries are not static; they probe, adapt, and develop novel tactics, techniques, and procedures (TTPs) specifically to circumvent existing defenses. A fixed set of automated responses, however sophisticated today, will eventually become predictable and exploitable. Therefore, the framework incorporates a robust feedback loop, where the efficacy of all response actions, both automated and human-directed, is continuously assessed. This learning process is not merely about identifying failures but also about recognizing and amplifying successes.

If an automated counter-drone protocol encounters a new jamming technique that renders it partially ineffective, this event is not simply logged as a failure. Instead, the raw data from the sensors detecting the jamming, the performance metrics of the counter-drone system, and the subsequent human intervention are fed back into the machine learning models. These models then work to develop new algorithms for jamming detection and, subsequently, new countermeasures. This iterative refinement might involve developing adaptive jamming frequencies, employing broader spectrum denial, or even leveraging advanced electronic warfare techniques to disable the adversarial jamming platform itself. The objective is to create a system that can rapidly adapt its defensive playbook based on real-world engagements.

Similarly, in the cyber domain, the continuous analysis of both successful and unsuccessful threat mitigation efforts informs the evolution of defense strategies. If a novel ransomware variant bypasses initial perimeter defenses, the system analyzes precisely how it propagated, what vulnerabilities it exploited, and how it was eventually contained. This information is used to retrain intrusion detection systems, update vulnerability assessment tools, and refine automated patching and isolation routines. The goal is to transform every adversarial encounter into a learning opportunity, hardening the installation's digital defenses against future incursions.

This capacity for adaptation extends to the physical security domain as well. As new physical breaching techniques emerge, or as adversaries develop more sophisticated means of evading surveillance, the SMART Installation can dynamically reconfigure its physical defenses and sensor deployments. For instance, if surveillance analytics reveal an increasing reliance on advanced camouflage or thermal cloaking by potential intruders, the framework can prioritize the deployment and integration of more sensitive thermal imaging, hyperspectral imaging, or even ground-penetrating radar systems along likely ingress routes. Automated physical barriers can also be dynamically reconfigured; if initial attempts to breach a specific gate are observed using specialized cutting tools, the system could automatically reinforce that gate with more resilient materials or increase the frequency of patrols by automated sentry systems in that vicinity.

The scalability of the SMART Installation framework is equally crucial. Threats can emerge at varying scales, from localized intrusions to large-scale, coordinated assaults. The architecture must be capable of scaling its sensing, analytics, and response capabilities proportionally to the perceived threat level. This means that individual modules must be capable of operating at different capacities, and the network infrastructure must support the surge in data traffic and processing demands during high-intensity events. For instance, during a period of heightened geopolitical tension, the installation might scale up its cyber monitoring to analyze significantly more network traffic for potential state-sponsored threats. Simultaneously, the physical sensing grid might increase its sampling rate and sensor fusion algorithms could be tasked with detecting a wider range of anomalous physical activities, from unusual vehicle movements to unauthorized drone activity.

Scalability implies the ability to expand the scope of the SMART Installation's security perimeter or to replicate its capabilities across multiple sites. A modular design facilitates this expansion. New sensors, analytics modules, and response subsystems can be added to extend the protected area or to establish a mirrored security posture at a different location, ensuring consistent levels of protection. This distributed scalability is vital for organizations with multiple critical facilities or for national defense strategies that require the deployment of similar advanced security frameworks across various operational theaters. The ability to seamlessly onboard new components and integrate them into the existing operational picture ensures that expansion does not compromise the integrity or performance of the overall system.

The framework's adaptability also encompasses its ability to integrate and leverage emerging technologies that might not yet be fully defined but show significant promise for enhancing security. This proactive stance requires an ongoing investment in research and development, as well as a culture that encourages experimentation and the adoption of novel solutions. For instance, the potential of advanced robotics for physical security, beyond simple sentry roles, is immense. The SMART Installation framework could be designed to integrate autonomous robotic units capable of conducting complex reconnaissance, de-escalation, or even direct intervention in hostile situations, all coordinated through the central intelligence platform. The ability to incorporate such platforms, even in their early stages of development, allows the installation to capitalize on technological breakthroughs as they occur.

The SMART Installation's adaptability is underpinned by its flexible and open architecture, which facilitates interoperability with external systems and the broader security ecosystem. This is particularly important in collaborative defense environments where installations must seamlessly share intelligence and coordinate responses with allied forces, civilian law enforcement, or other governmental agencies. By adhering to open standards and employing well-defined APIs (Application Programming Interfaces), the SMART Installation can effectively communicate and integrate with diverse external systems, enhancing its overall situational awareness and response capabilities beyond its immediate physical or digital boundaries. This interoperability allows for the aggregation of intelligence from a multitude of sources, enriching the analytical capabilities and enabling more comprehensive threat assessments.

The ongoing evolution of the framework is also driven by human expertise. While automation and AI are critical enablers, human intelligence remains indispensable. The system is designed to continuously ingest and analyze feedback from security personnel, analysts, and decision-makers. This qualitative input, combined with quantitative performance data, refines the algorithms, adjusts response priorities, and guides the development of new protocols. It fosters a symbiotic relationship between human operators and the intelligent system, where each complements the other's strengths. For example, experienced security officers might identify subtle behavioral anomalies or contextual clues that an AI, trained on historical data, might miss. This human insight can then be used to train the AI to recognize similar patterns in the future, thereby enhancing the system's predictive and analytical power.

In essence, the SMART Installation framework is conceived not as a static fortress, but as a living, breathing organism capable of growth, learning, and transformation. Its modular architecture ensures that technological obsolescence is continuously staved off through the seamless integration of new hardware and software. Its adaptive intelligence and response mechanisms provide a dynamic defense that can outmaneuver evolving adversarial TTPs. Its scalability ensures that it can meet the demands of threats both large and small, across various domains. This persistent state of evolution is not merely a desirable characteristic; it is an absolute prerequisite for maintaining security and operational superiority in a world where the only constant is change, and where the technological battlefield is in perpetual flux. The future threats, whether they manifest as hyper-advanced cyber warfare, sophisticated autonomous weapon systems, novel forms of electronic or directed energy attacks, or hybrid assaults that blend multiple domains, will be met not by a brittle, rigid defense, but by a resilient, intelligent, and ever-evolving SMART Installation.

Chapter 3: The S8S PRISM Methodology:

A Strategic Framework

The imperative for a comprehensive, integrated security posture has never been more pronounced. In an era characterized by rapidly evolving threats, the interconnectedness of critical infrastructure, and the pervasive influence of technology, a piecemeal or purely reactive approach to defense is no longer tenable. Installations, whether they be military bases, industrial complexes, or vital research facilities, are no longer isolated entities but complex systems-of-systems, each element intricately linked to the others. An adversary targeting one facet of an installation, be it its physical perimeter, its digital network, its operational technology, or its human element, can trigger cascading failures that compromise the entire system. Recognizing this profound interdependence, the Shield 8 Solutions (S8S) PRISM (Systems-of-Systems Protection, Resilience, Intelligence, and Mitigation) methodology has been developed as a strategic framework to address these multifaceted challenges. PRISM provides a structured, holistic paradigm for understanding, assessing, and actively mitigating the complex web of threats that modern installations face. It shifts the focus from isolated security measures to a unified, adaptive, and resilient defense strategy, designed to ensure the continued operational integrity and safety of the installation in the face of persistent and emerging dangers.

At its core, PRISM is predicated on a fundamental shift in perspective: viewing the installation not as a collection of discrete security components, but as a singular, interconnected "system-of-systems." This paradigm shift is crucial because vulnerabilities in one domain, for instance, a cyber intrusion, can directly impact the operational capacity of another, such as physical access control systems or even critical life support. Conversely, a physical breach could serve as an entry point for sophisticated cyber-espionage. PRISM acknowledges and leverages this interconnectedness, recognizing that true security and resilience arise from the synergistic interplay of all defense layers. The methodology is built upon several foundational principles, each contributing to its efficacy in fostering a robust and adaptive security ecosystem.

The first foundational principle of PRISM is *Holistic Integration*. This principle demands that all security elements, physical, cyber, personnel, operational technology (OT), and even the surrounding environment, be considered as integral parts of a single, unified defense system. No longer can physical security operate in a silo, with separate budgets, strategies, and personnel from cybersecurity or human resources. PRISM mandates the breaking down of these traditional departmental barriers. It requires the establishment of common operating pictures, shared intelligence platforms, and coordinated response protocols that span across all these domains. For example, a physical intrusion detection alarm, instead of merely triggering a local security response, should automatically initiate a parallel cyber alert, flagging unusual network activity from the suspected ingress point and potentially initiating lockdown procedures for adjacent sensitive data systems. This integration ensures that a threat detected in one domain immediately informs and influences the defensive posture in all other connected domains, creating a layered and mutually reinforcing defense.

The first core principle is *Proactive Resilience*. PRISM moves beyond a reactive "detect-and-respond" model. While reaction to immediate threats is a necessary component, the primary focus is on building inherent resilience into the system-of-systems. Resilience, in this context, means the ability of the installation to anticipate, withstand, absorb, adapt to, and rapidly recover from disruptive events, whether they are malicious attacks, natural disasters, or system failures. This proactive stance involves continuous risk assessment, vulnerability analysis, and the implementation of redundancy, fail-safe mechanisms, and robust contingency plans. It's about designing the system so that it can continue to operate, albeit potentially at a reduced capacity, even when parts of it are compromised or unavailable. This might involve having redundant power systems, multiple communication pathways, distributed data storage, and pre-trained personnel capable of operating in degraded modes. The goal is to minimize downtime and impact, ensuring that the essential functions of the installation can be maintained under duress.

Second, *Intelligence-Driven Operations* is central to PRISM. The methodology emphasizes the critical role of actionable intelligence in all aspects of security. This intelligence is not limited to the traditional definition of "threat intelligence" (i.e., information about adversaries and their capabilities). It encompasses a much broader spectrum, including environmental intelligence (weather patterns, seismic activity), operational intelligence (system performance metrics, resource availability), human intelligence (personnel behavior, insider threat indicators), and cyber intelligence (network traffic anomalies, known exploits). PRISM mandates the establishment of robust intelligence gathering, fusion, analysis, and dissemination capabilities. This intelligence must be timely, accurate, and directly relevant to decision-making at all levels, from strategic leadership to tactical response teams. The insights derived from this intelligence inform threat prioritization, resource allocation, the development of predictive defense strategies, and the refinement of response protocols.

The third guiding principle is Adaptive *Mitigation*. Recognizing that threats are dynamic and constantly evolving, PRISM advocates for mitigation strategies that are equally dynamic and adaptable. This means moving away from static, fixed defenses that can become obsolete or predictable over time. Mitigation efforts must be flexible, capable of being reconfigured, scaled, and redirected in response to changing threat landscapes and emerging vulnerabilities. This involves employing technologies and strategies that allow for rapid adjustments, such as dynamically reconfiguring network security policies, rerouting critical communications, or deploying specialized counter-measures based on real-time threat assessment. It also implies a continuous cycle of testing, evaluation, and refinement of mitigation techniques, ensuring they remain effective against the latest adversarial tactics, techniques, and procedures (TTPs).

Finally, *System-Level Understanding* underpins the entire PRISM methodology. Leaders and security professionals must develop a comprehensive understanding of how all the constituent systems of the installation interact and influence one another. This requires a deep dive into the dependencies, interconnections, and potential cascading effects within the installation's complex ecosystem. It involves mapping critical functions, identifying single points of failure, and understanding the flow of information and resources. Without this system-level perspective, efforts to enhance security in one area might inadvertently create new vulnerabilities in another, or mitigation efforts could be misdirected, failing to address the most critical systemic risks. PRISM thus encourages a holistic view, fostering an organizational culture that prioritizes cross-domain awareness and collaborative problem-solving.

The purpose of PRISM is multifaceted, yet unified. Primarily, it aims to equip leaders and security practitioners with a structured and comprehensive framework for understanding, assessing, and mitigating complex, interconnected threats. In a world where threats are no longer confined to a single domain, where a cyber-attack can disable physical infrastructure, or a physical infiltration can facilitate data exfiltration, a fragmented approach to security is insufficient. PRISM provides the intellectual architecture to move beyond this fragmentation, enabling organizations to view their security challenges through a holistic lens. It provides the tools and the mindset to analyze how different elements of the installation, its people, processes, technology, and physical infrastructure, interact and how these interactions create potential vulnerabilities and opportunities for adversaries.

A key objective of PRISM is to cultivate *proactive defense and resilience.* Traditional security models often operate on a reactive basis, waiting for an incident to occur before implementing a response. This is a costly and often ineffective strategy, as the damage may already be done. PRISM, conversely, emphasizes the proactive identification of potential threats and vulnerabilities, and the development of robust systems that can withstand and recover from disruptions. It focuses on building inherent resilience, ensuring that the installation can continue to function even under attack or during an unforeseen crisis. This involves not only hardening defenses but also building in redundancy, agility, and rapid recovery capabilities. The aim is to reduce the likelihood and impact of successful attacks, ensuring continuity of operations and minimizing disruption to critical functions.

PRISM seeks to enhance situational awareness across the entire installation. By integrating intelligence from disparate sources, physical sensors, cyber monitoring tools, human intelligence, and operational data, the methodology creates a unified, real-time picture of the security landscape. This enhanced situational awareness allows for better-informed decision-making, enabling leaders to prioritize threats, allocate resources effectively, and coordinate responses more efficiently. It ensures that all stakeholders have access to the most relevant and up-to-date information, fostering a shared understanding of the operational environment and potential risks.

Another crucial purpose of PRISM is to facilitate optimized resource allocation. Given the ever-increasing complexity and cost of security measures, it is imperative that resources are directed where they will have the greatest impact. By providing a structured method for assessing threats, vulnerabilities, and the potential impact of incidents, PRISM helps organizations to identify their most critical assets and the most significant risks they face. This allows for the strategic allocation of security investments, whether in technology, personnel, or training, to address the highest-priority risks and protect the most vital functions. It moves organizations away from diffuse, inefficient spending towards targeted, effective security solutions.

PRISM is designed to foster adaptability and continuous improvement. The threat landscape is not static; it is constantly evolving. Adversaries develop new tactics, techniques, and procedures, and new technologies emerge that can be exploited for malicious purposes. Therefore, security strategies must also evolve. PRISM builds in mechanisms for continuous learning and adaptation. By analyzing the effectiveness of responses, gathering feedback from incidents, and incorporating new intelligence, the methodology ensures that security protocols and systems are constantly refined and updated. This creates a dynamic defense that can keep pace with the evolving threat environment, ensuring long-term security and operational effectiveness.

The applicability of PRISM extends across a diverse range of installation environments. Whether the context is a forward operating base in a contested theater, a sprawling petrochemical complex, a critical national infrastructure hub, or a high-tech research and development facility, the principles of PRISM remain relevant. The core idea is that any complex, interconnected installation that relies on multiple overlapping systems for its functionality and security can benefit from this methodology. For example, on a military base, PRISM can integrate air defense systems, ground surveillance, cyber defense networks, personnel security protocols, and logistics management into a cohesive security strategy. For an industrial plant, it can connect physical security of the perimeter, safety systems, OT network security, supply chain integrity, and worker safety protocols. For a research facility, it can link the security of sensitive intellectual property, physical access controls to laboratories, cybersecurity of research networks, and insider threat monitoring. In each case, the methodology provides a structured approach to identifying systemic risks and developing integrated, resilient defenses tailored to the specific operational context.

The purpose of PRISM, therefore, is to provide a conceptual and practical toolkit that empowers organizations to confront the complexities of modern security. It moves beyond the limitations of siloed security approaches, offering a path towards a more integrated, intelligent, resilient, and adaptable defense posture. By embracing the PRISM methodology, organizations can transition from a state of constant reaction to a position of informed anticipation and enduring strength, safeguarding their critical assets and ensuring their sustained operational effectiveness against the myriad of threats they face today and will face tomorrow.

The introduction of the PRISM methodology represents a paradigm shift in how critical installations approach security and resilience. It is not merely a new set of tools or technologies, but a fundamental reorientation of strategic thinking. The very acronym, Systems-of-Systems Protection, Resilience, Intelligence, and Mitigation, encapsulates its comprehensive scope. The "Systems-of-Systems" aspect underscores the interconnected nature of modern installations, where physical, cyber, operational technology, and human elements are inextricably linked. PRISM recognizes that an attack on one system can have cascading effects across others, necessitating an integrated, holistic approach to defense. The "Protection" component signifies the traditional but essential function of safeguarding assets and personnel from harm. However, PRISM elevates protection by embedding it within a broader context of resilience. "Resilience" is the capacity of the installation to absorb, adapt to, and recover from disruptive events, whether they are malicious attacks, natural disasters, or system failures. This means designing the installation not just to resist an attack, but to continue functioning, perhaps at a reduced capacity, during and after an incident, and to recover quickly. This is a proactive stance, aiming to minimize the impact of any event.

"Intelligence" is the linchpin of the PRISM methodology. It emphasizes the critical role of actionable data and insights in informing all aspects of security. This intelligence is multi-faceted, encompassing threat intelligence, operational data, environmental factors, and human behavior analysis. The ability to gather, fuse, analyze, and disseminate relevant intelligence in real-time is crucial for effective decision-making and dynamic response. Finally, "Mitigation" refers to the strategies and actions taken to reduce the likelihood and impact of threats. PRISM advocates for adaptive mitigation, recognizing that static defenses can become obsolete and that responses must be flexible and capable of evolving as threats change.

The underlying purpose of PRISM is to equip leaders and security professionals with a structured framework for understanding, assessing, and managing complex, interconnected threats. In an increasingly volatile and unpredictable global landscape, installations are no longer isolated entities but nodes within larger networks, susceptible to a wide array of threats ranging from sophisticated cyber-attacks and advanced persistent threats (APTs) to physical sabotage, insider actions, and even the impacts of climate change or pandemics. A fragmented, siloed approach to security is insufficient to address this complexity. PRISM provides the conceptual architecture to break down these silos and foster a unified, coordinated defense.

One of the primary objectives of PRISM is to foster a transition from a purely reactive security posture to one of proactive defense and enhanced resilience. The traditional model of "detect and respond" often comes into play only after an incident has occurred, leading to significant damage, disruption, and loss. PRISM, conversely, emphasizes the continuous assessment of risks, vulnerabilities, and potential threats, enabling the anticipation of incidents. By integrating intelligence across all domains, installations can identify anomalies and predict potential threats before they materialize. This allows for the pre-emptive deployment of countermeasures, the hardening of critical assets, and the preparation of robust contingency plans. The focus on resilience means ensuring that the installation can withstand shocks, continue to perform its essential functions during disruptions, and recover rapidly afterward. This is achieved through redundancy, distributed systems, agile operational procedures, and well-rehearsed recovery plans.

PRISM aims to significantly improve situational awareness. By integrating data streams from diverse sources, such as physical security sensors (CCTV, radar, motion detectors), cyber intrusion detection systems, network traffic analyzers, operational technology monitoring tools, personnel tracking systems, and even external intelligence feeds, the methodology creates a comprehensive, real-time operational picture. This unified view allows decision-makers at all levels to understand the evolving security landscape, identify emerging threats, and assess their potential impact. Enhanced situational awareness is critical for effective threat prioritization, resource allocation, and the coordination of multi-domain response efforts. It transforms raw data into actionable insights, enabling smarter, faster decisions.

The PRISM methodology also serves the vital purpose of optimizing resource allocation. Security budgets are invariably constrained, and the cost of implementing comprehensive security measures can be substantial. PRISM provides a systematic approach to identifying and prioritizing risks, allowing organizations to allocate their resources, whether financial, human, or technological, to address the most critical vulnerabilities and protect the most essential functions. This data-driven approach ensures that investments are made where they will yield the greatest return in terms of enhanced security and resilience, moving away from inefficient, broad-spectrum spending towards targeted, effective security solutions.

Crucially, PRISM is designed to cultivate adaptability and continuous improvement in security operations. The adversary is not static; they constantly innovate and adapt their TTPs. New technologies emerge that can be exploited for both defense and offense. Therefore, security strategies must also be dynamic and capable of evolving. The "Intelligence" and "Mitigation" components of PRISM are intrinsically linked to this iterative process. By continuously gathering intelligence on evolving threats and assessing the effectiveness of current mitigation strategies, organizations can refine their defenses, update their protocols, and adapt their systems to remain effective against emerging challenges. This cyclical process of assessment, learning, and adaptation ensures that the installation's security posture remains robust and relevant over time. The applicability of the PRISM methodology is broad, transcending specific industry or sector boundaries. It is designed to be relevant for any complex, interconnected installation that relies on multiple overlapping systems for its functionality and security. This includes, but is not limited to:

Military Installations: From forward operating bases and command centers to naval vessels and airfields, PRISM can integrate physical security, cyber defense, electronic warfare, intelligence gathering, and personnel security into a cohesive defense strategy. This is particularly relevant in countering hybrid threats that blend conventional and unconventional tactics.

Critical National Infrastructure (CNI): Power grids, water treatment facilities, transportation networks, and communication hubs are prime targets for disruption. PRISM can help these installations develop resilience against both physical sabotage and cyber-attacks, ensuring continuity of essential services.

Industrial and Manufacturing Facilities: High-value manufacturing plants, petrochemical facilities, and sites handling hazardous materials face risks ranging from theft and industrial espionage to accidents and sabotage. PRISM can integrate safety systems, operational technology (OT) security, physical access controls, and supply chain integrity measures.

Research and Development Facilities: Laboratories and R&D; centers often house sensitive intellectual property and cutting-edge technologies. PRISM can secure these assets by integrating physical access, network security, data protection, and insider threat monitoring.

Government and Intelligence Agencies: The inherent interconnectedness of data systems and operational requirements within these organizations makes them ideal candidates for a PRISM-based approach to security and resilience.

Large-Scale Commercial Enterprises: Beyond CNI, large corporations with distributed operations, critical data centers, and significant physical footprints can also leverage PRISM to enhance their overall security posture and business continuity planning.

In essence, the PRISM methodology provides a strategic blueprint for organizations to move beyond fragmented security measures and embrace a unified, intelligent, and resilient approach. It empowers them to understand their installation as a complex system-of-systems, to anticipate and adapt to evolving threats, and to ensure the continuous protection and operational integrity of their most vital assets in an increasingly challenging security environment.

The cornerstone of the PRISM methodology, the 'Perceive' phase, is dedicated to building an unparalleled understanding of the operational environment and its inherent threats. This is not merely about knowing what is happening *now*, but about anticipating what *might* happen next. Effective perception is the bedrock upon which all subsequent defensive actions, Protection, Resilience, Intelligence, and Mitigation, are built. Without a clear, comprehensive, and dynamic understanding of the surrounding landscape, any security strategy, no matter how well-resourced or technologically advanced, risks being blind, reactive, and ultimately, ineffective. This phase is about establishing pervasive sensing capabilities across all critical domains: the physical, the cyber, the air (encompassing aerial and electromagnetic spectrums), and crucially, the human element. The objective is to move beyond discrete data points to a fused, integrated picture that reveals not just individual events, but patterns, trends, and potential trajectories of adversarial activity.

Achieving this pervasive sensing requires a multi-layered approach, beginning with the robust integration of existing and novel technologies. In the physical domain, this means extending beyond traditional perimeter security. It involves the strategic deployment of an array of sensors: advanced radar systems capable of detecting subtle movements in challenging terrain, high-resolution electro-optical and infrared (EO/IR) cameras offering persistent surveillance day and night, acoustic sensors to identify unusual sounds, seismic sensors to detect subterranean activity, and even environmental sensors that can monitor for changes in air quality or chemical signatures that might indicate unauthorized activity or a precursor to an incident. These sensors must be interconnected, feeding data into a common platform that can process and correlate information in real-time. For instance, a motion detection alert from a perimeter fence can be instantly cross-referenced with thermal imagery from an overhead drone and audio analysis from a nearby acoustic sensor. If all three systems indicate anomalous activity in the same sector, the confidence level of a potential intrusion skyrockets, prompting immediate, targeted investigation.

The cyber domain is equally, if not more, critical in today's interconnected world. Here, perception translates to deep visibility into the network's arteries and capillaries. This involves sophisticated Intrusion Detection and Prevention Systems (IDPS) that monitor network traffic for malicious patterns, analyze endpoint behavior for anomalies, and correlate alerts from various network segments. Beyond signature-based detection, modern cyber perception relies on behavioral analytics and machine learning to identify novel threats and insider activity that might evade traditional defenses. This includes User and Entity Behavior Analytics (UEBA) tools that establish baselines of normal activity for users and devices and flag deviations that could indicate compromised accounts or malicious intent. It necessitates continuous monitoring of the external digital landscape for indicators of compromise (IoCs), threat actor chatter on dark web forums, and vulnerabilities being exploited in software or hardware relevant to the installation's infrastructure. This external cyber intelligence provides an early warning system, allowing defensive measures to be put in place before an attack even reaches the installation's network.

The air domain, encompassing both the physical airspace above and the electromagnetic spectrum, is another vital area for perception. In terms of physical airspace, this means employing counter-unmanned aerial system (C-UAS) technologies that can detect, track, and identify small drones, and potentially disrupt their operation. This might involve radar, RF detection, optical sensors, and acoustic detection methods, all integrated to provide a comprehensive aerial picture. From an electromagnetic spectrum perspective, perception involves monitoring the radio frequency (RF) environment for unauthorized transmissions, jamming attempts, or the use of clandestine communication devices. This can reveal covert surveillance operations, attempts to disrupt command and control, or the use of unconventional communication channels by adversaries. Understanding the RF landscape is crucial, as it can provide indications of hostile intent long before physical actions are taken.

The most complex and often overlooked domain is the human element. Perceiving threats originating from or influenced by human behavior requires a nuanced approach that respects privacy while identifying significant risks. This involves understanding personnel security protocols, including vetting processes and ongoing monitoring for indicators of insider threats – such as sudden changes in financial status, expressions of grievance, or unusual access patterns. It also extends to understanding the broader human environment: social media sentiment analysis that might indicate unrest or radicalization in surrounding communities, public health data that could signal an impending pandemic, or even crowd dynamics at public access points that could indicate a planned disruption. This human intelligence, gathered through a combination of official channels, open-source analysis, and behavioral observation, is essential for a truly holistic perception.

The fusion of data from these disparate domains is where true situational awareness begins to coalesce. Raw data from individual sensors, network logs, and intelligence feeds is often voluminous, noisy, and lacks context. The 'Perceive' phase emphasizes the necessity of sophisticated data fusion engines and analytical platforms. These systems ingest data from all sensor types, correlate events across domains, identify relationships, and filter out noise. For example, a report of unusual vehicle activity near a sensitive physical boundary (physical sensor data) might be correlated with anomalous network access attempts from a device located near that boundary (cyber data) and a spike in local RF chatter (electromagnetic spectrum data). This triangulation of information elevates the alert from a minor anomaly to a high-priority incident requiring immediate attention.

This data fusion process is heavily reliant on advanced analytics, including artificial intelligence (AI) and machine learning (ML). These technologies are not merely about automation; they are about enhancing human cognitive capabilities to process information at a scale and speed that is otherwise impossible. AI algorithms can sift through terabytes of data to identify subtle patterns that human analysts might miss, predict potential threat vectors based on historical data and current intelligence, and even automate certain threat assessment and prioritization tasks. For instance, an ML model trained on past cyber-attack patterns can identify emerging attack methodologies in real-time, flagging them for human review and enabling a swift defensive response. Similarly, AI can analyze patterns in physical movement and sensor data to predict likely ingress or egress points for adversaries, allowing security forces to preposition assets proactively.

A critical component of the 'Perceive' phase is the leveraging of Open-Source Intelligence (OSINT). In the digital age, a vast amount of information is publicly available through social media, news outlets, academic research, government reports, and specialized forums. OSINT provides an invaluable, low-cost window into the operational environment, potential adversaries' intentions, capabilities, and locations. This can include monitoring public sentiment regarding the installation, identifying individuals or groups expressing hostile intent, tracking the movement of relevant geopolitical actors, or gleaning technical details about vulnerabilities being discussed in public forums. Effective OSINT collection requires sophisticated tools for scraping, filtering, and analyzing large volumes of unstructured data, as well as skilled analysts who can discern credible information from misinformation and disinformation. For example, by monitoring local news and social media in the vicinity of a critical infrastructure facility, security teams might detect early signs of public discontent or an organized protest that could escalate into a physical threat. Similarly, tracking online discussions among extremist groups could reveal chatter about potential targets or methods of attack directed at the installation.

The ultimate goal of the 'Perceive' phase is to create a dynamic, real-time Common Operational Picture (COP). This COP is not a static map or a dashboard; it is an evolving, multi-dimensional representation of the entire operational environment. It integrates all collected and fused intelligence, highlighting areas of concern, potential threats, ongoing incidents, and the status of defensive assets. The COP must be accessible to all relevant stakeholders, from the highest levels of leadership to tactical response teams, ensuring a shared understanding and enabling coordinated action. This shared awareness is crucial for effective decision-making, particularly in fast-moving, complex scenarios. For example, if a cyber-attack is detected targeting the installation's primary command and control network, the COP will immediately display this threat, along with any correlated physical or electromagnetic anomalies, and the status of available response teams, allowing leadership to make informed decisions on resource deployment and mitigation strategies.

The 'Perceive' phase is not a one-time event but a continuous cycle. The threat landscape is dynamic, and the operational environment is constantly changing. Therefore, perception capabilities must be continuously honed, sensors recalibrated, analytical models updated, and intelligence gathering strategies refined. This iterative process ensures that the installation remains aware of emerging threats and evolving vulnerabilities, allowing for proactive adaptation rather than reactive scrambling. This continuous learning loop is what imbues the PRISM methodology with its inherent adaptability, ensuring that the 'Perceive' phase remains relevant and effective over time, even as adversaries change their tactics, techniques, and procedures (TTPs).

The implementation of this comprehensive perception capability requires a strategic investment in technology, infrastructure, and human expertise. It necessitates breaking down traditional silos between physical security, cybersecurity, intelligence, and operations departments. Data sharing agreements, integrated command structures, and cross-training of personnel are essential to ensure that information flows freely and that different teams can collaborate effectively. Without this organizational and cultural alignment, even the most advanced technologies will struggle to provide the integrated, actionable intelligence required for true situational awareness. The 'Perceive' phase, therefore, is as much about organizational architecture and human collaboration as it is about technological prowess. It lays the essential foundation for understanding the complex web of threats and vulnerabilities that any modern installation faces, enabling the subsequent phases of Protection, Resilience, Intelligence, and Mitigation to be executed with precision and effectiveness.

The transition from a state of general awareness to specific threat understanding is the core of the 'Identify' phase within the S8S PRISM methodology. Having established a pervasive sensing capability in the 'Perceive' phase, the subsequent and equally critical step is to dissect the deluge of information generated, transforming raw data and nascent intelligence into actionable knowledge about specific threats. This is not a passive observation but an active, analytical process designed to characterize threats with sufficient granularity to enable effective prioritization and subsequent defensive actions. It moves beyond recognizing that *something* is happening to understanding *who* or *what* is behind it, *why* they are acting, *how* they might achieve their objectives, and crucially, *what* their potential impact could be.

The process of threat characterization begins with the aggregation and correlation of data points that have been flagged as anomalous or potentially significant during the perception phase. Consider a scenario where sensors detect unusual vehicle activity near a perimeter fence, correlating with an increase in specific types of network traffic originating from an external source, and a reported increase in social media chatter discussing local infrastructure vulnerabilities. Individually, these might be dismissed as low-level noise. However, within the 'Identify' phase, sophisticated analytical tools and human expertise work in concert to link these disparate signals. This linkage allows for the preliminary categorization of the threat. Is it a physical intrusion attempt, a cyber-attack, a reconnaissance operation, or a combination thereof? The initial characterization aims to answer these fundamental questions, providing a foundational understanding of the nature of the threat.

Central to this characterization is the identification of potential threat actors. This involves leveraging a multitude of intelligence sources, including the OSINT gathered during perception, classified intelligence feeds, and historical data on known adversaries. The objective is to attribute the detected activity, where possible, to specific groups, nations, or individuals. This attribution is not always definitive; often, it involves building a profile of the likely perpetrator based on their known capabilities, motivations, and modus operandi. For instance, if the detected cyber intrusion involves sophisticated, state-sponsored malware known to be employed by a particular nation-state actor, this becomes a primary line of inquiry. Similarly, if physical surveillance patterns mirror those of known extremist organizations, this intelligence informs the characterization. The process involves a constant interplay between observed activity and pre-existing intelligence, refining the understanding of the threat's origin and intent.

Understanding the capabilities of the identified threat actor is paramount. This involves assessing what resources, tools, and expertise they possess. In the cyber domain, this could mean evaluating the sophistication of their malware, their ability to bypass existing security controls, or their access to exploit kits. For physical threats, it might involve assessing their logistical capabilities, their training in relevant techniques (e.g., infiltration, sabotage), or their access to weaponry or specialized equipment. This assessment is crucial because an actor with limited capabilities poses a different level of risk than one with advanced, state-level resources. For example, a rudimentary phishing attempt, while still a threat, is characterized differently than a targeted Advanced Persistent Threat (APT) campaign designed to exfiltrate highly sensitive data over an extended period. The 'Identify' phase seeks to quantify these capabilities, moving beyond mere suspicion to a more concrete assessment of what the adversary is *able* to do.

Equally important is discerning the adversary's intentions. Why are they acting? What are their ultimate objectives? This is often the most challenging aspect of threat characterization, as intentions can be complex, multi-faceted, or deliberately obfuscated. Intelligence gathering at this stage aims to uncover the 'why' behind the 'what.' Are they seeking to disrupt operations, steal sensitive information, cause reputational damage, extort resources, or achieve a strategic political objective? Motivations can range from financial gain (cybercrime) to ideological extremism, geopolitical advantage (espionage, sabotage), or even simple mischief. Analyzing communication intercepts, studying adversary propaganda, understanding geopolitical contexts, and interpreting historical patterns of behavior all contribute to building a picture of their intent. For instance, a series of probes against a critical infrastructure's operational technology (OT) network, when combined with intelligence indicating a desire to destabilize a region, would strongly suggest an intent to disrupt critical services.

The identification of potential vectors of attack flows directly from the characterization of the actor, their capabilities, and their intentions. This involves mapping out the most probable pathways through which the threat could manifest and achieve its objectives. For a cyber threat actor intending to steal intellectual property, the vectors might include spear-phishing emails targeting key personnel, exploitation of unpatched vulnerabilities in external-facing systems, or the compromise of third-party vendors with privileged access. For a physical threat actor aiming to disrupt operations, vectors could include insider collusion, a coordinated physical assault on entry points, or the sabotage of critical infrastructure components through clandestine means. This detailed mapping of potential attack pathways is essential for effective defensive planning. It allows security teams to anticipate where and how an attack is likely to occur, enabling the proactive reinforcement of those specific points of vulnerability.

Once threats have been characterized, the subsequent and equally vital step within the 'Identify' phase is threat prioritization. Not all threats are created equal, and resources for defense are finite. Therefore, a systematic methodology for prioritizing threats based on their potential impact is essential. This involves assessing the criticality of identified threats to the installation's core mission, operational continuity, personnel safety, and overall security posture. A multi-faceted impact assessment is required, considering various dimensions:

First, the operational impact: How would a successful execution of this threat affect the ability of the installation to perform its designated functions? For a military base, this could mean the inability to launch aircraft, communicate with deployed forces, or process critical intelligence. For a critical infrastructure facility, it might mean the cessation of power generation, water supply, or transportation services. This assessment often involves quantifying the potential downtime, the scale of operational disruption, and the cascading effects on other interconnected systems or entities.

Second, the safety and security impact on personnel: This is often the most critical factor. What is the potential for loss of life, injury, or compromise of personnel safety? Threats that pose an immediate and direct risk to human life, such as a direct assault, the deployment of explosives, or the release of hazardous materials, will naturally receive the highest priority. This assessment considers not only direct casualties but also potential long-term health effects or the psychological impact of a major security breach.

Third, the economic impact: While often secondary to personnel safety, the financial implications of a successful threat can be substantial. This includes the cost of direct damage, the expense of recovery and restoration, lost revenue due to operational downtime, and potential fines or penalties for regulatory non-compliance. For businesses or government agencies, this can also encompass the loss of competitive advantage or significant damage to market reputation.

Fourth, the reputational and trust impact: In today's interconnected world, the damage to an organization's reputation and the erosion of public trust can be as devastating as direct physical or financial losses. A significant security breach, especially one involving the compromise of sensitive data or a failure to protect personnel, can lead to a loss of confidence from stakeholders, partners, and the public, which can be exceedingly difficult and costly to rebuild.

To facilitate this prioritization, robust frameworks and scoring mechanisms are employed. These can range from simple high-medium-low classifications to more complex matrix-based approaches that weigh likelihood against impact. For instance, a threat characterized as having a high probability of occurring and a catastrophic impact on personnel safety would be assigned the highest priority, demanding immediate and extensive resource allocation for mitigation and defense. Conversely, a threat with low probability and minimal impact might be placed lower on the list, requiring only a baseline level of monitoring and preparedness.

The 'Identify' phase also necessitates understanding the "attack surface", the sum of the different points where an unauthorized user can try to enter or extract data from an environment. This involves a comprehensive inventory of all accessible systems, networks, physical locations, and even personnel who might be exploited. By mapping the attack surface, organizations can more effectively identify where vulnerabilities lie and how threat actors might exploit them. This mapping is dynamic, as new systems are introduced, configurations change, and software is updated, expanding or contracting the attack surface. Continuous reassessment of the attack surface is therefore integral to the 'Identify' phase, ensuring that the prioritization remains relevant.

The characterization and prioritization must be a continuous, iterative process. The threat landscape is not static; it evolves daily. New actors emerge, existing ones change their tactics, techniques, and procedures (TTPs), and vulnerabilities are discovered and patched (or exploited). Therefore, the 'Identify' phase cannot be a one-off exercise. It requires constant vigilance, ongoing intelligence analysis, and regular re-evaluation of identified threats. This iterative nature ensures that defensive strategies remain aligned with the current threat environment, preventing complacency and ensuring that resources are always directed towards the most pressing risks. This continuous feedback loop from 'Identify' back to 'Perceive' is crucial, as new threat intelligence gathered might necessitate a recalibration of sensing efforts or a deeper dive into specific areas of the operational environment.

The output of the 'Identify' phase is a refined, prioritized list of credible threats, each characterized with as much detail as possible regarding the actor, their capabilities, intentions, and probable vectors of attack. This intelligence product is not merely an academic exercise; it serves as the direct input for the subsequent phases of the PRISM methodology. It provides the actionable intelligence necessary for the 'Protect' phase to implement targeted defenses, for the 'Resilience' phase to build robust recovery plans, for the 'Intelligence' phase to focus its collection efforts, and for the 'Mitigation' phase to develop strategies for managing residual risks. Without this granular understanding and rigorous prioritization, any subsequent defensive efforts would be akin to shooting in the dark, allocating resources indiscriminately rather than strategically focusing on where they can have the most significant impact in safeguarding the installation and its mission.

The effectiveness of the entire PRISM framework hinges on the accuracy, depth, and actionable nature of the threat identification and prioritization conducted at this critical juncture. This deep dive into threat characterization and prioritization allows for a highly granular understanding, moving beyond general awareness to specific, actionable intelligence that directly informs risk management decisions and the allocation of precious defensive resources. It is the intellectual engine that powers the entire defensive apparatus.

The transition from understanding *what* the threats are to developing concrete, integrated plans to counter them marks the commencement of the 'Plan & Prepare' phase. This is where the actionable intelligence painstakingly gathered and prioritized in the 'Identify' phase is transformed into a tangible defensive architecture. It is not enough to know an adversary's intent, capabilities, and likely attack vectors; one must proactively build the shields and prepare the responses that will nullify or mitigate those threats before they materialize or at least contain their impact should they succeed. This phase is about strategic foresight, operational readiness, and the synchronized application of diverse defensive capabilities across all domains.

Developing integrated defensive strategies requires a holistic perspective, recognizing that threats rarely operate in a single domain. A sophisticated adversary might employ a cyber-attack to disable physical security systems or use physical reconnaissance to inform a cyber intrusion. Therefore, the defensive strategy must mirror this complexity by weaving together physical security, cybersecurity, counter-unmanned aircraft systems (C-UAS), and human resilience initiatives into a cohesive and mutually reinforcing network of defenses. This integration is not simply about having separate plans for each domain, but about ensuring these plans are synchronized, interoperable, and capable of supporting each other during an incident. For instance, a cyber intrusion detection system might trigger an alert that initiates a physical lockdown of specific areas, while also flagging a potential need for airborne surveillance to detect any accompanying physical infiltration or escape routes. Similarly, the failure of a critical communication network during a cyber-attack could necessitate a pre-defined manual fallback procedure for physical security personnel.

The foundation of this integrated strategy lies in translating the threat assessments from the 'Identify' phase into specific, measurable, achievable, relevant, and time-bound (SMART) defensive objectives. If threat intelligence indicates a high probability of state-sponsored cyber espionage targeting sensitive data hosted on a particular network segment, the planning must articulate clear objectives like "Reduce the attack surface of the identified network segment by 70% within 30 days," or "Implement multi-factor authentication for all access points to the target data repository within 15 days," and "Achieve a 99% detection rate for known state-sponsored malware signatures within 7 days." These objectives then drive the selection and configuration of specific defensive measures.

Physical security measures form a critical, often visible, layer of defense. This includes not only traditional elements like robust perimeter fencing, access control points, surveillance cameras, and trained security personnel, but also more advanced technologies. Motion sensors, biometric scanners, and intelligent video analytics that can automatically detect anomalies (e.g., loitering, unauthorized entry attempts, unattended packages) are essential. Furthermore, the integration of these physical systems with command and control centers is paramount. An alert from a perimeter sensor should not just trigger an alarm; it should automatically display relevant camera feeds, provide information about the specific sector under threat, and potentially initiate automated responses like the activation of public address systems or the deployment of mobile response units.

This pre-planned integration ensures that the human element, when alerted, has all necessary context and tools at their immediate disposal, minimizing reaction time and maximizing the effectiveness of their response. The design of these physical defenses must consider the ingress and egress points identified as high-risk vectors in the 'Identify' phase, ensuring these are disproportionately hardened and monitored.

Cyber defense strategies must be equally robust and integrated. This involves a multi-layered approach that encompasses network segmentation to limit lateral movement of attackers, intrusion detection and prevention systems (IDPS) that are constantly updated with the latest threat intelligence, endpoint detection and response (EDR) solutions, and secure configurations across all systems. Crucially, the planning must go beyond static defenses. It must include proactive measures such as regular vulnerability scanning and penetration testing, threat hunting operations to find adversaries already within the network, and robust security awareness training for all personnel, as human error remains a significant vector. The integration aspect here is vital: cyber defense systems must be able to share threat indicators and alerts with physical security systems and C-UAS platforms. For instance, if a cyber-attack attempts to disable communication channels, the cybersecurity team should be able to rapidly inform physical security to revert to pre-determined communication protocols.

The advent of increasingly sophisticated and accessible unmanned aerial systems (UAS), commonly known as drones, necessitates dedicated C-UAS capabilities as a core component of modern defensive planning. Threats can range from malicious payload delivery (explosives, chemical agents) to surveillance and intelligence gathering. Integrated C-UAS strategies involve a combination of detection (radar, acoustic sensors, optical sensors, RF detection), identification and tracking, and mitigation (jamming, spoofing, kinetic defeat mechanisms, or soft-kill electronic countermeasures). The planning must specify the zones of operation for C-UAS, the types of threats they are designed to counter, and how their operational status is maintained. Integration with other domains is key: the detection of an unidentified drone could trigger an alert for physical security to secure sensitive areas and initiate public announcements, while also flagging the need for cyber defenses to monitor for potential drone-based command-and-control signals or payloads. The C-UAS response plan must also consider legal and ethical implications, as well as deconfliction with friendly air traffic.

Human resilience is the often-overlooked but fundamentally critical element of any defensive strategy. This encompasses not only the physical well-being and security of personnel but also their psychological preparedness, training, and awareness. In the context of integrated defense, it means ensuring that individuals are trained to recognize and report suspicious activities, understand their roles during an incident, and are psychologically resilient enough to function effectively under duress. This involves realistic scenario-based training exercises that simulate complex, multi-domain attacks, allowing personnel to practice their responses and identify gaps in coordination. It also includes developing robust support mechanisms for personnel who may be affected by an incident. The planning must ensure that training regimens are not static but evolve in parallel with the threat landscape and the technological capabilities deployed. A well-trained and vigilant workforce can act as an early warning system, a critical link in the detection chain, and a force multiplier for any defensive action.

Contingency planning is a cornerstone of the 'Plan & Prepare' phase. This involves developing detailed, pre-defined courses of action for a range of anticipated scenarios, from minor security breaches to full-scale hybrid attacks.

These plans must address specific threat scenarios identified in the previous phase, outlining step-by-step procedures for response, communication protocols, command and control structures, and resource deployment. Importantly, contingency plans must account for potential failures of primary systems. What happens if the primary communication network goes down during a cyber-attack? What if key personnel are incapacitated? What if physical access points are compromised simultaneously? These "what-if" scenarios require the development of redundant systems, alternative operational procedures, and clearly defined succession plans for leadership roles. A robust contingency plan doesn't just dictate actions; it builds adaptability and provides frameworks for decision-making in uncertain and rapidly evolving situations. This also extends to pre-identifying and establishing mutual aid agreements with external agencies, ensuring that the necessary support can be brought to bear quickly during a crisis.

Effective resource allocation is intrinsically linked to contingency planning and the overall defensive strategy. The insights gained from threat prioritization must guide the distribution of financial, technological, and human resources. This means investing in the technologies and training that address the most probable and impactful threats, rather than spreading resources too thinly across every conceivable risk. The plan must clearly delineate budget allocations for physical security upgrades, cybersecurity software and hardware, C-UAS systems, training programs, and personnel. It also involves optimizing the deployment of human assets, ensuring that skilled personnel are positioned where they can have the greatest impact, both in routine operations and during an incident. This might involve shifting personnel from less critical roles to front-line defense or augmenting surveillance teams during periods of heightened threat intelligence. The allocation process should be dynamic, allowing for adjustments based on evolving threat assessments and operational realities.

Pre-positioning of assets is a critical operational element of the 'Plan & Prepare' phase, particularly for rapid response capabilities. This involves strategically locating equipment, personnel, and supplies in advance of potential incidents. For physical security, this could mean deploying mobile surveillance units or rapid response teams to areas identified as potential flashpoints. For cyber defense, it might involve ensuring that backup systems and forensic analysis tools are readily accessible and in a state of readiness. For C-UAS, it could mean pre-deploying sensor arrays or mitigation equipment to vulnerable locations. The principle is to minimize the time required to bring critical capabilities to bear when an incident occurs. This pre-positioning must be balanced with security considerations to prevent the assets themselves from becoming targets or being compromised. The plan must clearly define the triggers for pre-positioning, the duration for which assets will remain in place, and the procedures for their subsequent redeployment or stand-down.

The concept of a layered defense posture, often referred to as "defense in depth," is the culmination of these planning efforts. It means creating multiple barriers and independent layers of security, so that if one layer fails, another is in place to detect, delay, or prevent the threat from achieving its objectives. This layered approach extends across all domains. For example, an external network firewall (cyber) protects against initial intrusion attempts, followed by an intrusion prevention system on the internal network (cyber), then strict access controls to sensitive data (cyber/physical), coupled with employee awareness training (human), and physical security measures guarding the server rooms (physical). If an attacker bypasses the firewall, the IDPS should detect them. If they manage to breach the internal network, access controls should limit their movement. If they attempt to physically access a server room, guards and cameras should detect them. Each layer contributes to the overall security, making it significantly harder and more time-consuming for an adversary to succeed.

This layered defense must also consider the 'Resilience' aspect of the PRISM methodology, albeit with a focus on preparedness here. Plans must include not only how to stop an attack but also how to maintain critical functions during an attack and how to recover quickly afterwards. This means developing business continuity and disaster recovery plans that are tightly integrated with the defensive strategy. For instance, if a cyber-attack targets the primary operational network, the contingency plan might involve shifting operations to a secure, isolated backup network, ensuring that essential services can continue uninterrupted. This requires pre-planning and testing of these failover mechanisms.

The development of integrated defensive strategies is an iterative and dynamic process. It cannot be a static document produced once and then filed away. The threat intelligence is constantly evolving, new technologies are emerging, and the operational environment itself is subject to change. Therefore, the plans developed in this phase must be regularly reviewed, tested, and updated. This involves conducting periodic exercises and drills, analyzing the results of these exercises, and incorporating lessons learned back into the defensive plans. Post-incident reviews are also critical, providing invaluable real-world data to refine defensive strategies and resource allocation. The 'Plan & Prepare' phase is not a destination; it is an ongoing commitment to readiness, ensuring that the organization is as agile and adaptable as the threats it faces. The output of this phase is not just a set of documents, but a state of preparedness, where capabilities are synchronized, personnel are trained, and the organization is postured to respond effectively to a wide spectrum of potential threats, thereby fulfilling the promise of a truly strategic and integrated defense.

The transition from meticulously laid plans to decisive, synchronized action defines the 'Execute & Respond' phase of the PRISM methodology. This is where the foresight developed in the preceding 'Plan & Prepare' stage is tested and proven against the realities of an active threat or incident. It is the operational arm of strategic defense, demanding agility, clear communication, and the seamless integration of diverse capabilities. This phase is not merely about reacting; it is about executing a pre-defined, yet flexible, response designed to neutralize threats, minimize impact, and restore normalcy with maximum efficiency. The core of this phase lies in achieving coordinated action across all relevant security domains and implementing effective mitigation strategies, ultimately showcasing the organization's resilience.

Coordinated action during an incident is the linchpin of an effective response. In a complex environment, threats rarely adhere to single-domain boundaries, and neither can a response. Imagine a scenario where a sophisticated adversary initiates a cyber-attack aimed at disrupting critical infrastructure communications, while simultaneously employing a physical infiltration attempt. Without a pre-established framework for coordination, the cybersecurity team might focus solely on network anomalies, while the physical security team remains unaware of the broader context or the potential for concurrent threats. The S8S PRISM methodology, by emphasizing integration in the planning phase, sets the stage for this coordinated action.

The execution of coordinated responses often hinges on sophisticated command and control (C2) structures. These structures must be designed to provide a unified operational picture, enabling decision-makers to comprehend the full scope of an incident, allocate resources effectively, and direct actions across disparate teams. Modern C2 centers are increasingly leveraging technology to achieve this, integrating data feeds from physical security sensors, cybersecurity monitoring tools, C-UAS platforms, and human intelligence reporting into a single, intuitive dashboard. This fusion of data allows for real-time situational awareness, critical for informed decision-making under pressure. For instance, if a network intrusion detection system flags unusual activity on a segment controlling physical access, the C2 system can simultaneously pull up camera feeds from the relevant access points, display the status of network connections, and alert the physical security response team to potential simultaneous physical breaches or attempted overrides. This cross-domain visibility ensures that responses are not siloed but synergistic, amplifying their overall effectiveness.

Automated response mechanisms play a crucial role in the speed and efficiency of coordinated action. While human oversight and decision-making remain paramount, certain pre-defined actions can be automated to address immediate threats or to buy valuable time for human responders. In the cyber domain, this might involve automatically isolating compromised network segments, blocking malicious IP addresses, or initiating endpoint containment procedures based on specific threat signatures detected by IDPS or EDR systems. Similarly, in physical security, an automated response could trigger lockdown procedures for specific zones, activate emergency lighting, or deploy mobile response units to pre-determined locations based on sensor alerts. For C-UAS, automated systems can be programmed to detect, track, and potentially initiate defensive measures against unauthorized aerial intrusions, such as jamming frequencies or activating localized denial-of-service countermeasures. The key to effective automation lies in robust testing and validation during the 'Plan & Prepare' phase, ensuring that automated actions are accurate, proportionate, and do not inadvertently escalate a situation or create unintended consequences. Each automated action must be clearly logged and auditable, providing a trail for post-incident analysis and continuous improvement.

De-escalation procedures are an integral part of coordinated response, particularly when dealing with dynamic situations that might involve human actors or the potential for unintended harm. While the primary objective is to neutralize a threat, the method of doing so must consider the broader context and potential ramifications. This includes developing clear protocols for communication with individuals involved in an incident, whether they are potential perpetrators, victims, or uninvolved parties. For example, if a physical security team confronts an individual who is acting suspiciously but has not yet committed a hostile act, de-escalation tactics, such as verbal commands, non-confrontational positioning, and the establishment of communication channels, would be prioritized over immediate forceful intervention. In a cyber context, de-escalation might involve targeted actions to disrupt an adversary's operations without causing collateral damage to critical systems or data or providing clear communication channels to facilitate negotiation or cessation of hostilities, where appropriate and feasible. The planning must also incorporate procedures for managing public perception and communication during a crisis, ensuring that official information is disseminated accurately and promptly to counter misinformation and maintain public trust.

Mitigation strategies are deployed concurrently with the initial response actions. The goal here is to minimize the damage caused by an incident, prevent its further spread, and preserve critical functions. This involves a multi-faceted approach tailored to the specific nature of the threat. In the event of a cyber breach, mitigation might include activating incident response plans to contain the breach, performing forensic analysis to understand the extent of the compromise, and initiating recovery procedures from secure backups. This could involve the temporary shutdown of non-essential systems, the redirection of network traffic, and the deployment of specialized cybersecurity teams to eradicate the threat and patch vulnerabilities. The speed at which these actions are taken is critical; every minute of exposure can lead to significant data loss or operational disruption. Pre-defined playbooks for common cyber threats, developed during the planning phase, are invaluable here, guiding the incident response team through a structured process of containment and eradication.

For physical security incidents, mitigation strategies focus on limiting the physical scope of the threat and protecting personnel and assets. This could involve establishing security perimeters, evacuating affected areas, and deploying specialized response teams to neutralize any immediate physical threats. For instance, in the case of an active shooter incident, the immediate mitigation steps would be to secure surviving personnel, provide medical aid to the injured, and systematically clear the area. For less severe incidents, such as unauthorized access to a facility, mitigation might involve securing the breached area, assessing the extent of any unauthorized access or tampering, and initiating repair or replacement of damaged infrastructure. The integration of physical and cyber defense means that during a physical intrusion, cybersecurity measures would be heightened to prevent any attempt by the intruder to leverage the physical breach for cyber espionage or sabotage.

When dealing with C-UAS threats, mitigation strategies are geared towards neutralizing the aerial threat and preventing it from achieving its objective. This could involve employing electronic countermeasures to disrupt the drone's command and control link, employing kinetic measures to physically disable the drone if authorized and necessary, or implementing soft-kill techniques to force the drone to land or return to its point of origin. The choice of mitigation tactic is heavily influenced by the type of drone, its payload, the operational environment, and legal/regulatory constraints. For instance, using jamming techniques might be preferable in an urban environment to avoid unintended collateral damage from kinetic engagement. The plan must clearly delineate the authorized use of different mitigation technologies and the escalation procedures for their deployment, ensuring compliance with airspace regulations and minimizing risks to civilian populations.

Restoration of operations is the ultimate objective following an incident, and this is where the resilience aspect of the PRISM methodology is truly demonstrated. It is not enough to simply neutralize a threat; the organization must be able to resume its critical functions as quickly and as seamlessly as possible. This requires well-rehearsed business continuity and disaster recovery plans that are directly linked to the incident response protocols. For a cyber incident, restoration might involve bringing systems back online from clean backups, validating data integrity, and re-establishing secure network connectivity. This process should be methodical and thorough, ensuring that the recovered systems are not re-infected or compromised. The 'Plan & Prepare' phase would have identified critical systems and prioritized their restoration, ensuring that the most essential functions are brought back first.

In the context of physical security, restoration might involve repairing damaged infrastructure, re-establishing access control systems, and bringing security personnel back to their operational posts. This also includes debriefing personnel, providing psychological support where needed, and conducting a thorough review of the incident to identify lessons learned for future preparedness. For C-UAS incidents, restoration may involve resuming normal aerial operations once the threat has been neutralized and the airspace declared safe or implementing new operational procedures or technological enhancements to prevent recurrence.

The process of restoration is often iterative, with organizations gradually bringing services back online, monitoring their performance, and addressing any emergent issues. This phase is heavily supported by the communication protocols established during the planning stage, ensuring that all stakeholders, internal personnel, external partners, and potentially the public, are kept informed about the progress of restoration efforts. Transparent and timely communication can help to manage expectations, build confidence, and mitigate the negative impact of the incident on the organization's reputation and operations.

Throughout the 'Execute & Respond' phase, continuous monitoring and feedback loops are essential. As actions are taken and mitigation strategies are deployed, their effectiveness must be continuously assessed. This involves analyzing real-time data from security systems, performance metrics of restored services, and human intelligence reports. If a particular response action is proving ineffective, or if a mitigation strategy is creating unforeseen problems, the incident response team must be empowered to adapt and adjust their approach. This adaptability is a hallmark of a resilient organization. The data gathered during an incident response and restoration effort is invaluable for refining the

'Plan & Prepare' phase, informing updates to threat assessments, defensive strategies, and contingency plans. Every incident, regardless of its severity, represents a learning opportunity.

The coordination of efforts often involves multi-agency collaboration, especially for large-scale or complex incidents. This could include partnerships with law enforcement, emergency services, cybersecurity agencies, and even international partners. The 'Plan & Prepare' phase would have established protocols and points of contact for such collaborations. During an incident, clear communication channels and a shared understanding of roles and responsibilities are critical to ensure that these external resources are integrated effectively into the overall response effort. For example, a major cyber-attack that impacts national infrastructure might require the involvement of national cybersecurity agencies to provide specialized expertise, threat intelligence, and coordinated response efforts across multiple organizations. Similarly, a physical security breach involving potential criminal activity would necessitate immediate collaboration with law enforcement.

The human element remains central to the 'Execute & Respond' phase. While technology and automation play vital roles, it is the training, judgment, and courage of individuals that often determine the outcome of an incident. Security personnel, IT professionals, and indeed all employees must be equipped to recognize threats, follow established protocols, and contribute to the overall response. Regular drills and exercises, conducted during the 'Plan & Prepare' phase, ensure that personnel are familiar with their roles and responsibilities, and can execute them effectively under pressure. The psychological resilience of responders is also a critical factor, as they may face stressful and dangerous situations. Providing adequate support mechanisms, including stress management resources and post-incident counseling, is an essential component of a comprehensive response strategy.

In essence, the 'Execute & Respond' phase is a dynamic interplay of strategy, technology, and human action. It is the critical juncture where the preparedness of an organization is put to the test. By fostering coordinated action across all security domains, implementing swift and effective mitigation strategies, and prioritizing the restoration of critical functions, organizations can navigate even the most challenging incidents. This phase is not an endpoint but a continuous cycle of action, assessment, and adaptation, ensuring that the organization not only survives an incident but emerges stronger and more resilient, ready to face future threats. The successful execution of this phase directly validates the strategic investments and planning efforts undertaken previously, reinforcing the iterative and evolving nature of the PRISM methodology.

The 'Sustain & Improve' phase is the cornerstone of a truly robust and forward-looking security posture. It transforms every incident, every drill, and every technological advancement into a valuable learning opportunity, ensuring that the PRISM methodology is not a static document but a living, breathing framework that evolves alongside threats and capabilities. This final pillar is where resilience is not just demonstrated but actively cultivated and strengthened. It is about moving beyond merely reacting to incidents and towards a proactive, adaptive approach that anticipates future challenges and continuously refines defensive measures. The ultimate aim is to foster a perpetual cycle of enhancement, ensuring that the SMART Installation's security remains not just adequate, but consistently ahead of the curve.

At the heart of this phase lies the critical process of post-incident analysis. Once an incident has been contained, mitigated, and operations have been restored, a thorough and objective review is paramount. This is not a perfunctory exercise but a deep dive into the entirety of the response. It begins with a comprehensive data collection effort, gathering all logs, reports, sensor data, communication records, and witness statements related to the event. The objective is to reconstruct a precise timeline of the incident, from initial detection to final resolution. This detailed reconstruction allows for the identification of key moments, decision points, and the precise sequence of events. Crucially, this analysis must extend beyond the immediate response to encompass the entire lifecycle of the incident, including any pre-incident indicators that may have been missed or misinterpreted.

Performance evaluation within this analysis is multifaceted. It requires assessing the effectiveness of the 'Execute & Respond' phase. Were the pre-defined protocols followed? Were they adequate? Did command and control structures function as intended? How effectively were resources allocated and managed? The speed and accuracy of threat identification and response are scrutinized. Were there any delays? Where did they occur and why? For automated systems, their performance is assessed: did they trigger correctly? Did they operate within expected parameters? Did they contribute positively to the response or inadvertently complicate it? Human performance is equally important, focusing on adherence to training, decision-making under pressure, and effective communication. This evaluation must be conducted without assigning blame, fostering an environment where honest assessment and constructive criticism can flourish. The goal is to identify what worked well and should be reinforced, and what did not work well and requires modification.

The incorporation of lessons learned is the actionable output of this analysis. These insights are not to be filed away and forgotten but actively integrated into the fabric of the organization's security strategy. This means revisiting and updating the 'Plan & Prepare' phase of the PRISM methodology. Threat assessments are refined based on the specifics of the incident. New vulnerabilities identified during the event are cataloged and addressed. Response playbooks are revised to reflect successful tactics and to incorporate solutions for identified shortcomings. For example, if a particular phishing campaign bypassed existing email filters, the lesson learned might be to enhance anti-phishing training for personnel and to invest in more advanced email security solutions, updating the relevant sections of the 'Plan & Prepare' documentation accordingly. Similarly, if communication breakdowns were identified during a multi-agency response, protocols for inter-agency liaison and information sharing would be reviewed and strengthened.

Technology adoption is also heavily influenced by the 'Sustain & Improve' phase. Post-incident analysis often reveals gaps in current technological capabilities or highlights emerging technologies that could offer significant advantages. This might involve the evaluation of new cybersecurity tools for threat detection and response, advanced physical security sensors, or enhanced C-UAS countermeasures. The decision to adopt new technology should be data-driven, directly linked to the lessons learned from past events and the evolving threat landscape. This process requires a rigorous assessment of potential solutions, considering their effectiveness, cost, integration challenges, and the training required for personnel. The introduction of new technologies must be carefully managed, ensuring they are properly implemented, tested, and integrated into existing operational workflows. For instance, if an incident highlighted the difficulty in tracking rapidly moving physical threats, the analysis might lead to the evaluation and subsequent adoption of AI-powered video analytics capable of real-time object tracking and anomaly detection.

Continuous training forms a vital component of this improvement cycle. Lessons learned are translated into updated training programs for all relevant personnel. This training should go beyond theoretical knowledge and focus on practical application, ensuring that individuals can effectively execute revised procedures and utilize new technologies. Regular drills and exercises are indispensable for reinforcing this training. These are not mere simulations but realistic simulations designed to test the updated plans, procedures, and technological capabilities. Tabletop exercises can be used to walk through hypothetical scenarios and discuss response strategies, while more complex full-scale exercises can involve actual deployment of resources and simulated operational environments. The frequency and complexity of these drills should be increased over time, mirroring the evolving threat landscape and the increasing sophistication of the organization's defense mechanisms. For example, after a simulated cyber-attack involving ransomware, a follow-up drill might focus on the speed and integrity of data restoration from immutable backups, specifically testing the procedures that were updated based on lessons from the initial event.

Adapting defense strategies based on an evolving threat landscape is not a reactive measure but a proactive necessity. The adversaries are constantly innovating, and so too must the defenders. This requires ongoing intelligence gathering and threat analysis, not just from internal incidents, but from external sources as well. Subscribing to threat intelligence feeds, participating in industry information-sharing groups, and maintaining relationships with relevant government agencies are crucial for staying abreast of emerging threats, tactics, techniques, and procedures (TTPs).

This intelligence should then be fed directly back into the 'Plan & Prepare' phase, informing adjustments to threat assessments, risk analyses, and defensive strategies. The PRISM methodology's inherent flexibility allows for these strategic adjustments to be made without requiring a complete overhaul, ensuring agility in the face of a dynamic threat environment. This might involve re-prioritizing certain defensive measures, allocating more resources to combat specific types of threats, or developing entirely new operational concepts.

The culture of perpetual security enhancement is perhaps the most profound outcome of the 'Sustain & Improve' phase. It shifts the organizational mindset from viewing security as a compliance requirement or a discrete set of procedures to recognizing it as an ongoing, dynamic process. This culture is fostered by leadership that champions continuous learning, encourages open communication about security challenges, and provides the resources necessary for improvement. It is a culture where every individual understands their role in maintaining and enhancing security, and where feedback is welcomed and acted upon. This permeates all levels of the organization, from the executive suite to frontline personnel. It means that security is not an afterthought but an integrated component of every decision and every operation.

The SMART Installation, by embedding the 'Sustain & Improve' pillar into its operational DNA, ensures that its security posture is not static but dynamic and resilient. This continuous learning and adaptation are what truly elevate the PRISM methodology from a comprehensive framework to a strategic advantage. It is the mechanism by which the organization remains not only secure but also progressively more secure, a vital characteristic in an era of persistent and evolving threats. The investment in robust post-incident analysis, performance evaluation, and the subsequent integration of lessons learned through training, technology adoption, and strategic adaptation ensures that the security framework itself is as agile and responsive as the threats it is designed to counter. This creates a virtuous cycle where each challenge overcome makes the organization stronger and better prepared for the next.

This iterative refinement process means that the 'Plan & Prepare' phase is constantly being informed by the realities of the 'Execute & Respond' phase. Intelligence gathered from real-world incidents, even minor ones, provides invaluable data for anticipating future attacks. For example, a phishing attempt that is successfully identified and reported by an employee, even if it doesn't lead to a compromise, provides crucial data on the evolving tactics of adversaries. This data can then be used to refine employee awareness training, update email filtering rules, and potentially even inform the development of new detection algorithms. The feedback loop is direct and impactful, ensuring that the planning remains relevant and grounded in practical experience rather than theoretical assumptions.

The 'Sustain & Improve' phase encourages a proactive approach to identifying potential weaknesses before they can be exploited. Regular vulnerability assessments and penetration testing, conducted as part of this continuous improvement cycle, act as crucial stress tests for the entire security apparatus. These tests, informed by the latest threat intelligence and designed to emulate sophisticated adversary tactics, help to uncover previously unknown vulnerabilities in systems, networks, and even procedural workflows. The findings from these assessments are then treated with the same rigor as lessons learned from actual incidents, leading to targeted improvements and updates to the 'Plan & Prepare' and 'Execute & Respond' phases. This proactive stance is essential in outpacing adversaries who are continuously seeking new avenues of exploitation.

The integration of C-UAS capabilities within the 'Sustain & Improve' framework also deserves particular attention. As drone technology advances and their potential applications, both legitimate and malicious, expand, so too must the capabilities for detecting, tracking, and responding to them. Post-incident analysis from any drone-related event, whether it's an unauthorized drone intrusion or the successful deployment of countermeasures, provides critical data. This data can inform the refinement of detection algorithms, the calibration of sensor arrays, and the optimization of engagement protocols. Continuous training for personnel operating C-UAS systems is also vital, ensuring they remain proficient with evolving technologies and tactical approaches. Regular exercises that simulate various drone threat scenarios, from simple surveillance drones to more complex, weaponized platforms, allow for the testing and refinement of response strategies.

This ensures that the C-UAS capabilities are not only technologically advanced but also operationally effective and adaptable to the dynamic nature of the aerial threat landscape.

The human element in 'Sustain & Improve' is as critical as in any other phase. Continuous professional development for security personnel is a key aspect. This includes staying abreast of new cybersecurity threats, advancements in physical security technologies, and evolving best practices in incident management. Certifications, advanced training courses, and participation in professional conferences are all part of this ongoing learning process. Moreover, fostering a culture of knowledge sharing within the security team and across relevant departments is essential. Regular debriefings, internal workshops, and the development of internal knowledge bases ensure that lessons learned are disseminated effectively and that best practices become ingrained in the operational procedures of all personnel. This continuous upskilling ensures that the human capital within the SMART Installation is always prepared to meet the challenges posed by an evolving threat environment.

The 'Sustain & Improve' phase necessitates a commitment to understanding and adapting to the broader socio-technical landscape. As new technologies become integrated into the SMART Installation's operations, their potential security implications must be rigorously assessed. This includes not only direct cyber or physical threats but also the potential for cascading failures, unintended consequences of interconnected systems, and the impact of human factors on system performance. For instance, the increasing reliance on artificial intelligence (AI) in various security functions requires ongoing evaluation of AI biases, robustness against adversarial attacks, and ethical considerations. Lessons learned from the implementation and operation of AI systems must be fed back into their development and deployment, ensuring they remain effective, reliable, and aligned with organizational values.

In essence, the 'Sustain & Improve' phase encapsulates the dynamic and adaptive nature of modern security. It recognizes that security is not a destination but a journey, characterized by continuous learning, rigorous evaluation, and constant adaptation. By diligently applying the principles of post-incident analysis, performance evaluation, lessons learned incorporation, technology adoption, continuous training, and strategic adaptation, the SMART Installation, guided by the S8S PRISM methodology, solidifies its position as a leader in resilient and evolving security. This commitment to perpetual enhancement ensures that the organization is not merely prepared for today's threats but is actively shaping its defense to meet the challenges of tomorrow. The cyclical nature of the PRISM methodology, with 'Sustain & Improve' feeding directly back into 'Plan & Prepare', guarantees a security posture that is perpetually optimized, resilient, and ultimately, more effective in safeguarding the organization's assets and objectives.

Chapter 4: Advanced Sensing and Situational Awareness

INTEGRATED SENSOR NETWORK
COMMON OPERATIONAL PICTURE

The efficacy of any advanced security strategy hinges upon its ability to perceive, understand, and react to its operating environment. This perception is fundamentally enabled by a sophisticated sensor network, a critical component that moves beyond simple detection to provide a rich, nuanced understanding of the installation's physical and digital landscapes. The architecture of this network is not a monolithic entity but a carefully orchestrated symphony of diverse sensing modalities, each contributing a unique perspective to a unified operational picture. The goal is to create a comprehensive, multi-layered system that offers total installation coverage, ensuring that no blind spots remain and that every potential threat vector is continuously monitored. This is achieved through the strategic integration of numerous sensor types, meticulously positioned and interconnected to provide overlapping fields of detection and validation, thereby fostering a robust and resilient security fabric.

At the forefront of modern threat detection, particularly against the burgeoning challenge of Unmanned Aircraft Systems (UAS), is advanced radar technology. This is not the traditional radar of military aviation but highly specialized systems designed to detect, track, and classify small, often low-flying, and maneuverable aerial threats. These systems employ sophisticated signal processing techniques to differentiate drones from natural clutter such as birds or atmospheric disturbances, and to provide crucial telemetry like speed, altitude, and direction. The deployment of these radar systems is typically strategic, often positioned at elevated points or distributed across key sectors to maximize their line of sight and coverage area. Their ability to operate effectively in various weather conditions and at day or night makes them an indispensable component of the perimeter and aerial defense.

Complementing radar's capabilities are advanced optical and thermal imagers. High-definition visible light cameras, equipped with powerful zoom lenses and pan-tilt-zoom (PTZ) capabilities, provide detailed visual identification of potential intruders or anomalous activities. These cameras are often integrated with intelligent video analytics (IVA) software, which can automatically detect and flag suspicious behaviors such as loitering, unauthorized entry, or unusual movement patterns. Thermal imagers, on the other hand, detect heat signatures, allowing for the identification of individuals or vehicles obscured by darkness, camouflage, or environmental obscurants like fog or smoke. This dual-spectrum imaging provides a more complete picture, enabling security personnel to confirm visual observations and gather crucial identification details that might otherwise be missed. The placement of these imagers is crucial, often overlapping with radar coverage zones and strategically located to monitor entry points, critical infrastructure, and vulnerable areas.

Acoustic sensors play a crucial, albeit often overlooked, role in the layered defense. These sensors are designed to detect and analyze sounds, ranging from the distinct whine of a drone's rotors to the distinct sound of approaching footsteps or the detonation of an explosive device. Advanced acoustic sensor networks can triangulate the source of a sound with remarkable accuracy, providing an alert and directional cue even before a visual or radar detection is made. This is particularly valuable for identifying low-flying drones or ground-based threats that may be moving through vegetated or otherwise obscured areas. The integration of acoustic data with other sensor inputs can significantly reduce false alarms and accelerate the identification of genuine threats.

Ground-based radar systems are essential for monitoring the immediate vicinity of the installation and the approaches to its perimeter. Unlike airborne radar, these systems are optimized for detecting ground vehicles, individuals on foot, and even changes in terrain that might indicate tunneling or clandestine activity. They provide a persistent surveillance capability over large areas, offering robust detection and tracking of terrestrial movement. Their integration with optical and thermal sensors allows for rapid verification of radar contacts, providing immediate visual confirmation of the nature of the detected activity.

Perimeter intrusion detection systems (PIDS) form the first physical line of defense. These can range from buried fiber-optic cables that detect vibrations caused by digging or climbing, to microwave barriers, infrared beams, and electrified fences. Each technology has its strengths, and a comprehensive PIDS often employs a combination to create redundancy and mitigate the vulnerabilities of any single system. For instance, buried sensors can detect attempts to breach the perimeter from below, while above-ground systems can detect attempts to scale or cross it. The data from these PIDS is critical, providing immediate alerts that initiate a response, and crucially, offering precise location information for responding security forces.

Beyond the physical realm, cyber network monitoring tools are indispensable components of the modern sensor network. The digital infrastructure of an installation is as critical as its physical boundaries, and it presents a unique set of vulnerabilities. Intrusion detection and prevention systems (IDPS), security information and event management (SIEM) systems, and network traffic analysis tools constantly monitor network activity for signs of compromise, unauthorized access, or malicious activity. These systems analyze data flows, log events, and system behaviors to identify anomalies and potential cyber threats in real-time. The integration of cyber sensor data with physical security alerts can reveal sophisticated, multi-pronged attacks where cyber intrusion is used to disable physical defenses or to facilitate physical access.

The true power of this multi-layered sensor network lies not in the individual capabilities of each component, but in their seamless integration. This creates a unified, 360-degree view of the installation's environment, offering not just detection, but deep situational awareness. Data from disparate sensors is fused together through sophisticated command and control (C2) platforms. For example, a radar contact detected at the perimeter might be immediately correlated with optical camera feeds and acoustic sensor data. If the optical camera confirms a human presence and the acoustic sensor identifies footsteps, the confidence level of a genuine intrusion alert is significantly heightened. Conversely, a radar alert that is not corroborated by other sensor modalities might be flagged as a low-confidence event, reducing the likelihood of unnecessary response. This fusion of data enables automated cross-validation, significantly reducing the number of false positives and allowing security personnel to focus on genuine threats.

This intelligent correlation and fusion of data allows for a dynamic prioritization of alerts. The C2 system, informed by the criticality of the asset being monitored and the characteristics of the detected threat, can automatically escalate alerts. A drone detected within a sensitive airspace, for instance, would trigger a higher-priority response than a similar detection at a less critical perimeter sector. This ensures that resources are allocated efficiently and that the most immediate threats receive the swiftest attention. The system can also learn and adapt, refining its detection algorithms and alert prioritization based on historical data and the outcomes of past events.

The network architecture itself is designed for resilience and redundancy. Rather than relying on a single central processing hub, data is often processed at distributed nodes, with robust communication links ensuring that the loss of one component does not cripple the entire system. Secure, encrypted communication channels are paramount to prevent adversaries from intercepting or manipulating sensor data.

The physical placement of sensors often incorporates overlapping fields of detection. This means that if one sensor is damaged or its field of view is obstructed, another sensor can still provide coverage of the same area, ensuring continuity of surveillance. This redundancy is a cornerstone of robust situational awareness, guaranteeing that the security posture remains effective even under duress.

The deployment of such a comprehensive network requires meticulous planning. Site surveys are conducted to identify optimal sensor locations, considering factors such as terrain, existing infrastructure, potential environmental interference, and the need for clear lines of sight or signal propagation. The types of sensors deployed are tailored to the specific threats anticipated for each sector of the installation. For example, areas with high air traffic density will prioritize advanced C-UAS radar and optical systems, while border areas or vulnerable access points might see a greater concentration of PIDS and ground-based radar.

The human-machine interface is equally critical. Sensor data, even when fused and analyzed, must be presented to human operators in a clear, intuitive, and actionable manner. Modern C2 platforms utilize sophisticated graphical user interfaces (GUIs) that overlay sensor data onto detailed site maps, providing operators with a real-time, bird's-eye view of the situation. Alerts are visually highlighted, and relevant data from multiple sensors is presented in a consolidated format, enabling rapid comprehension and decision-making. Training for operators focuses not just on understanding the technology but on interpreting the data, recognizing subtle indicators of threat, and effectively managing the response.

The evolution of this sensor network is an ongoing process, driven by continuous advancements in sensor technology and the ever-changing threat landscape. As new types of threats emerge and existing ones become more sophisticated, the network must adapt. This includes the integration of novel sensing modalities, such as chemical or biological sensors for detecting WMD threats, or advanced materials analysis for identifying disguised explosives. It also involves leveraging artificial intelligence and machine learning more deeply, not just for anomaly detection, but for predictive analysis, forecasting potential threat vectors and enabling proactive defensive measures.

The multi-layered sensor network, therefore, is not a static installation but a dynamic, evolving ecosystem of interconnected intelligence, providing the foundational layer for comprehensive security and unparalleled situational awareness. This pervasive sensing capability ensures that the installation remains vigilant, prepared, and resilient against a spectrum of threats, from the skies to the earth, and into the digital domain. The persistent challenge posed by the ubiquitous and rapidly evolving threat landscape of Unmanned Aircraft Systems (UAS) necessitates a dedicated focus on the sophisticated technologies employed for their detection and tracking. This is not merely an extension of existing surveillance capabilities but a specialized domain addressing the unique characteristics of drones, which often present as small, low-flying, highly maneuverable, and sometimes stealthy aerial platforms. The effectiveness of any C-UAS strategy is fundamentally predicated on its ability to achieve reliable and timely detection, forming the critical first step in a cascading chain of defensive actions. Without accurate and early detection, even the most robust countermeasure systems would be rendered ineffective, leaving installations vulnerable to a myriad of potential threats, from aerial reconnaissance and surveillance to the delivery of ordnance or the disruption of critical operations.

Advancements in radar technology have been central to the development of effective C-UAS detection. Traditional military radar systems, designed for large, high-altitude aircraft, often struggle with the diminutive size and low flight profiles of many drones. Consequently, specialized C-UAS radars have emerged, characterized by their high sensitivity, rapid scanning capabilities, and sophisticated signal processing algorithms. These systems are engineered to detect small radar cross-sections (RCS) that can be as small as that of a bird. Techniques such as inverse synthetic aperture radar (ISAR) imaging are employed to help classify targets based on their physical characteristics, differentiating between a drone and more benign aerial objects like birds or atmospheric phenomena. Doppler processing is crucial for discerning the distinct movement signatures of rotorcraft and fixed-wing drones from the clutter of wind-blown debris or migrating flocks.

Phased-array and multi-function radar technologies allow for rapid electronic beam steering, enabling continuous tracking of multiple targets simultaneously across a wide surveillance volume. The challenge of low-altitude detection is addressed through radar designs that minimize ground clutter interference, often employing bistatic or multistatic configurations where transmit and receive antennas are separated, or by utilizing advanced clutter suppression techniques that dynamically adapt to the surrounding environment. The development of solid-state transmit modules has also improved radar reliability and reduced maintenance requirements, making these systems more practical for persistent deployment.

The integration of artificial intelligence and machine learning into radar processing is further enhancing the ability to accurately classify targets and reduce false alarm rates, a persistent issue in C-UAS operations due to the sheer volume of small aerial objects in the operational environment. Complementing radar, electro-optical and infrared (EO/IR) systems provide crucial visual confirmation and detailed identification capabilities for C-UAS operations.

High-definition visible-light cameras, equipped with advanced zoom lenses and stabilized gimbals, offer the ability to visually acquire and track drones at significant distances. When combined with intelligent video analytics (IVA), these systems can automatically detect anomalies in the sky, such as objects exhibiting flight characteristics inconsistent with natural phenomena or known aircraft. IVA can be trained to identify specific drone shapes, sizes, and movement patterns. Thermal imagers, or infrared cameras, are particularly effective during periods of low light, at night, or in conditions of reduced visibility such as fog or smoke. They detect the heat signatures emitted by drone motors, electronics, and even the airframe itself due to aerodynamic heating.

This capability allows for the detection of drones that might otherwise be invisible to the naked eye or standard radar. The fusion of data from EO and IR sensors provides a more robust detection capability, allowing operators to confirm a threat visually and gather critical intelligence about the drone's configuration, potential payload, and flight path. Advanced EO/IR systems are increasingly incorporating sensor fusion algorithms that automatically correlate radar tracks with visual or thermal signatures, significantly improving situational awareness and reducing operator workload. The development of cooled infrared detectors has further enhanced sensitivity, enabling the detection of smaller thermal signatures at longer ranges. The challenge for EO/IR systems remains their reliance on line-of-sight and their susceptibility to atmospheric conditions, which can degrade performance.

Acoustic sensing offers a complementary and often overlooked layer of C-UAS detection. Drones, particularly rotorcraft, generate a distinct acoustic signature, the characteristic hum or whine of their propellers. Advanced acoustic sensor networks utilize arrays of microphones to detect, triangulate, and classify these sounds. By analyzing the frequency, amplitude, and temporal characteristics of the detected sound, sophisticated algorithms can differentiate drone noise from ambient background noise and even identify the type of drone based on its propulsion system. Triangulation allows for the determination of the sound's origin, providing a directional cue that can cue other sensors, such as EO/IR cameras, to focus on the potential threat location. This is especially valuable for detecting low-flying drones that may be emerging from behind terrain or foliage, where radar and optical systems might have a delayed or obscured view.

The integration of acoustic data into a multi-sensor fusion system can provide an early warning, often preceding other detection modalities. However, acoustic sensors are susceptible to interference from other noise sources, and their effective range can be limited by environmental factors like wind and foliage.

Nevertheless, their ability to provide an independent detection modality and their relatively low cost make them a valuable component in a layered C-UAS defense strategy.

Radio Frequency (RF) detection systems have become increasingly vital in C-UAS operations, particularly against drones that rely on remote control or data links for operation. These systems monitor the electromagnetic spectrum for the characteristic signals emitted by drones and their ground control stations. This includes detecting the control signals used to fly the drone, as well as any data streams, such as video feeds, being transmitted. By analyzing the frequency, modulation, and signal patterns, RF detection systems can identify the presence of active drones, determine their approximate location, and even, in some cases, identify the type of drone and its controller. This technology is particularly effective against commercial drones that operate on common ISM bands (e.g., 2.4 GHz, 5.8 GHz) or use proprietary communication protocols.

Advanced RF detection systems employ techniques like direction finding (DF) to pinpoint the source of the RF emissions, providing a location for the drone or its controller. They can also detect unauthorized or anomalous RF activity in restricted airspace. The challenge for RF detection lies in the increasing use of frequency hopping, encrypted communication, and directional antennas by sophisticated adversaries, which can make signals harder to detect and geolocate. Furthermore, the sheer volume of legitimate RF traffic in the environment can lead to false positives, requiring advanced signal processing and threat assessment capabilities. The integration of RF detection with other sensor data allows for correlation; for instance, an RF signal detected in a specific direction can be used to cue an EO/IR camera or radar.

The challenge of detecting small, low-flying, or stealthy drones is multifaceted and requires a synergistic approach. Small drones have reduced radar cross-sections, making them difficult to detect by conventional radar. Low-flying drones are often obscured by terrain and can be masked by ground clutter. Stealthy drones may employ materials that absorb radar waves or use quiet propulsion systems, further complicating detection. To overcome these challenges, C-UAS technologies are increasingly employing sensor fusion. This involves integrating data from multiple, diverse sensor types, radar, EO/IR, acoustic, and RF, into a unified operational picture. By combining the strengths of each sensor modality and compensating for their individual weaknesses, a more comprehensive and reliable detection and tracking capability is achieved. For example, radar might detect an object, acoustic sensors might pick up its distinct sound, and RF sensors might identify its control signal. This corroboration significantly increases the confidence in a detected threat and reduces the likelihood of false alarms.

Differentiating between benign and malicious UAS is a critical aspect of C-UAS detection and tracking. The airspace is increasingly populated by commercial drones used for photography, delivery, infrastructure inspection, and recreational purposes. A robust C-UAS system must be able to distinguish these legitimate uses from potentially hostile activities. This is achieved through a combination of technological capabilities and operational protocols. Advanced classification algorithms, often powered by machine learning, analyze sensor data to identify characteristics associated with malicious drones, such as flight patterns deviating from expected norms, payload indicators, or operation in restricted or sensitive areas. Geofencing capabilities, where predefined virtual boundaries are established, can automatically flag any drone entering a prohibited zone. Intelligence databases, containing information on known drone models, flight characteristics, and common operational patterns, are continuously updated to aid in identification.

The concept of "persistent surveillance" is key. By continuously monitoring an area, security forces can observe the behavior of drones over time, identifying patterns that might indicate malicious intent. For instance, a drone that repeatedly flies over a sensitive facility, loiters, or exhibits evasive maneuvers might be flagged for closer scrutiny, even if its initial detection did not raise an immediate alarm. The integration of human operators remains crucial in this process. While automation can significantly enhance detection and initial classification, human expertise is often required for final threat assessment and decision-making, especially in ambiguous situations. The development of "digital battle management systems" that integrate all sensor inputs and present actionable intelligence to operators is central to this endeavor, enabling faster and more informed responses.

The operational environment significantly influences the choice and deployment of C-UAS detection technologies. Urban settings, with their complex clutter, numerous RF signals, and dense population, present different challenges than open rural areas or maritime environments. In urban environments, radar systems may need to employ advanced clutter rejection techniques, and EO/IR systems might be integrated with building-mounted sensors to overcome line-of-sight limitations. RF detection systems must be adept at filtering out legitimate signals from the vast electromagnetic spectrum. In open areas, longer-range radar and acoustic detection capabilities become more critical, while maritime operations may require specialized radar systems that can differentiate drones from sea clutter and employ specialized tracking algorithms for surface-following targets. The littoral zone, where land and sea meet, presents a complex hybrid environment requiring a combination of land-and sea-based C-UAS assets.

The continuous evolution of drone technology, including the advent of autonomous flight capabilities and the increasing sophistication of jamming and spoofing countermeasures, demands a perpetual cycle of innovation in detection and tracking technologies. This includes research into novel sensing modalities, such as laser-based detection systems or advanced waveform radar, as well as the refinement of artificial intelligence and machine learning algorithms to improve classification accuracy and reduce false alarm rates. The goal is to create a layered, resilient, and adaptive C-UAS detection architecture that can effectively counter the ever-expanding array of threats posed by unmanned aircraft systems. This layered approach, encompassing diverse technologies and intelligent fusion, is the cornerstone of maintaining airspace security against these increasingly pervasive aerial platforms.

The proliferation of digital infrastructure and the increasing reliance on networked systems for critical operations underscore the imperative of robust cyber domain monitoring and anomaly detection. This is not merely a technical consideration but a strategic necessity for any entity seeking to maintain operational integrity and security in the face of ever-evolving cyber threats. The cyber domain, encompassing all interconnected digital systems, networks, and the data they process, has become a primary battleground, susceptible to intrusions, data exfiltration, disruption, and manipulation. Effective defense hinges on the ability to not only prevent known threats but also to identify and respond to novel or sophisticated attacks that may bypass traditional signature-based defenses. This necessitates a paradigm shift from static defense postures to dynamic, continuously adaptive monitoring that can discern subtle deviations from normal operational behavior, which often serve as harbingers of malicious activity.

At the core of proactive cyber defense lies real-time network traffic analysis. This involves the continuous inspection and logging of data packets traversing an organization's networks. By examining the volume, origin, destination, protocol, and content of this traffic, security analysts can gain invaluable insights into network activity. Advanced Network Intrusion Detection and Prevention Systems (NIDPS) are at the forefront of this capability. Unlike passive Intrusion Detection Systems (IDS) that merely alert on suspicious activity, NIDPS actively intervene to block or mitigate detected threats in real-time. These systems employ a variety of techniques, including signature-based detection, which compares network traffic against a database of known attack patterns, and anomaly-based detection, which establishes a baseline of normal network behavior and flags significant deviations.

The latter is particularly crucial for identifying zero-day exploits or novel attack vectors that lack pre-defined signatures. Modern NIDPS leverage sophisticated deep packet inspection (DPI) capabilities, allowing them to examine the payload of data packets, not just their headers, to identify malicious code, unauthorized data transfers, or policy violations. The integration of machine learning and artificial intelligence is enhancing the efficacy of NIDPS, enabling them to adapt to evolving threat landscapes and reduce false positives by learning complex patterns of normal and malicious traffic. For instance, a sudden surge in outbound traffic to an unusual geographic location, utilizing an unexpected protocol, or the transfer of unusually large files, could all be indicative of data exfiltration attempts. Similarly, a proliferation of failed login attempts from an internal host to critical servers might signal a brute-force attack or an attempt to gain lateral movement within the network.

Beyond network-level monitoring, Endpoint Detection and Response (EDR) solutions provide deep visibility into the activity occurring on individual devices, such as servers, workstations, and mobile devices. In today's distributed and hybrid work environments, where the traditional network perimeter has become increasingly porous, endpoints represent critical points of vulnerability. EDR systems continuously collect and analyze data from endpoints, including process execution, file system activity, registry changes, and network connections. This telemetry is then correlated and analyzed to detect suspicious behaviors that might indicate the presence of malware, advanced persistent threats (APTs), or insider misuse. EDR solutions go beyond traditional antivirus software by not only detecting known threats but also by identifying unknown malicious activities through behavioral analysis.

When a potential threat is identified, EDR systems enable security teams to perform rapid investigations, understand the scope of the compromise, and execute remediation actions directly from the endpoint, such as isolating the device from the network, terminating malicious processes, or deleting infected files. For example, if an EDR system detects a previously unknown executable file attempting to modify critical system files, encrypt user data, or establish communication with a known command-and-control server, it can trigger an alert, allowing security personnel to investigate and respond. The ability to reconstruct the sequence of events leading up to and following a detected anomaly is paramount for understanding the attack methodology and preventing future occurrences.

Behavioral analytics forms the bedrock of effective anomaly detection in the cyber domain. Instead of relying solely on predefined rules or signatures, behavioral analytics focuses on understanding what constitutes "normal" behavior for users, devices, and applications within a given environment. This baseline is established through continuous monitoring and the application of statistical models and machine learning algorithms. Once a baseline is defined, any significant deviation from it can be flagged as a potential anomaly.

This approach is particularly effective against sophisticated threats that may not exhibit easily recognizable signatures. For example, a user who typically accesses only internal HR documents suddenly begins attempting to access sensitive financial records at odd hours, or a server that normally handles routine database queries starts making numerous outbound connections to unfamiliar external IP addresses, would both represent deviations from established behavioral patterns.

User and Entity Behavior Analytics (UEBA) platforms are specifically designed to aggregate data from various sources, including logs from firewalls, NIDPS, EDR systems, authentication servers, and even cloud applications, to build comprehensive profiles of user and system behavior. These platforms can detect subtle indicators of compromise, such as credential stuffing attacks, insider threats, or account takeovers, which might otherwise go unnoticed. The key challenge in behavioral analytics is the fine-tuning of models to minimize false positives while maximizing the detection of genuine threats. This often involves a collaborative effort between automated systems and human analysts who can provide context and validate alerts.

The implementation of these monitoring and detection capabilities must be tailored to the specific operational environment and threat profile of the installation. For a military installation, this might involve monitoring the convergence of operational technology (OT) and information technology (IT) networks. OT networks, which control physical processes like power grids, weapon systems, or environmental controls, often have different security requirements and legacy systems that may be more vulnerable to cyber-attack. Monitoring these interfaces and ensuring that they are not exploited as entry points into critical IT systems is paramount. Similarly, the monitoring of Industrial Control Systems (ICS) and Supervisory Control and Data Acquisition (SCADA) systems requires specialized tools and expertise, as a compromise in these areas could have devastating physical consequences.

The concept of "least privilege" is also critical. By ensuring that users and systems only have the access necessary to perform their functions, the potential attack surface is reduced, and anomalous behavior that indicates privilege escalation becomes more conspicuous. Furthermore, the dynamic nature of cyber threats necessitates continuous adaptation and updating of detection mechanisms.

Threat intelligence feeds, which provide real-time information on emerging threats, vulnerabilities, and attacker tactics, techniques, and procedures (TTPs), are essential for keeping monitoring systems relevant and effective. The integration of Security Orchestration, Automation, and Response (SOAR) platforms can further enhance the response to detected anomalies by automating routine tasks, enabling faster incident triage, and streamlining the investigation process. Ultimately, effective cyber domain monitoring and anomaly detection is a continuous cycle of observation, analysis, and adaptation, designed to identify and neutralize threats before they can cause significant damage or compromise critical operations.

The granularity of monitoring can be further enhanced through the diligent analysis of system logs and event data. Every interaction, transaction, and operation within an IT environment generates logs, records of what happened, when it happened, and who or what was involved. These logs, originating from operating systems, applications, security devices, and network infrastructure, represent a rich source of information for detecting anomalies. However, the sheer volume of log data generated by large and complex systems can be overwhelming without proper management and analysis tools. Security Information and Event Management (SIEM) systems play a pivotal role in this regard. SIEM platforms aggregate, correlate, and analyze log data from a multitude of sources, providing a centralized view of security events. By establishing correlation rules, SIEM systems can link seemingly disparate events into a coherent picture of a potential attack. For instance, a series of failed login attempts followed by a successful login from an unusual IP address, coupled with an elevated number of file access operations on sensitive data, could be correlated by a SIEM to identify a compromised account.

The effectiveness of SIEM systems is greatly amplified when integrated with advanced analytics, including machine learning, to identify patterns that might not be captured by static correlation rules. This allows for the detection of more sophisticated and subtle anomalies that indicate advanced persistent threats or insider misuse. The proactive analysis of these logs allows for the identification of precursor activities to an attack, enabling intervention before the actual exploitation occurs. For example, the discovery of reconnaissance activities, such as port scanning or vulnerability probing, within log data can serve as an early warning signal, prompting enhanced security measures.

The evolving threat landscape also necessitates a focus on proactive threat hunting. While detection systems are designed to flag known or anomalous activities, threat hunting involves the deliberate, iterative search through networks and systems for signs of malicious activity that may have evaded automated defenses. This is a proactive, hypothesis-driven process where security analysts, armed with their knowledge of attacker TTPs and advanced analytical tools, actively seek out threats. Threat hunting goes beyond simply responding to alerts; it involves actively exploring data for subtle indicators of compromise. This could involve searching for specific file hashes associated with known malware, identifying unusual registry modifications, or tracing the execution paths of suspicious processes.

The process often begins with a hypothesis, such as "an adversary may have gained initial access through a phishing email and is now attempting to move laterally." The analyst then uses various tools and data sources, including endpoint telemetry, network traffic logs, and threat intelligence, to validate or refute this hypothesis. Effective threat hunting requires a deep understanding of system internals, network protocols, and attacker methodologies. It also relies on the availability of rich, historical data that can be queried and analyzed. The insights gained from threat hunting exercises are invaluable, not only for discovering and eradicating existing threats but also for improving the organization's overall security posture by identifying gaps in existing defenses and refining detection capabilities. For instance, a successful threat hunt might uncover a previously unknown variant of malware or a novel lateral movement technique, which can then be used to update signature-based detection rules or enhance behavioral analytics models.

The integration of cloud security monitoring is also paramount in contemporary cyber defense. As organizations increasingly adopt cloud computing services, the cyber domain expands to encompass these distributed environments. Cloud-native security tools and services, offered by cloud providers, alongside third-party cloud security solutions, are essential for monitoring cloud infrastructure, applications, and data. This includes monitoring access logs, configuration changes, network flows within virtual private clouds (VPCs), and the security posture of cloud-based workloads. Anomalies in the cloud environment can manifest as unauthorized access to sensitive data stored in cloud storage, the deployment of unauthorized virtual machines, or unusual API call patterns. Cloud Security Posture Management (CSPM) tools, for example, continuously assess cloud environments for misconfigurations and compliance risks, which can be significant entry points for attackers. Similarly, Cloud Workload Protection Platforms (CWPP) focus on securing the workloads running in the cloud, providing visibility and threat detection at the instance or container level. The ability to correlate activity across on-premises and cloud environments is crucial for a comprehensive understanding of the overall cyber threat landscape, especially in hybrid cloud architectures. An anomaly detected in a cloud service, such as a sudden spike in outbound data transfer from a sensitive data repository, could be a critical indicator of a data breach.

The human element remains an indispensable component of cyber domain monitoring and anomaly detection. While technology provides the tools and capabilities, it is the skilled cybersecurity professionals who interpret the data, validate alerts, conduct investigations, and make critical decisions. Continuous training and skill development are essential to keep pace with the rapidly evolving threat landscape. This includes training in areas such as digital forensics, incident response, malware analysis, and threat intelligence analysis. Fostering a culture of security awareness among all personnel is also crucial, as many cyber-attacks begin with social engineering tactics targeting individuals. By combining advanced technological solutions with skilled human expertise and a strong security culture, organizations can build a robust and resilient cyber defense that can effectively monitor their digital domain, detect anomalies, and respond decisively to emerging threats. The objective is to create a state of persistent vigilance, where the cyber domain is continuously scrutinized for deviations from normal behavior, allowing for swift and effective mitigation of potential compromises.

The integration of Artificial Intelligence (AI) and Machine Learning (ML) represents a profound evolution in the domain of threat identification, fundamentally reshaping how sensors collect, process, and interpret data. These advanced computational techniques move beyond the limitations of traditional, rule-based systems, enabling a more dynamic, adaptive, and predictive approach to discerning malicious activities from benign signals. The sheer volume and velocity of data generated by modern sensor networks, ranging from sophisticated radar and acoustic arrays to cyber-monitoring tools and even passive visual sensors, have rendered manual analysis increasingly untenable. AI and ML offer the promise of automating much of this analysis, accelerating the identification, classification, and tracking of threats with a level of speed and accuracy previously unattainable, thereby significantly reducing the cognitive load on human operators and enhancing overall situational awareness.

At its core, AI/ML-driven threat identification leverages algorithms that can learn from vast datasets to identify patterns, anomalies, and specific signatures indicative of threats. Unlike conventional systems that rely on predefined rules or known threat signatures, ML models can discern subtle correlations and emergent behaviors that might elude human analysts or static detection mechanisms. This learning capability is particularly crucial in dynamic environments where threat actors constantly adapt their tactics, techniques, and procedures (TTPs). For instance, in the realm of drone detection, AI algorithms trained on diverse datasets of aerial objects can learn to differentiate between common objects like birds, weather balloons, or commercial aircraft and the more illicit presence of unmanned aerial systems (UAS).

These algorithms can analyze characteristics such as flight path predictability, acoustic signatures, thermal profiles, and radar cross-sections. A flapping wing pattern and erratic flight would be recognized as avian, whereas a consistent, albeit sometimes unpredictable, vector and a distinct rotor or jet sound profile could flag a drone. ML can be employed to classify the type of drone based on its observed characteristics, aiding in the assessment of its potential threat level, distinguishing a small, recreational drone from a larger, more sophisticated military-grade UAS. This level of nuanced classification is critical for prioritizing responses and allocating resources effectively.

The application of AI/ML extends powerfully into the cyber domain, complementing the network and endpoint monitoring discussed previously. In this context, AI algorithms can analyze network traffic, system logs, and user behavior for subtle indicators of compromise that may not trigger traditional alerts. For example, ML models can establish a baseline of normal network communication patterns, identifying deviations such as unusual data exfiltration routes, the emergence of covert channels, or anomalous communication protocols used by malware. By continuously learning and adapting to the network's specific traffic flows and user activities, these models can detect sophisticated, zero-day exploits or novel attack vectors that lack known signatures.

One practical application involves the identification of phishing attempts or social engineering tactics. AI can analyze email content, sender reputation, linguistic patterns, and link destinations with greater speed and scale than human review. It can identify subtle linguistic anomalies, unusual requests, or suspicious URLs that might indicate a phishing email. Moreover, ML can analyze the sequence of user actions following an initial interaction. If a user clicks on a suspicious link and subsequently exhibits unusual file access patterns or attempts to establish unauthorized network connections, an ML model can correlate these events, raising a higher-fidelity alert for a potential compromise. This proactive identification of cyber threats, based on learned patterns of malicious activity, significantly enhances an organization's resilience against evolving cyber warfare tactics.

Beyond classifying known threats, AI and ML are revolutionizing the identification of novel or unknown threats by focusing on anomalous behavior. This is particularly vital in sensor fusion scenarios where data from multiple disparate sources needs to be integrated and analyzed holistically. For instance, consider a scenario involving a large military installation. Acoustic sensors might pick up unusual sounds in a restricted area, while thermal cameras detect an anomaly at the perimeter, and motion sensors register unexpected activity. Individually, each of these alerts might be low-priority or even a false positive. However, an AI system, capable of fusing and analyzing these disparate data streams in real-time, can identify the correlation between these events. The acoustic anomaly might be identified as the sound of a non-standard engine, the thermal signature could correspond to a person or a small vehicle operating outside designated hours, and the motion detection confirms movement. The AI can then assess the spatial and temporal proximity of these events and based on learned patterns of adversarial reconnaissance or intrusion, flag this confluence as a high-confidence threat. This ability to correlate seemingly unrelated sensor inputs and identify emergent anomalous patterns is a significant leap forward from traditional, siloed alert systems.

The accuracy and speed offered by AI/ML are particularly impactful in time-critical scenarios. In a contested airspace or a naval environment, the ability to rapidly distinguish between friendly, neutral, and hostile entities is paramount. Radar systems, for example, generate vast amounts of data regarding the size, speed, altitude, and trajectory of objects. ML algorithms can process this data far more quickly than human operators, identifying subtle anomalies in radar signatures that might indicate the presence of stealthy aircraft or unmanned vehicles designed to evade traditional detection methods. AI can be trained to recognize characteristic movement patterns associated with different types of platforms. A predictable, steady flight path might indicate a commercial aircraft, while a highly agile, evasive maneuver could suggest a military jet or a drone employing electronic countermeasures. The classification and tracking of these objects are then continuously refined by the AI, providing operators with a more reliable and actionable understanding of the operational picture. This is not about replacing human judgment but about augmenting it, by filtering out noise, highlighting potential threats, and presenting information in a clear, concise manner that allows human decision-makers to focus on strategic response rather than minutiae of data processing.

The challenge of distinguishing between legitimate activity and malicious intent is also addressed by ML's capacity for learning context. In communication networks, for example, an ML model can learn the typical communication patterns of specific units or individuals. A sudden, unexplained surge in communication traffic from a particular node, or an unusual frequency of data transfers to an external entity, can be flagged. This is especially relevant when considering insider threats or compromised accounts. If a user who typically accesses only administrative documents suddenly begins downloading large volumes of classified intelligence, an ML system, having learned the user's normal behavior profile, can identify this deviation as highly anomalous and indicative of potential malicious activity or a compromised credential. The system can then initiate a more detailed investigation, potentially isolating the user's account or device pending human review. This contextual understanding allows for a reduction in false positives, as the AI can differentiate between a genuine emergency requiring unusual data access and a deliberate attempt to exfiltrate sensitive information.

AI and ML are instrumental in optimizing the performance and efficiency of sensor networks themselves. Predictive maintenance algorithms can analyze sensor data to identify potential malfunctions or degradation before they impact performance, ensuring the continuous availability of critical surveillance capabilities. ML can also be used to dynamically adjust sensor parameters based on the prevailing environment and identified threats. For instance, in a noisy electromagnetic spectrum, an AI could optimize the settings of a radio frequency detection system to improve signal-to-noise ratio and enhance the detection of covert transmissions. Similarly, in an optical surveillance scenario, an AI could dynamically adjust camera focus, zoom, and filtering based on atmospheric conditions and the type of object being tracked, ensuring the clearest possible imagery for identification. This adaptive optimization of sensor capabilities contributes to a more robust and resilient threat identification framework.

The application of AI/ML in threat identification also necessitates careful consideration of the data used for training these models. Bias in training data can lead to skewed outcomes, where the AI might misclassify certain objects or activities, potentially overlooking specific types of threats or wrongly flagging benign ones. For instance, if a drone detection system is primarily trained on data from a specific geographic region with a particular set of drone models, it might struggle to accurately identify novel drone designs encountered elsewhere. Therefore, the ongoing curation and expansion of diverse, representative datasets are crucial for ensuring the accuracy and reliability of AI/ML-powered threat identification systems. This involves continuously feeding new data, including adversarial examples and real-world operational data, into the training pipelines to allow the models to adapt and improve over time. The development of adversarial ML techniques, which aim to trick AI systems into misclassifying data, also highlights the need for robust defenses and continuous retraining of models to counter such sophisticated attacks.

The infusion of AI and ML into sensor-based threat identification represents a paradigm shift, moving from reactive, signature-based detection to proactive, behavior-based identification and prediction. These technologies enable systems to process and interpret vast quantities of sensor data with unprecedented speed and accuracy, distinguishing between friendly, neutral, and hostile entities, identifying novel threats, and recognizing subtle indicators of compromise across physical and cyber domains. By automating complex analytical tasks, reducing operator workload, and enhancing the precision of threat classification and tracking, AI/ML empowers more effective and efficient responses, ultimately bolstering the security posture and operational effectiveness of any organization reliant on advanced situational awareness. The continued research and development in this field promise even more sophisticated capabilities, further solidifying AI/ML as indispensable tools in the modern threat identification landscape.

The aggregation and synthesis of disparate data streams from advanced sensor networks converge on a singular, critical objective: the creation of a Common Operational Picture (COP). This COP is not merely a collection of raw data points; rather, it is a dynamic, integrated, and continuously updated representation of the entire operational environment, offering a unified and unambiguous understanding of the security status of an installation, a battlespace, or any area of interest. It represents the apex of advanced sensing capabilities, transforming the deluge of information from individual sensors into actionable intelligence readily accessible to decision-makers. The journey from myriad, often independently operating, sensors to a coherent COP involves sophisticated data fusion techniques, a process that transcends simple aggregation to achieve a synergistic understanding far greater than the sum of its individual parts.

Data fusion, in the context of developing a COP, is the process of combining data and information from multiple sources to achieve improved accuracy and more definitive conclusions than would be possible when these sources were used individually. This process can be broken down into several levels, each building upon the last to progressively refine the understanding of the environment. At the most fundamental level is signal-level fusion, where raw data from sensors is combined. For instance, multiple acoustic sensors detecting faint sounds might have their signals amplified and combined to discern a pattern that would be lost if analyzed in isolation. This is often followed by feature-level fusion, where extracted features from different sensor types are combined. A radar might provide range and bearing, while an infrared sensor offers a thermal signature, and an optical camera provides a visual confirmation. Fusing these features allows for a more robust identification of an object, as cross-referencing thermal characteristics with visual morphology and radar profile can confirm or deny initial identifications with higher confidence.

Moving up the hierarchy, decision-level fusion or object-level fusion involves combining the outputs of individual target detection and classification algorithms from various sensors. If a radar identifies a fast-moving object, an electro-optical sensor classifies it as a drone, and an electronic intelligence system detects a specific drone communication frequency, these independent decisions can be fused. This fusion process, often orchestrated by AI and machine learning algorithms, assesses the consistency and credibility of these individual reports. For example, if all sensors independently point to the same object and agree on its trajectory and classification, the confidence level in that fused track increases dramatically. Conversely, discrepancies might trigger further scrutiny or highlight potential sensor errors or spoofing attempts. The goal here is to create a single, coherent track for each entity of interest, minimizing duplication and reducing the ambiguity that can arise from single-source reporting.

The ultimate aim of these fusion processes is the creation of the Common Operational Picture. The COP is the visual manifestation of this fused data, presented on a user-friendly interface that allows commanders and operators to comprehend the complex tapestry of their environment at a glance. It is a digital map or display that overlays information from all contributing sensor domains, radar, sonar, electro-optical, infrared, signals intelligence, cyber monitoring, and even human intelligence reports, onto a common geospatial reference. This unified display eliminates the need for operators to mentally correlate information from multiple, disparate screens or reports, a process that is not only time-consuming but also prone to error, especially under the pressures of high-stakes operations.

The COP is designed to provide an intuitive and comprehensive overview. Imagine a scenario at a critical infrastructure facility. The COP might display the perimeter fence, with sensors indicating its integrity. Motion detectors at specific points might show activity, with alphanumeric codes identifying the sensor. Thermal cameras could highlight heat signatures near a vulnerable access point, perhaps indicating a human presence obscured by foliage. Radar could show an unidentified aerial object approaching the airspace, while sonar might detect unusual underwater activity near a water intake. Cyber sensors could be flagging anomalous network traffic originating from within the facility's IT infrastructure. All of this information is not presented as a chaotic jumble of alerts. Instead, it is intelligently integrated. The radar track of the aerial object would be displayed as a moving icon, its trajectory and predicted path clearly indicated. The thermal anomaly would be depicted as a distinct colored area on the ground, with associated data on its size and intensity. The sonar contacts would appear as symbols on the water surface or subsurface, showing their movement patterns. The network anomalies would be represented by alerts or status indicators on a digital representation of the facility's network architecture.

A crucial aspect of an effective COP is its user-centric design. The "common" in Common Operational Picture refers not only to the shared data but also to the shared understanding fostered by a well-designed interface. Decision-makers at different levels require different levels of detail and different perspectives. A tactical commander on the ground might need a highly detailed, localized view showing immediate threats and personnel locations, while a strategic commander overseeing a much larger area might require a broader overview, focusing on trends, major force dispositions, and strategic vulnerabilities. Therefore, the COP must be highly customizable. Users should be able to tailor the display to their specific needs, selecting which sensor feeds are displayed, adjusting the level of detail, and choosing the types of information prioritized. This might involve filtering out low-priority alerts to reduce cognitive clutter, focusing only on credible threats, or highlighting specific types of activity, such as unauthorized vehicular movement or the presence of specific electronic emissions.

The ability to zoom in on specific areas of concern is essential. If the radar detects a potential incoming threat, the operator can zoom into that sector of the COP, bringing up higher-resolution imagery from electro-optical and infrared sensors, along with detailed tracking data, and potentially even signals intelligence information that might help identify the object's origin or intent. The interface should allow for the rapid display of associated metadata for any displayed object or alert. Clicking on a radar track, for instance, could bring up a pop-up window detailing its speed, altitude, course, estimated size, and the confidence level of the track. Similarly, clicking on a cyber alert might reveal the source IP address, the type of anomaly detected, the affected systems, and the potential impact.

The COP must facilitate situational understanding, not just situational awareness. Awareness is knowing that something is happening; understanding is knowing what it means and what the implications are. This is where AI and ML play an increasingly vital role within the COP environment. Beyond simply displaying fused data, the COP can leverage AI to provide context and predictive analysis. For example, if multiple sensors indicate the movement of an unknown entity towards a sensitive area, the AI integrated into the COP might not only highlight the threat but also predict its likely course of action, potential targets, and the associated risk level. It could also suggest potential countermeasures or alert relevant response teams. The AI can correlate the detected activity with known threat patterns, intelligence databases, and even historical data to provide a richer, more insightful understanding of the situation.

The concept of "persistence" is also critical for a functional COP. The operational environment is not static. Threats evolve, movements occur, and conditions change. The COP must reflect this dynamism in real-time. Updates from sensors need to be processed and integrated instantaneously, ensuring that the picture remains current. This requires robust communication networks capable of handling high volumes of data and powerful processing capabilities to manage the fusion and display. Delays in data processing or transmission can render the COP obsolete, leading to critical decision-making based on outdated or incomplete information. The COP, therefore, acts as a living document, constantly being rewritten by the flow of real-time data.

The development of a COP is not a one-size-fits-all endeavor. The specific requirements will vary depending on the mission, the environment, and the resources available. For a forward operating base, the COP might focus on immediate perimeter security, entry control points, and the immediate surrounding terrain. For a naval vessel, it would encompass air, surface, and subsurface threats, as well as the vessel's own operational status and the status of supporting assets. In a cyber operations center, the COP would be a visualization of the network infrastructure, the flow of data, and the status of security controls, highlighting anomalies and potential intrusion points. Regardless of the specific application, the underlying principles of data fusion, integration, and user-focused presentation remain constant.

The importance of a well-executed COP cannot be overstated. It is the foundation upon which effective command and control are built. It empowers commanders to make informed decisions rapidly, allocate resources effectively, and direct operations with confidence. In an era of increasingly complex and rapidly evolving threats, the ability to see, understand, and act upon the operational environment through a unified and comprehensive COP is no longer a luxury; it is an absolute necessity for maintaining security and achieving mission success. The constant drive for more sophisticated sensors, advanced algorithms for data fusion, and intuitive interfaces for visualization are all aimed at perfecting this critical capability, ensuring that the human element remains at the center of decision-making, armed with the most complete and accurate understanding possible. The future of situational awareness lies in the seamless integration of technology to provide that perfect, real-time clarity.

Chapter 5: Defensive Systems: Countering Diverse Threats

The escalating proliferation of Unmanned Aircraft Systems (UAS), commonly referred to as drones, has introduced a multifaceted and increasingly sophisticated threat landscape. These aerial platforms, ranging from hobbyist quadcopters to advanced military-grade systems, possess the capability to conduct reconnaissance, deliver payloads, and even engage in swarm tactics, presenting significant challenges to traditional air defense architectures. Consequently, the development and integration of effective Counter-Unmanned Aircraft Systems (C-UAS) have become a paramount concern for military and security organizations worldwide. The efficacy of C-UAS operations hinges not on a single technology, but on the synergistic deployment of an array of integrated systems, designed to detect, track, identify, and neutralize UAS threats across the entire spectrum of their operational envelope.

The strategic imperative for integrated C-UAS systems arises from the inherent limitations of any single-point solution. A UAS, particularly a small or medium-sized one, presents a difficult target for conventional radar systems designed for larger aircraft. Its low radar cross-section, slow speed, and often erratic flight paths can allow it to evade detection or be misclassified as a bird or other environmental clutter. Similarly, optical or infrared sensors, while effective in certain conditions, can be hampered by weather, camouflage, or the sheer visual disparity of a small drone against a complex background. Electronic warfare systems might be adept at disrupting communications, but a pre-programmed or autonomous drone might not be susceptible to such measures. This necessitates a layered approach, where different sensor and effector technologies complement each other to create a robust and resilient defense network.

The foundation of any effective C-UAS strategy lies in comprehensive detection and tracking. This often begins with radar systems, specifically those optimized for detecting small, low-flying targets. Advanced multi-mode radars, capable of operating in various frequencies and modes, can be employed to scan designated airspace volumes. These radars are often augmented by specialized C-UAS software that employs sophisticated algorithms to distinguish drone signatures from other airborne objects. Complementing radar are electro-optical (EO) and infrared (IR) sensors. These visual spectrum and thermal imaging systems can provide positive identification of detected objects, crucial for differentiating between a drone and a bird or other natural phenomena. High-resolution cameras with advanced zoom capabilities can provide detailed imagery, while thermal sensors can detect the heat signature of the drone's motors and electronics, even in low-light conditions or against complex backgrounds.

Acoustic sensors also play a role, particularly for detecting the characteristic sound signatures of UAS rotors. While individual acoustic sensors might have limited range, a distributed network of microphones can triangulate the source of the sound, providing an additional cue for other sensor systems. Radio Frequency (RF) detection systems are equally vital, as many UAS rely on radio links for control and data transmission. These systems can detect the presence of RF signals associated with common drone control frequencies and telemetry. By analyzing the direction, type, and intensity of these signals, RF detection can provide early warning and help pinpoint the location of the UAS operator or the drone itself. The fusion of data from these disparate sensor types is critical, as it allows for a more confident and accurate assessment of potential threats. A radar detection might be corroborated by an RF signal and a visual confirmation from an EO camera, significantly increasing the probability that an actual UAS threat is present and providing precise location and trajectory data.

Once a UAS is detected and tracked, the next critical phase is identification and classification. This is where the distinction between a friendly drone, a commercial drone operating in controlled airspace, and a hostile threat becomes paramount. Data fusion algorithms, often powered by artificial intelligence (AI) and machine learning (ML), are indispensable in this process. By correlating sensor data with known UAS profiles, flight behaviors, and intelligence databases, these algorithms can rapidly classify a detected object. This classification might include the type of drone, its potential capabilities (e.g., payload capacity), and its likely intent based on its flight path and behavior. For instance, a drone loitering near a sensitive area might be flagged as a higher-priority threat than one simply transiting through an open area.

With a confirmed threat identified, the C-UAS system must then employ an appropriate effector to neutralize it. The range of effector technologies is diverse, encompassing both non-kinetic and kinetic solutions, each with its own advantages and disadvantages. Non-kinetic effectors focus on disrupting the drone's ability to operate without physically destroying it. Electronic jamming is a common tactic, where the C-UAS system broadcasts radio frequency signals to interfere with the drone's control link or GPS navigation. This can cause the drone to lose its connection to the operator, return to its launch point (if equipped with a "return-to-home" function), or land in place. Jamming can have unintended consequences, potentially disrupting legitimate communications in the vicinity, and is often less effective against drones operating autonomously or on pre-programmed flight paths.

A more sophisticated non-kinetic approach is spoofing. This involves transmitting false GPS signals to the drone, tricking it into believing it is somewhere else, or broadcasting counterfeit control signals that allow the C-UAS operator to take control of the drone or redirect it. Spoofing requires a deep understanding of drone communication protocols and navigation systems and can be highly effective but also technically complex to implement. Another non-kinetic method involves directed energy, specifically high-power microwaves (HPM). HPM weapons emit focused beams of microwave energy that can overload and damage the drone's electronic components, rendering it inoperable. These systems offer a rapid, "soft kill" capability that can neutralize multiple drones simultaneously within their effective range.

Kinetic effectors, on the other hand, aim to physically destroy the UAS. This can range from traditional methods adapted for C-UAS to highly specialized systems. Interceptor drones are a rapidly developing option, where a C-UAS drone is launched to intercept and physically disable or destroy the threat drone, often through a mid-air collision or by deploying a net. This offers a mobile and flexible kinetic solution. Specialized munitions, such as networked or guided munitions designed to engage small, fast-moving aerial targets, can also be employed. These might include airburst munitions that detonate above a drone, showering it with shrapnel, or precision-guided missiles.

Perhaps the most cutting-edge kinetic C-UAS technology is directed energy weapons (DEWs) in the form of lasers. High-energy lasers (HEL) can deliver a concentrated beam of light to a specific point on the drone, rapidly heating and burning through its airframe or critical components, such as wings or control surfaces. Lasers offer the advantage of speed-of-light engagement, virtually unlimited magazine depth (as long as power is available), and high precision, minimizing collateral damage. Their effectiveness can be degraded by atmospheric conditions like fog, rain, or smoke, and they typically require a precise and sustained aim on the target. The integration of these diverse effectors into a cohesive C-UAS system is crucial. For instance, a system might first attempt to disrupt a drone with electronic jamming. If jamming proves ineffective, it could then transition to a laser system for a kinetic neutralization. This layered approach ensures that the most appropriate and effective countermeasure is applied based on the specific threat and environmental conditions.

The strategic considerations for selecting and integrating these C-UAS systems are multifaceted. Layered defense is the cornerstone principle. This means establishing overlapping fields of detection, tracking, and engagement that cover all potential ingress routes and altitudes. A typical layered defense might include long-range surveillance radars and RF sensors to provide early warning, followed by medium-range EO/IR and acoustic sensors for closer-in detection and identification. The effector layer would then be positioned to engage threats identified by the sensor network, with different effectors optimized for different ranges and threat types. For example, long-range effectors like HPM or certain missile systems might be used to engage threats at a distance, while close-in defense might rely on lasers or interceptor drones.

Operational effectiveness is paramount. This involves ensuring that the integrated C-UAS system can reliably detect and neutralize threats in the specific operational environment. Factors such as the size of the area to be protected, the expected types of UAS threats, the density of civilian air traffic, and the surrounding terrain all influence system selection and deployment. For instance, defending a large, open airfield will require different systems and deployment strategies than protecting a densely populated urban center or a forward operating base in a mountainous region. The ability of the system to operate autonomously or with minimal operator intervention is also increasingly important, especially in scenarios where rapid response is critical.

Minimizing collateral damage is a non-negotiable requirement, especially in civilian or mixed-use environments. Kinetic effectors, if not precisely controlled, pose a risk of dropping debris or impacting unintended targets. Therefore, C-UAS systems must incorporate advanced targeting and fail-safe mechanisms. Directed energy weapons, with their inherent precision, often offer an advantage in this regard, as they can neutralize a threat without creating falling debris. Non-kinetic methods, such as jamming or spoofing, are generally considered to have a lower risk of collateral damage, although their effectiveness can be limited. The integration of robust identification friend or foe (IFF) systems and continuous monitoring of the airspace to avoid engaging friendly or civilian drones is also crucial for responsible C-UAS operations.

The integration of C-UAS systems is not a static undertaking; it is a continuous process of adaptation and evolution. As UAS technology advances, so too must the counter-measures. The emergence of sophisticated autonomous drones, AI-driven swarming capabilities, and novel flight platforms necessitates ongoing research and development in C-UAS technologies. Furthermore, the legal and ethical frameworks governing the use of C-UAS systems, particularly concerning their employment in civilian airspace, must be carefully considered and continuously refined. The goal is to create a defense that is both technologically capable and operationally responsible, ensuring the security of critical assets and personnel without compromising broader safety and security objectives.

The tactical employment of integrated C-UAS systems often involves a combination of fixed and mobile assets. Fixed installations, such as military bases, airports, or critical infrastructure sites, can be protected by permanently emplaced sensor suites and effector systems, offering continuous surveillance and defense. Mobile C-UAS platforms, mounted on vehicles, vessels, or even carried by personnel, provide flexibility and the ability to rapidly deploy defenses to areas of immediate concern or to accompany moving forces. This hybrid approach ensures comprehensive coverage, adapting to the dynamic nature of modern security challenges.

The operational doctrine for integrated C-UAS often emphasizes a "detect-decide-act" loop, where the speed and accuracy of each step are critical. Advanced command and control (C2) systems are vital for orchestrating the symphony of sensors and effectors. These C2 systems ingest data from all detection sources, fuse it into a coherent operational picture, and present threat information to operators. Based on pre-defined rules of engagement and real-time threat assessment, the C2 system can then recommend or automatically initiate the appropriate countermeasure. This automation is key to overcoming the speed at which many UAS threats can operate, ensuring that a response is initiated before a drone can achieve its objective.

The integration of C-UAS into broader air defense networks is becoming increasingly important. By sharing data and coordinating responses with traditional air defense systems, C-UAS can enhance overall airspace security. This integration allows for a more efficient allocation of resources, ensuring that high-value assets are protected by the most appropriate systems and that limited resources are not wasted on engaging low-priority threats with high-end weaponry. The C-UAS capability serves as a vital lower-tier defense, filtering out simpler threats and allowing traditional air defense systems to focus on more significant aerial adversaries.

The spectrum of UAS threats is not monolithic. It includes everything from commercial off-the-shelf (COTS) drones modified for malicious purposes, to sophisticated state-sponsored systems designed for espionage or attack. Each type of threat demands a tailored response. COTS drones, often controlled via Wi-Fi or Bluetooth, are susceptible to jamming and spoofing. More advanced drones, employing encrypted communication links or operating autonomously, require more sophisticated EW capabilities or kinetic neutralization. Swarming UAS present a particularly daunting challenge, as they can overwhelm traditional single-target engagement systems. Integrated C-UAS strategies must therefore incorporate the capability to detect, track, and engage multiple targets simultaneously, often employing area-effect effectors or high-volume kinetic responses.

The development of C-UAS technologies is in a state of rapid evolution, driven by continuous innovation in drone technology itself. The miniaturization of sensors and actuators, the advancement of battery technology, and the increasing autonomy and intelligence of UAS platforms all contribute to the escalating challenge. In response, C-UAS systems are also becoming more sophisticated, leveraging AI for improved detection and classification, developing more precise and efficient directed energy weapons, and exploring novel countermeasures such as cyber-attack vectors against UAS command and control systems. The ongoing arms race between UAS and C-UAS developers ensures that the landscape of aerial threats and defenses will remain dynamic and challenging for the foreseeable future. The success of future C-UAS operations will depend on the ability to anticipate these technological advancements and integrate them into robust, adaptable, and layered defense architectures.

Directed energy (DE) weapons represent a paradigm shift in defensive capabilities, moving beyond traditional kinetic or electronic warfare methods to offer novel and often highly precise means of neutralizing threats. These systems harness concentrated forms of energy – typically electromagnetic radiation or particle beams – to inflict damage or disrupt the function of targets. Within the context of installation protection, DE technologies, primarily high-energy lasers (HEL) and high-power microwaves (HPM), are emerging as critical components of layered defense strategies. Their unique characteristics offer distinct advantages over conventional countermeasures, particularly against the growing threat posed by unmanned aerial systems (UAS) but also present their own set of operational considerations.

The core appeal of directed energy weapons lies in their fundamental operational principles. Laser systems, for instance, deliver a concentrated beam of photons that, when focused on a specific point on a target, rapidly transfer energy. This energy absorption leads to a dramatic increase in temperature, causing materials to melt, burn, or vaporize. The effectiveness of a laser system is contingent on several factors, including the power output of the laser, the wavelength of the light (which affects absorption by different materials), the beam quality (how tightly focused the beam can be), and atmospheric conditions that can scatter or absorb the laser energy. For anti-UAS applications, a HEL system can be aimed at critical components of a drone, such as its wings, control surfaces, or sensors. A sustained, precise beam can cause structural failure or disable navigation and targeting systems, leading to the drone's loss of control and subsequent incapacitation. The speed of light engagement is a significant tactical advantage;

once the laser is fired, the energy reaches the target almost instantaneously, drastically reducing the time between detection and effect compared to projectile-based systems. This is particularly crucial for rapidly moving or agile threats.

High-power microwave (HPM) weapons, on the other hand, operate on a different principle. Instead of a focused beam of light, HPM systems generate intense bursts of microwave radiation. This energy can induce damaging electrical currents in conductive materials, particularly in electronic circuits. When an HPM beam is directed at a drone, it can overwhelm and damage the sensitive electronic components within its control systems, navigation equipment, sensors, or even its power supply. This effectively results in an electronic "kill" of the system, rendering it inoperable without necessarily causing physical destruction to the drone's airframe. HPM weapons can be particularly effective against multiple targets simultaneously or against targets that are difficult to physically engage with lasers or projectiles, such as swarms of smaller drones. The energy pulse can propagate through the airframe and directly interfere with internal electronics.

The applications of DE weapons for installation protection are diverse and expanding. One of the most prominent use cases is countering the ever-present threat of drones. Drones, from small commercial models to larger military variants, can be employed for reconnaissance, surveillance, payload delivery (including explosive devices), or even as swarming attackers. Traditional defense systems can struggle to effectively and cost-efficiently counter these threats. Kinetic interceptors, such as missiles or bullets, are expensive on a per-shot basis and can create collateral damage from falling debris. Electronic jamming, while effective against some drones, is often restricted in its operational range and can be ineffective against autonomous or pre-programmed systems. DE weapons offer a compelling alternative. A HEL system can precisely target and neutralize a single drone, while an HPM weapon can potentially disrupt multiple drones within its coverage area. The "magazine depth" of DE weapons is a significant advantage; unlike kinetic weapons that are limited by the number of rounds carried, DE systems are primarily constrained by their power supply. As long as there is energy available, they can continue to engage targets. This makes them highly suitable for sustained defense operations or against persistent threats.

Beyond drones, DE technologies are being explored for their potential against other threats. Advanced surveillance and targeting sensors, crucial for adversary operations, could be vulnerable to DE effects. A precisely aimed laser could blind or damage optical sensors, rendering them useless. Similarly, HPM energy could disrupt or disable electronic reconnaissance equipment. While current capabilities are largely focused on UAS, the research and development trajectory suggests future applications against more substantial airborne threats, potentially including cruise missiles or even certain types of aircraft, though this would require significantly higher power levels and more sophisticated targeting. The ability to selectively engage threats, minimizing collateral damage, is a key selling point for DE systems in protecting sensitive installations. A laser can be aimed with extreme precision, ensuring that only the intended target is affected, a critical factor when operating in or near civilian airspace or populated areas.

The deployment and operational effectiveness of DE weapons are not without their challenges. Atmospheric conditions represent a significant operational consideration. For HEL systems, phenomena such as fog, rain, dust, smoke, and even turbulence can scatter, absorb, or refract the laser beam, significantly reducing its power and effectiveness at the target. This means that laser systems may perform optimally in clear, dry weather but can be degraded in adverse conditions. While advanced beam control technologies and adaptive optics are being developed to mitigate these effects, they remain a limitation. HPM weapons are generally less susceptible to atmospheric degradation than lasers, but their effectiveness can still be influenced by environmental factors and the specific shielding or construction of the target.

Another key challenge is the power requirement. High-energy lasers and HPM systems demand substantial amounts of electrical power, often necessitating robust and dedicated power generation and distribution infrastructure. This can limit the mobility and deploy-ability of such systems, making them more suited for fixed or semi-fixed installations rather than highly mobile battlefield roles, though advancements in compact power sources are continually being made. The thermal management of DE weapons is also critical. High-power energy generation produces significant heat, requiring effective cooling systems to prevent the weapon from overheating and to maintain optimal operational performance.

The cost of DE weapon systems, particularly in their current developmental stages, can also be a factor. While the per-engagement cost might be low compared to traditional munitions, the initial acquisition and integration costs of sophisticated DE systems can be substantial. Furthermore, the training of personnel to operate and maintain these complex systems is an ongoing requirement. Safety protocols are also paramount. The intense energy output of DE weapons necessitates stringent safety measures to protect operators, support personnel, and civilians from accidental exposure to laser radiation or microwave energy.

Despite these challenges, the trajectory of DE technology is one of rapid advancement. Researchers are continuously improving laser efficiency, increasing power outputs, and developing more robust beam control systems. Similarly, HPM technology is benefiting from advances in solid-state electronics and pulsed power technology, leading to more compact and effective systems. The integration of DE weapons into existing air defense networks is also a key area of development. By fusing data from various sensors and coordinating DE engagement with other defensive assets, a more comprehensive and resilient protection capability can be achieved. For example, a DE system might be tasked with neutralizing drones that evade or saturate initial electronic warfare defenses, or it might be used to disable sensors on a more significant threat to allow kinetic systems to engage more effectively. The ongoing evolution of DE technology promises to make it an indispensable element of future defensive architectures, offering a versatile, precise, and powerful means of countering a wide spectrum of emerging threats. The capability for "soft kill" (disabling without destruction) also offers advantages in situations where complete destruction might be undesirable, such as when attempting to capture intact enemy technology or avoid creating hazardous debris. As DE systems mature, their cost-effectiveness is expected to improve, making them increasingly viable for a broader range of applications and operational environments.

The imperative for a resilient installation in the modern security landscape is inextricably linked to the strength and sophistication of its cyber defenses. As threats evolve from physical intrusions to sophisticated digital assaults, the architecture of an installation's cyber defenses must transcend basic perimeter protection and embrace a multi-layered, adaptive approach. This requires not merely deploying individual security tools, but meticulously designing and implementing a cohesive architectural framework that anticipates, detects, and neutralizes a broad spectrum of cyber threats. Such robustness is not a static achievement but a dynamic process, demanding continuous vigilance, strategic adaptation, and an unwavering commitment to operational integrity.

A cornerstone of any robust cyber defense architecture is network segmentation. This principle involves dividing a larger network into smaller, isolated subnetworks, or segments. The primary goal is to limit the lateral movement of threats. If an attacker manages to breach one segment, the segmentation acts as a barrier, preventing them from easily accessing other, potentially more sensitive, parts of the network. Imagine a large, sprawling castle. Network segmentation is akin to building sturdy internal walls and doors, ensuring that even if an enemy breaches the outer walls, they cannot immediately rampage through the entire fortress. This isolation is achieved through various technological means, including Virtual Local Area Networks (VLANs), firewalls, and Access Control Lists (ACLs). VLANs allow for the logical separation of network traffic, even if devices are physically connected to the same switch.

Firewalls, acting as digital gatekeepers, then enforce strict rules about what traffic is allowed to pass between these segments. ACLs provide granular control over which users or systems can access specific network resources. For instance, critical operational technology (OT) networks that control physical infrastructure, such as power grids or life support systems, should be rigorously segmented from standard information technology (IT) networks. This prevents a ransomware attack on a user's workstation from cascading into a system-wide outage of essential services. The segmentation strategy must be carefully planned, considering the flow of data, the criticality of systems, and the potential impact of a breach. Regular review and adjustment of these segments are crucial as the network evolves and new threats emerge.

Building upon the principle of segmentation, the Zero Trust Architecture (ZTA) represents a fundamental paradigm shift in how we approach network security. Traditionally, security models operated on a "trust but verify" principle, where systems and users within the network perimeter were implicitly trusted.

ZTA, conversely, operates on the premise of "never trust, always verify." This means that every access request, regardless of its origin (inside or outside the network perimeter), must be authenticated, authorized, and continuously validated. Think of a highly secure government facility where every individual, even senior officials, must present their credentials and undergo scrutiny at every internal checkpoint, not just at the main entrance. ZTA enforces this strict verification through a combination of strong identity management, micro-segmentation (an even more granular form of segmentation), and least privilege access controls.

Identity and Access Management (IAM) systems become paramount, ensuring that only authenticated and authorized users and devices can access specific resources. Micro-segmentation further restricts access to only the absolute necessary resources for a given task. Least privilege ensures that users and systems are granted only the minimum permissions required to perform their functions, thereby minimizing the potential damage if an account or system is compromised. For example, a maintenance technician might be granted access to specific diagnostic tools on a server but not to sensitive data stored on that same server. Continuous monitoring and real-time risk assessment are also integral to ZTA, allowing for dynamic adjustments to access policies based on changing threat landscapes or user behavior. If a user suddenly exhibits unusual access patterns, their access could be immediately revoked or escalated for further review.

Advanced firewalls are no longer just simple packet filters; they have evolved into sophisticated network security devices capable of deep inspection and intelligent threat detection. Next-Generation Firewalls (NGFWs) and Unified Threat Management (UTM) devices integrate a suite of security functions beyond basic stateful inspection. These include Intrusion Prevention Systems (IPS), deep packet inspection (DPI) to analyze the content of network traffic for malicious payloads, application awareness to control specific applications regardless of their port or protocol, and often secure web gateways to filter malicious URLs and content.

NGFWs can identify and block malware attempting to move laterally within the network, detect command-and-control communications, and prevent the exfiltration of sensitive data. For instance, an NGFW could detect an attempt by a compromised endpoint to communicate with a known malicious IP address and immediately block that traffic, even if it's disguised within a seemingly legitimate protocol like HTTP. The strategic placement of firewalls at critical junctures within the network, at the perimeter, between network segments, and in front of critical application servers, creates multiple layers of defense. Web Application Firewalls (WAFs) are specifically designed to protect web applications from a range of attacks, including SQL injection, cross-site scripting (XSS), and other common web exploits, by filtering and monitoring HTTP traffic between a web application and the internet.

Complementing firewalls, Intrusion Prevention Systems (IPS) act as proactive guardians, not only detecting but also actively blocking malicious activity in real-time. Unlike Intrusion Detection Systems (IDS), which merely alert administrators to suspicious activity, IPS takes a more assertive stance by automatically responding to threats. This response can include dropping malicious packets, blocking traffic from offending IP addresses, or resetting connections. IPS systems utilize a variety of detection methods, including signature-based detection (comparing network traffic against a database of known attack patterns), anomaly-based detection (identifying deviations from normal network behavior), and protocol analysis to detect malformed or suspicious protocol usage. In an installation, an IPS could detect a rapidly propagating exploit attempting to compromise multiple systems and immediately quarantine the affected devices or block the malicious traffic before it can spread widely. The effectiveness of IPS relies heavily on up-to-date signature databases and intelligent tuning to minimize false positives, which can disrupt legitimate network operations. Behavioral analysis capabilities are increasingly being integrated into IPS to detect novel threats that lack known signatures.

The endpoint, whether it be a workstation, server, or mobile device, is often the initial point of compromise. Therefore, endpoint security solutions are a critical component of a robust cyber defense architecture. Modern endpoint security goes far beyond traditional antivirus software. Endpoint Detection and Response (EDR) solutions provide advanced threat detection, investigation capabilities, and automated response actions. EDR systems continuously monitor endpoint activity, collecting vast amounts of data on processes, network connections, file system changes, and registry modifications. This telemetry is then analyzed using a combination of signature-based, heuristic, and machine learning techniques to identify sophisticated threats, including fileless malware and advanced persistent threats (APTs).

When a threat is detected, EDR can automatically isolate the endpoint from the network, terminate malicious processes, and provide detailed forensic data for incident responders. Endpoint hardening, which involves configuring endpoints with security best practices, disabling unnecessary services, and enforcing strong password policies, is also a vital proactive measure. Mobile Device Management (MDM) solutions are essential for securing the growing number of mobile devices accessing organizational networks, enforcing policies such as remote wipe, encryption, and secure access. The integration of endpoint security with broader network security systems, creating a unified security fabric, enhances the ability to detect and respond to threats across the entire digital estate.

Beyond reactive and preventative measures, proactive threat hunting is an essential element of a mature cyber defense strategy. Threat hunting involves actively searching for undetected threats within the network that may have bypassed existing security controls. This is a human-driven, intelligence-led process that goes beyond automated alerts. Skilled security analysts use a combination of advanced tools, threat intelligence, and deep knowledge of adversary tactics, techniques, and procedures (TTPs) to hunt for subtle indicators of compromise. This could involve searching for unusual process execution patterns, anomalous network traffic flows, or signs of persistence mechanisms that automated systems might miss. For example, a threat hunter might investigate a sudden increase in PowerShell activity on multiple servers, looking for evidence of malicious scripting rather than waiting for an alert.

This proactive approach allows for the discovery and neutralization of threats before they can cause significant damage or achieve their objectives. Establishing a dedicated threat hunting team or integrating threat hunting methodologies into the Security Operations Center (SOC) is crucial for installations facing persistent and sophisticated adversaries. The process of threat hunting often leads to the discovery of new vulnerabilities or gaps in existing defenses, which can then be addressed to further strengthen the overall security posture.

The effectiveness of any cyber defense architecture hinges on its ability to remain vigilant and responsive. Continuous monitoring of the network and its assets is paramount. This involves deploying a comprehensive suite of monitoring tools, including Security Information and Event Management (SIEM) systems, network traffic analysis (NTA) tools, and log management solutions. SIEM systems aggregate security logs from various sources across the network, firewalls, servers, endpoints, applications, and correlate these events to detect suspicious patterns and potential security incidents. NTA tools analyze network traffic in real-time, identifying anomalies, policy violations, and potential threats that might not be visible in log data alone. Effective log management ensures that critical security logs are collected, stored securely, and retained for a sufficient period to support investigations and forensic analysis. The insights gained from continuous monitoring enable the rapid detection of security incidents, allowing for a swift and effective response. This is not simply about collecting data; it's about transforming raw data into actionable intelligence.

In the face of a constantly evolving threat landscape, the ability to rapidly patch vulnerabilities is non-negotiable. Software and hardware vulnerabilities are constantly being discovered, and adversaries are adept at exploiting them. A robust patch management program is essential to ensure that all systems are updated with the latest security patches and firmware. This involves a systematic process of identifying vulnerabilities, prioritizing patching based on risk, testing patches in a controlled environment before deployment, and then applying them across the network. Automation plays a key role in efficient patch management, allowing for the rapid deployment of patches to large numbers of systems.

Careful planning is required to avoid disrupting critical operations, especially in environments with specialized or legacy systems. For systems that cannot be immediately patched, compensating controls, such as network segmentation or IPS rules, should be implemented to mitigate the risk. Regular vulnerability scanning and penetration testing are vital to identify any unpatched systems or newly discovered vulnerabilities.

A well-defined and regularly practiced incident response (IR) capability is the last line of defense against catastrophic cyber events. An incident response plan outlines the procedures to be followed when a security incident occurs, from initial detection and containment to eradication, recovery, and post-incident analysis. A typical IR plan includes defined roles and responsibilities, communication protocols, forensic investigation procedures, and legal considerations. It is crucial that this plan is not just a document but a living entity that is regularly reviewed, updated, and exercised through tabletop simulations or full-scale drills.

Effective incident response minimizes the damage caused by a breach, reduces downtime, and helps restore normal operations as quickly as possible. For example, if ransomware encrypts critical data, a well-rehearsed incident response plan will guide the team through isolating the infected systems, assessing the scope of the encryption, and initiating recovery from secure backups. The post-incident review is equally important, providing lessons learned that can be used to improve defenses and update the incident response plan for future events. The integration of threat intelligence into the incident response process can also help responders anticipate adversary actions and improve their effectiveness. The overall goal is to move from a reactive stance to a proactive and resilient posture, where cyber incidents are managed efficiently and their impact is minimized.

The evolution of defensive strategies for modern installations necessitates a parallel advancement in physical security measures, even as the digital domain becomes increasingly complex. While sophisticated cyber defenses address the intangible threats that traverse networks, the tangible threat of physical intrusion, sabotage, or unauthorized access to critical infrastructure remains a persistent and often foundational risk. Therefore, a robust physical security posture is not an anachronism but a fundamental complement to any advanced security architecture, serving as the initial, and often most visible, deterrent and barrier. This section delves into the contemporary enhancements and methodologies employed to fortify physical perimeters, control access, and integrate these tangible defenses into the overarching security framework of a SMART Installation.

Intelligent surveillance systems represent a significant leap beyond traditional closed-circuit television (CCTV). These modern systems leverage artificial intelligence (AI) and machine learning (ML) to move from passive recording to active analysis and threat identification. High-resolution cameras, equipped with advanced thermal imaging, low-light capabilities, and often integrated with radar or lidar for comprehensive environmental sensing, form the bedrock of these systems. The true intelligence lies in the software that processes the raw data.

AI-powered video analytics can perform a multitude of functions: object detection and classification (distinguishing between humans, vehicles, animals, and potential threats like drones); behavior analysis (identifying loitering, unusual movement patterns, or signs of distress); facial recognition for authorized personnel verification; and anomaly detection (flagging deviations from established norms, such as a vehicle entering a restricted area at an unusual hour). For instance, at a critical facility, an AI surveillance system could detect a person attempting to scale a fence in a dimly lit area and automatically alert security personnel, providing real-time video feeds and suspect location data, while simultaneously initiating lockdown procedures in nearby sensitive zones. This proactive identification capability allows for a more rapid and precise response, shifting security from a reactive to a predictive posture.

These systems can be integrated with acoustic sensors to detect unusual noises, such as gunshots or explosions, providing a multi-modal sensor fusion approach to threat detection. The continuous learning capability of ML algorithms means that these systems become more adept at identifying threats over time, adapting to evolving adversary tactics and local environmental conditions. The sheer volume of data generated by such comprehensive surveillance networks necessitates sophisticated data management and analysis platforms, often integrated with SIEM systems to correlate physical events with potential cyber indicators.

Automated access control systems are equally crucial in managing the flow of personnel and vehicles, ensuring that only authorized entities can enter specific zones within an installation. These systems have evolved beyond simple keycards. Biometric authentication, such as fingerprint scanners, iris recognition, and even facial recognition, offers a higher level of assurance by verifying identity based on unique physiological characteristics. For high-security areas, multi-factor authentication, combining a physical token (like a smart card) with a biometric credential, becomes standard.

Within a SMART Installation, these systems are deeply integrated. An employee's biometric data, stored securely and linked to their access privileges, can be verified at multiple points: a vehicle gate, a building entrance, and even internal doors leading to sensitive equipment rooms. If an individual's access is revoked for any reason, this change is instantaneously propagated across all connected access points, preventing unauthorized entry. Advanced access control can also incorporate behavioral analytics. For example, a system might flag an access attempt if an individual is detected attempting to access multiple high-security areas in quick succession, which could indicate a compromised credential or a deliberate attempt to exploit system loopholes.

For vehicle access, automated license plate recognition (ALPR) systems, integrated with lists of authorized and unauthorized vehicles, can streamline entry while simultaneously flagging any potential security risks. The system can also trigger additional checks for vehicles flagged as suspicious, such as diverting them for a physical inspection. The management of these access control systems often resides within a centralized security operations center (SOC), allowing for real-time monitoring of all entry points and immediate response to any access violations or system anomalies. The data generated by access control systems , who entered where, when, and through which method, is invaluable for post-incident investigations and for auditing compliance with security protocols.

Hardened infrastructure forms the immutable foundation of physical security. This involves fortifying the built environment against a variety of threats, from ballistics and explosive breaching to environmental sabotage. Structures may be designed with reinforced concrete, blast-resistant materials, and ballistic-rated glazing. Critical infrastructure elements, such as power generation, communication hubs, and server rooms, are often housed in subterranean bunkers or specially constructed, shielded facilities. Beyond structural integrity, internal defenses are paramount. For example, server rooms might feature redundant power supplies, environmental controls (temperature, humidity), and advanced fire suppression systems that are designed to protect sensitive electronics.

Access to these critical zones is further restricted through multiple layers of security, often involving mantrap doors—a security vestibule with two doors where only one can be open at a time, preventing tailgating and unauthorized passage. In a SMART Installation, the hardening extends to the integration of sensors within the infrastructure itself. Vibration sensors on walls or floors could detect tunneling attempts. Environmental sensors can monitor for unauthorized chemical or biological agents. The design philosophy emphasizes resilience and redundancy, ensuring that even if one layer of defense is breached or compromised, secondary and tertiary barriers prevent catastrophic failure or unauthorized access to the core assets. This also includes considerations for protecting against electromagnetic pulse (EMP) attacks, with specialized shielding for sensitive electronic components and infrastructure.

Advanced perimeter defense technologies are designed to detect, deter, and delay intrusions at the outermost boundaries of an installation. These technologies go beyond simple fences and guards. Integrated sensor networks, incorporating buried seismic sensors, fence-mounted vibration detectors, and microwave or infrared beams, create an invisible, multi-layered shield. When an intrusion attempt is detected by any of these sensors, the system can initiate a layered response. This might begin with automated visual confirmation via intelligent surveillance, followed by the activation of acoustic deterrents or directed energy non-lethal systems to dissuade the intruder. For instance, a perimeter breach detected by a seismic sensor in the ground, coupled with a vibration alert on the fence line, would trigger PTZ (Pan-Tilt-Zoom) cameras to focus on the area, while simultaneously alerting security personnel and potentially activating floodlights or warning sirens.

In more advanced scenarios, drones equipped with thermal cameras can be automatically launched to patrol the perimeter or track fleeing suspects, providing a dynamic aerial perspective that complements ground-based defenses. The perimeter itself might be enhanced with anti-climb coatings, reinforced fencing materials, or even strategically placed obstacles designed to slow down any physical penetration. The concept of a "hardened perimeter" is not solely about preventing entry, but about creating significant barriers and delays that provide ample time for response forces to intercept any unauthorized intrusion. This is crucial for installations that house high-value assets or are deemed critical national infrastructure. The continuous integration of threat intelligence allows these systems to adapt, for example, by adjusting sensor sensitivity or patrol patterns based on known adversary reconnaissance activities or observed vulnerabilities. The data from these perimeter defenses is fed into the central security management platform, providing a comprehensive operational picture.

The integration of these physical security enhancements with the broader SMART Installation framework is paramount. Physical security is no longer an isolated discipline but a critical component of a unified defense posture. The data streams from intelligent surveillance, automated access control, and perimeter sensors are fed into the central command and control system. This allows for a holistic view of the installation's security status, enabling faster and more informed decision-making. For example, if a cyber-attack is detected within the network, the physical security system can automatically restrict access to critical server rooms or data centers, preventing any immediate physical exploitation of the digital vulnerability. Conversely, if a physical intrusion is detected, the cyber defense systems can be immediately alerted to implement heightened monitoring, isolate potentially compromised network segments, or increase authentication requirements for personnel attempting to access digital resources from within the affected area. This interoperability ensures that physical and cyber defenses act in concert, creating a synergistic effect that is far more potent than either could achieve in isolation.

The SMART Installation framework facilitates this by providing a common data architecture and communication protocols that allow diverse security systems to share information and coordinate responses. This seamless integration is what elevates a collection of security tools into a truly intelligent and adaptive defense mechanism, capable of detecting, deterring, and responding to a wide spectrum of threats, both physical and digital. The principle of least privilege also extends to physical access, ensuring that personnel are only granted access to areas necessary for their duties, thereby minimizing the potential impact of a compromised physical credential or a disgruntled insider. The maintenance and regular testing of these physical security systems are as critical as their initial deployment. A hardened door is only effective if its locking mechanisms are functional, and an intelligent camera system is only valuable if its analytics are calibrated and its data is being actively monitored. This leads to the ongoing need for rigorous security auditing, vulnerability assessments, and regular drills that test the efficacy of both the physical and integrated cyber defenses. The physical security layer, when intelligently designed and integrated, serves as a tangible testament to an installation's commitment to security, acting as a potent deterrent and a robust first line of defense against a world of increasingly complex threats.

The efficacy of any advanced defensive system hinges not merely on its ability to detect and deter threats, but equally on its capacity to orchestrate a swift, coherent, and proportionate response. This is where integrated response and de-escalation technologies become paramount. These systems bridge the gap between identifying a potential breach or threat and neutralizing it effectively, while simultaneously striving to minimize collateral damage and prevent unnecessary escalation. At the core of this capability lies sophisticated command and control (C2) systems, designed to act as the central nervous system for the entire security apparatus.

These C2 platforms consolidate information streams from all deployed sensors, be they intelligent surveillance cameras, perimeter intrusion detection systems, access control logs, or even environmental and acoustic sensors. They process this data, correlate events, and present a unified, real-time operational picture to security personnel. Instead of sifting through disparate alerts from multiple systems, security operators receive a consolidated view that prioritizes threats, identifies their likely nature, and suggests or initiates appropriate responses. For instance, if a perimeter sensor detects an intrusion, the C2 system can automatically task surveillance cameras to focus on the incident location, cross-reference vehicle or personnel data against known watchlists, and assess the proximity of the threat to critical assets. This intelligent fusion of data allows for significantly faster decision-making and a more accurate understanding of the situation on the ground, transforming raw sensor data into actionable intelligence.

The concept of a synchronized response is fundamental to modern security operations. In a traditional setup, a breach detected by a fence alarm might trigger a manual alert to a guard, who then might dispatch another guard to investigate. This process can be time-consuming and prone to miscommunication. In a SMART Installation, however, the C2 system can initiate a pre-programmed, multi-layered response automatically. This might include not only alerting personnel but also activating directed lighting to illuminate the area, broadcasting pre-recorded warning messages, or even deploying automated drone patrols to provide aerial reconnaissance. The C2 system can manage the engagement sequence. For example, it might first direct non-lethal deterrents to be employed, such as a high-intensity strobe light or an acoustic device, to disorient and deter unauthorized individuals without causing permanent harm. Only if these de-escalation measures prove ineffective and the threat persists or escalates would the system authorize or escalate to more forceful responses, following strict rules of engagement.

This layered approach ensures that the response is always calibrated to the perceived threat level, minimizing the risk of an overreaction that could have unintended consequences. The integration extends to personnel mobilization, with the C2 system able to dispatch the nearest and most appropriate response teams, providing them with real-time updates and situational awareness en route. This ensures that by the time a response team arrives, they have a comprehensive understanding of the threat and the environment, allowing them to act decisively and effectively. The C2 systems also incorporate robust communication protocols, ensuring that secure and reliable voice and data links are maintained between all elements of the security force, from the central command to individual response officers and automated systems. This interoperability is crucial for maintaining situational awareness and coordinating complex operations involving multiple units and diverse assets.

Alert and notification systems form a critical component of integrated response, ensuring that the right people are informed at the right time with the right information. These systems are designed to move beyond simple audible alarms, delivering precise, context-aware alerts through various channels. For personnel within the installation, this can range from immediate text messages or app notifications on their personal devices to voice announcements over an integrated public address system or even flashing visual indicators in specific zones. The content of these alerts is dynamic and tailored to the recipient's role and location. For example, an alert notifying security personnel might include a live video feed of the incident, the precise location, the type of threat detected, and suggested initial actions. For general personnel in a nearby area, the alert might simply instruct them to shelter in place or evacuate a specific zone, without providing details that could cause unnecessary panic. The sophistication of these systems allows for tiered notifications, ensuring that higher-priority alerts reach key decision-makers and response teams first, while broader notifications are disseminated as needed. For critical incidents, the system can also facilitate two-way communication, allowing personnel on the ground to report back to the C2 center, provide updates, and request specific resources.

This immediate feedback loop is invaluable for dynamically adjusting response strategies. Moreover, these systems can be integrated with personnel tracking technologies, such as RFID badges or GPS locators within vehicles, to confirm that all personnel are accounted for during an incident and to direct them to safety if necessary. The ability to push detailed safety instructions, including escape routes or designated safe zones, directly to individuals' devices enhances the overall survivability and safety of the installation's occupants. The underlying infrastructure for these alert systems is designed with redundancy and resilience in mind, ensuring that notifications can be delivered even if primary communication networks are disrupted. This might involve utilizing multiple cellular networks, satellite communication, or even dedicated secure radio channels for critical alerts. The objective is to guarantee that critical information reaches its intended audience, irrespective of the prevailing conditions, thereby enabling swift and coordinated action to mitigate the impact of any security event.

The development and deployment of non-lethal or de-escalation tools represent a significant advancement in the pursuit of proportionate responses. While lethal force remains a necessary option in extreme circumstances, a robust defense strategy prioritizes the neutralization of threats with the minimum necessary force. Non-lethal technologies offer a spectrum of capabilities designed to incapacitate, deter, or disrupt without causing lasting harm. This can include directed energy systems, such as pulsed laser dazzlers that temporarily impair vision, or acoustic devices that emit disorienting sound frequencies. For instance, if a potential intruder is detected approaching a restricted area, security personnel might first activate a low-level acoustic deterrent to signal their presence and warn the individual away. If this fails, they might escalate to a focused light beam to deter further advance. In situations involving active threats, advanced non-lethal technologies can include less-lethal projectile systems that deploy beanbags, rubber bullets, or incapacitating agents like pepper spray or incapacitating foam from a distance.

These are designed to temporarily incapacitate an individual, allowing security forces to apprehend them safely. Drones themselves can be equipped with these non-lethal payloads, enabling remote deployment and reducing the risk to ground personnel. Beyond direct physical intervention, de-escalation technologies also encompass systems designed for environmental control and psychological deterrence. This can involve the use of specialized lighting, such as intensely bright or disorienting strobes, to disrupt an intruder's senses and make navigation difficult. Similarly, automated systems can deploy obscuring agents, like dense smoke or foam, to create temporary visual barriers and impede movement. The effective deployment of these non-lethal tools requires careful training and strict adherence to protocols. Security personnel must understand the capabilities and limitations of each technology, as well as the legal and ethical considerations surrounding their use. The integration of these tools into the C2 system is crucial. The system can provide real-time feedback on the effectiveness of a deployed non-lethal measure, allowing operators to adjust the intensity or type of response as needed. For example, if a particular acoustic frequency is proving ineffective, the system could suggest an alternative or prompt the operator to consider a different approach. This ensures that the response remains adaptive and proportionate throughout the incident.

The concept of controlled escalation is intricately linked to the effective use of de-escalation technologies. The goal is to create a phased response where each step is designed to resolve the situation before it necessitates more forceful measures. This approach not only enhances safety but also minimizes the legal and public relations ramifications of security incidents. For example, when an unauthorized drone enters a protected airspace, the initial response might involve passive detection and tracking. If the drone continues to approach critical infrastructure, the system could then trigger an active warning, perhaps via directed radio frequency jamming or a visual warning broadcast. If the drone remains a direct threat, the C2 system might authorize the use of a specialized counter-drone system designed to disable or capture the drone, such as a net-deploying drone or a directed energy system. Throughout this process, the C2 system logs all actions, sensor data, and communication, creating an irrefutable audit trail. This is vital for post-incident analysis, legal proceedings, and continuous improvement of security protocols. The data gathered from these de-escalation attempts provides invaluable insights into the effectiveness of different technologies and tactics against various types of threats.

This information can then be used to refine threat detection algorithms, update response playbooks, and even inform the development of new de-escalation technologies. In essence, the integrated response and de-escalation framework creates a feedback loop that continuously enhances the installation's overall security posture. The ability to precisely control the level of response, from passive observation to active intervention, is a hallmark of a truly advanced and responsible security architecture. This meticulous calibration ensures that the installation is protected effectively, while also upholding principles of proportionality and minimizing harm.

The technologies discussed are not merely tools for confrontation; they are instruments for intelligent management of security risks, prioritizing de-escalation and controlled resolution to safeguard assets and personnel alike. This holistic approach, combining advanced detection with sophisticated command, communication, and precisely calibrated response capabilities, forms the bedrock of a resilient and adaptive defense strategy in the face of diverse and evolving threats. The continuous learning embedded within these systems, fueled by data from real-world incidents and simulations, ensures that the installation's response capabilities remain at the cutting edge, ready to adapt to new challenges and adversary tactics. The emphasis is always on achieving the desired security outcome with the least intrusive and least harmful means possible, a testament to the maturity and sophistication of modern defense strategies. The effectiveness of these integrated systems is not solely measured by their ability to stop an attack, but by their capacity to manage a situation, de-escalate tension, and restore normalcy with minimal disruption and maximum safety for all involved parties.

Chapter 6: The Human Layer: Training, Readiness, and Resilience

The intricate tapestry of a SMART Installation, woven with threads of cutting-edge artificial intelligence, sophisticated sensor networks, and automated response protocols, ultimately finds its anchor in the indispensable human operator. While the preceding discussions have illuminated the remarkable capabilities of these technological systems, it is crucial to underscore that their efficacy, adaptability, and ultimate success in safeguarding an installation hinge not on the algorithms alone, but on the skilled individuals who command, interpret, and synergize them. Technology, however advanced, is an instrument; the human operator is the maestro, conducting the symphony of security with nuanced understanding, critical judgment, and decisive action.

The sheer complexity of modern defense systems necessitates a human layer of oversight and control that transcends mere technical proficiency. Operators are not simply button-pushers; they are the cognitive bridge between the raw data churned out by sensors and the nuanced, context-dependent decisions required to neutralize a threat effectively and proportionately. In the dynamic and often chaotic environment of a security incident, automated systems, while adept at pattern recognition and pre-programmed responses, can falter when faced with ambiguity, novel tactics, or situations that fall outside their established parameters. It is in these critical junctures that human vigilance, intuition, and experience become irreplaceable. The ability to perceive subtle anomalies that might elude an algorithm, to assess the intent behind an action, and to weigh the multifaceted implications of a response, these are uniquely human attributes that form the bedrock of robust security.

Consider the scenario of an unidentified aerial object detected approaching the perimeter. While an automated system might flag it as a potential drone threat based on its flight profile and size, a human operator possesses the capacity for deeper analysis. They can cross-reference the object's trajectory with known flight paths, consider local weather conditions, and analyze its behavior against historical data, all within moments. Furthermore, they can access live, high-resolution video feeds, not just to confirm the object's presence, but to discern its purpose. Is it a recreational drone straying off course, a research apparatus, or a hostile unmanned aerial system? The distinction is critical, and while AI can assist, the final judgment often rests with the operator, who can then initiate a response tailored to the assessed threat level, from a simple warning broadcast to a more assertive countermeasure, thereby avoiding unnecessary escalation against a benign entity.

The maintenance and continuous improvement of these sophisticated systems also fall squarely on the shoulders of human operators. They are responsible for not only the day-to-day operation but also for the ongoing calibration, testing, and upkeep of the technological infrastructure. This involves everything from performing routine diagnostics on sensor arrays and command and control (C2) platforms to updating software, replacing faulty hardware, and ensuring the seamless integration of new technologies. The very intelligence of a SMART Installation is a living entity, constantly requiring tending and refinement. Operators must possess a deep understanding of the underlying architecture, the interconnectedness of its various components, and the potential failure points. This proactive maintenance, driven by human expertise, prevents minor technical glitches from cascading into significant security vulnerabilities.

The human operator serves as the crucial nexus for information fusion and analysis, transforming a deluge of data into actionable intelligence. While C2 systems consolidate information streams, it is the operator who synthesizes these disparate inputs, drawing connections that might not be immediately apparent to a machine. They can overlay sensor data with human intelligence reports, correlate access control logs with observed activity, and interpret the subtle cues from thermal imaging or acoustic sensors. This holistic understanding allows for a more accurate assessment of the threat landscape and informs the most effective course of action. For instance, a perimeter intrusion alert might be corroborated by unusual electromagnetic spectrum activity detected by specialized sensors, or by a sudden shift in wildlife behavior observed by wildlife monitoring systems. It is the operator's ability to recognize this confluence of indicators, rather than isolated events, that can signal a sophisticated, multi-pronged attack or a covert infiltration attempt that might otherwise go undetected by purely automated analysis.

The nuanced decision-making required in dynamic threat environments is a domain where human operators excel. Automated systems are programmed with predefined rules of engagement, which are essential for efficiency and consistency. However, the reality of a security incident is rarely as clear-cut as a flowchart.

Human operators can exercise judgment and discretion, adapting responses to unforeseen circumstances. They can account for non-combatants in the vicinity, assess the potential for collateral damage, and consider the broader implications of their actions beyond the immediate tactical objective. This capacity for ethical reasoning and contextual awareness is vital for ensuring that responses are not only effective but also proportionate and legally sound, upholding principles of minimizing harm and respecting human rights. A situation might appear to be a straightforward intrusion, but a skilled operator might recognize signs of duress or a humanitarian crisis prompting a different approach than a simple apprehension.

The process of training and readiness for these human operators is as critical as the technological development itself. It is not enough to equip an installation with advanced systems; personnel must be thoroughly trained to operate, maintain, and leverage these tools to their fullest potential. This training must go beyond the technical operation of specific hardware and software. It needs to encompass comprehensive scenario-based exercises, simulated threat environments, and realistic drills that challenge operators to think critically under pressure. This includes developing their decision-making skills, their ability to communicate effectively with other team members and command elements, and their capacity for rapid adaptation to evolving situations. The goal is to foster a culture of continuous learning and improvement, where operators are not only proficient in current procedures but are also prepared to anticipate and counter emerging threats and evolving adversary tactics.

Building resilience within the human layer is paramount. Security operations can be mentally and physically demanding. Operators may face extended periods of high alert, followed by sudden, intense periods of action. They must be trained to manage stress, maintain focus, and recover from fatigue. Psychological resilience training, including stress management techniques, situational awareness reinforcement, and robust debriefing protocols after incidents, is essential for ensuring that operators can perform optimally even in the most challenging circumstances. The ability to maintain composure and make sound judgments when faced with extreme pressure is a hallmark of a highly effective security professional. This psychological preparedness is as vital as any technological defense mechanism.

The integration of human operators into the security architecture is not merely about having people oversee machines; it is about creating a symbiotic relationship where technology augments human capabilities, and human insight guides technological application. For example, AI-powered predictive analytics can highlight potential vulnerabilities or unusual patterns, flagging them for human review. This allows operators to focus their attention on the most critical areas, rather than being overwhelmed by vast amounts of data. Similarly, augmented reality (AR) systems can overlay real-time sensor data and threat information onto an operator's field of view, providing instant situational awareness during patrols or response operations. The operator can see not only what is in front of them but also what is happening behind walls or in adjacent areas, guided by the technology.

The constant evolution of threats demands a parallel evolution in the human operator's skillset and mindset. Adversaries are continuously adapting their tactics, employing novel methods to circumvent even the most sophisticated defenses. This necessitates a proactive approach to training and development, ensuring that operators are equipped with the knowledge and skills to counter these emerging threats. This might involve specialized training in counter-drone operations, cyber warfare defense, or responding to unconventional attack vectors. The human operator must remain a step ahead, anticipating the adversary's next move through continuous learning, intelligence analysis, and adaptation of operational strategies.

The role of the human operator extends to the ethical and legal dimensions of security operations. While automated systems can be programmed with rules, they lack the capacity for nuanced ethical judgment. Operators must understand the legal frameworks governing the use of force, the principles of proportionality, and the human rights implications of their actions. This requires ongoing training in legal compliance and ethical decision-making, ensuring that all responses are not only tactically sound but also legally defensible and morally responsible. This is particularly critical in de-escalation scenarios, where the precise application of force must be carefully calibrated to avoid unintended harm.

The SMART Installation, for all its technological prowess, remains fundamentally dependent on the skill, judgment, and resilience of its human operators. They are the guardians of the complex systems, the interpreters of ambiguous data, and the ultimate decision-makers in critical moments. Investing in their training, well-being, and continuous development is not merely an operational necessity; it is a strategic imperative. The human layer is not a legacy component to be phased out by automation, but rather the indispensable core around which all technology revolves, ensuring that defense remains intelligent, adaptable, and ultimately, humane. The synergy between advanced technology and skilled human operators forms the most robust defense, capable of navigating the complexities of the modern threat landscape with foresight, precision, and unwavering commitment. Without this human element, even the most advanced technological infrastructure would be a collection of inert components, lacking the essential spark of awareness, judgment, and decisive action that defines true security. The ongoing commitment to cultivating and empowering these human sentinels is, therefore, as vital to the installation's security as any physical barrier or digital defense system.

The efficacy of any advanced security system, regardless of its technological sophistication, is inextricably linked to the human element. While automated systems can process vast datasets and execute pre-programmed responses with incredible speed, it is the human operator who provides the critical layers of cognitive processing, contextual understanding, and adaptable decision-making necessary to navigate the complexities of modern security challenges. This necessitates a rigorous and multifaceted approach to training, designed not merely to impart technical knowledge but to cultivate a profound sense of threat recognition and a robust capacity for rapid, effective response.

Developing these specialized skills begins with understanding the nature of contemporary threats. Adversaries are no longer confined to traditional kinetic attacks; they operate across multiple domains, employing sophisticated cyber tactics, leveraging unmanned aerial systems (UAS) with increasing autonomy, and exploiting human vulnerabilities through social engineering. Consequently, training programs must be dynamic and all-encompassing, preparing personnel to identify subtle indicators that might elude automated systems. For instance, in the realm of cyber intrusion, training must move beyond basic network monitoring. Operators need to be educated on the nuanced signs of advanced persistent threats

(APTs), such as anomalous data exfiltration patterns that might masquerade as legitimate traffic, unusual command-and-control communications disguised within encrypted channels, or even subtle shifts in system behavior that indicate lateral movement within the network. This involves not just understanding the technical signatures of malware but also recognizing the strategic intent behind seemingly minor anomalies.

Training scenarios should incorporate realistic simulations where trainees must sift through immense volumes of network traffic, identify covert channels, and trace the progression of an attack vector from initial compromise to potential system disruption. This hands-on experience, coupled with theoretical instruction on attacker methodologies and evolving threat landscapes, is crucial for fostering a sharp, discerning eye.

Beyond the digital realm, the proliferation of drones presents a significant and evolving challenge. Training for UAS threat recognition must equip personnel to identify a wide range of aerial anomalies, from small, commercially available drones to more sophisticated military-grade platforms. This involves developing skills in visual identification, understanding flight characteristics, and recognizing the operational patterns associated with various UAS types. Operators need to be trained on the use of specialized sensor systems, such as radar, electro-optical, and acoustic sensors, and how to interpret the data they provide to detect and track airborne threats. Crucially, training should emphasize the importance of distinguishing between benign drone activity and malicious intent.

A drone survey mission for infrastructure assessment, for example, might exhibit similar radar signatures to a surveillance platform. It is the operator's ability to integrate information from multiple sources, visual confirmation, flight path analysis, local airspace regulations, and intelligence reports, that allows for an accurate threat assessment. Simulation exercises can recreate scenarios involving swarms of drones, drones operating in challenging weather conditions, or drones attempting to circumvent detection systems, pushing trainees to refine their observational and analytical capabilities under pressure.

Social engineering, a consistently potent weapon in an adversary's arsenal, also demands specialized training. This aspect of security focuses on exploiting human psychology to gain unauthorized access to information or systems. Personnel must be trained to recognize common social engineering tactics, such as phishing emails that mimic legitimate communications, vishing (voice phishing) attempts that impersonate trusted authorities, or baiting schemes that entice individuals to compromise security. Training should go beyond simply identifying suspicious emails; it should foster a critical mindset that questions unsolicited communications, verifies identities through independent channels, and understands the psychological triggers that adversaries exploit. Role-playing exercises can be highly effective, allowing trainees to practice responding to simulated social engineering attempts, thereby developing the confidence and composure needed to resist such manipulations in real-world situations. Educating personnel on the importance of adhering to strict verification protocols for sensitive information requests, regardless of the perceived authority of the requester, is fundamental.

A cornerstone of effective threat recognition and response is the understanding of integrated system operations. SMART Installations are complex ecosystems where various technological components, sensors, C2 systems, communication networks, cyber defense platforms, and even physical security measures, work in concert. Training must ensure that operators understand how these systems interrelate, how data flows between them, and how their individual functions contribute to the overall security posture. This holistic perspective is vital for interpreting complex threat scenarios. For example, an alert from a perimeter intrusion detection system might be meaningless in isolation. However, if it is correlated with unusual network traffic detected by the cyber defense system and a lack of expected radio frequency (RF) emissions from authorized communication channels, it could indicate a sophisticated, multi-pronged attack. Training programs must therefore incorporate modules that provide a deep dive into the architecture of the installation's security infrastructure, emphasizing the interconnectedness of its various elements.

Moreover, effective response protocols are not static blueprints; they are dynamic strategies that must be adapted to the specific nature and context of a threat. Training must therefore focus on developing personnel's ability to execute these protocols with precision and flexibility. This involves not only understanding the procedural steps for different threat scenarios but also cultivating the judgment needed to deviate from standard procedures when circumstances warrant it. For instance, a protocol for responding to a minor cyber anomaly might involve automated isolation of the affected system. However, if intelligence suggests that isolating the system would prematurely alert a sophisticated adversary to their detection and cause them to abort a larger operation, a human operator might opt for a more nuanced approach, such as covert monitoring or subtle disruption, to gather more intelligence. Training should thus emphasize critical thinking and problem-solving under pressure, encouraging operators to analyze the immediate situation, consider the broader strategic implications, and make informed decisions about the most appropriate response.

Scenario-based training is paramount in developing these skills. These exercises should simulate a wide array of potential threats, ranging from routine security incidents to highly complex, multi-domain attacks. They should progressively increase in difficulty, requiring trainees to not only identify threats but also to coordinate responses, communicate effectively with other team members and external agencies, and adapt their strategies as the scenario evolves. For example, a scenario might begin with a single, ambiguous sensor alert, escalating to involve a coordinated cyber-physical attack, the deployment of UAS, and a social engineering attempt targeting key personnel. Such exercises test the limits of an operator's training, pushing them to think critically, apply their knowledge in novel situations, and hone their instinctive reactions.

The process of threat recognition and response training must also be iterative and continuous. The threat landscape is in constant flux, with adversaries developing new tactics, techniques, and procedures (TTPs) at an accelerated pace. Therefore, training programs cannot be a one-time event. They must be regularly updated to reflect the latest intelligence on emerging threats and to incorporate lessons learned from real-world incidents and exercises. This might involve incorporating newly developed TTPs into simulation scenarios, updating training modules with information on novel malware or drone capabilities, or conducting periodic refresher courses to reinforce critical skills. A robust feedback mechanism, including detailed after-action reviews following all exercises and incidents, is essential for identifying areas for improvement in both the training curriculum and individual operator performance.

The development of threat recognition and response skills extends to fostering a proactive security culture. Personnel should be encouraged to report any unusual observations or potential security concerns, no matter how minor they may seem. This requires creating an environment where reporting is not penalized but is instead seen as a vital contribution to collective security.

Training should emphasize the importance of 'seeing something, say something,' and provide clear, accessible channels for reporting. This can include empowering junior personnel to question procedures or raise concerns without fear of reproach, thereby cultivating a distributed intelligence network where every member of the installation contributes to identifying potential vulnerabilities and threats. This democratized approach to security awareness ensures that potential threats are not missed due to hierarchical barriers or a reluctance to speak up.

In essence, the objective of this specialized training is to transform operators from passive observers into active, intelligent defenders. It is about equipping them with the cognitive tools and practical experience to anticipate, identify, and neutralize threats across all domains, ensuring the integrity and operational readiness of the installation. This requires a commitment to continuous learning, a deep understanding of integrated systems, and a constant awareness of the evolving nature of security challenges. By investing in such comprehensive training, the human layer becomes not just a component of the security architecture, but its most dynamic and adaptable defense. This meticulous preparation ensures that when a threat materializes, the response is not one of surprise and confusion, but one of practiced proficiency and decisive action, grounded in a profound understanding of the situation and a mastery of the available tools and protocols. The ability to recognize a threat at its nascent stage, to understand its potential trajectory and impact, and to initiate the correct, proportionate response, is the hallmark of a truly resilient and secure installation.

The adversarial landscape has evolved dramatically, moving beyond brute-force attacks to sophisticated manipulations of the human psyche. Adversaries understand that bypassing technological defenses can be exceedingly difficult, and therefore, they often turn their attention to the "human layer", the individuals who operate within an installation. This focus on psychological manipulation manifests in various forms, including social engineering, deception, and influence operations. Building resilience against these insidious tactics is paramount, transforming personnel from potential vulnerabilities into an active and informed line of defense. This requires a deliberate and continuous effort to inoculate individuals against manipulation, fostering a security-conscious culture that recognizes and resists these threats.

Social engineering, at its core, is the art of exploiting human psychology to gain access to information, systems, or physical locations. It relies on deception, manipulation, and persuasion to trick individuals into divulging sensitive data or performing actions that compromise security. Phishing, a ubiquitous form of social engineering, continues to be a highly effective vector for initial compromise. attackers craft emails, text messages, or other communications that appear legitimate, often mimicking trusted organizations or individuals. These messages typically contain a sense of urgency or a compelling offer, designed to bypass critical thinking and prompt an immediate, often ill-considered, response. For instance, an employee might receive an email seemingly from IT support requesting them to click a link to "verify their account details" due to a "security breach." This link, however, leads to a fake login page designed to steal credentials.

Alternatively, an urgent notification about an unpaid invoice, complete with a convincing invoice attachment, might trick a finance department employee into opening malware-laden documents. Training must go beyond simply recognizing a suspicious sender's email address. It must instill a deep understanding of the psychological triggers attackers exploit: fear, greed, curiosity, and the desire to be helpful. Personnel need to be educated on common phishing lures, the subtle grammatical errors or formatting inconsistencies that often betray fake communications, and, most importantly, the principle of verifying requests through independent, pre-established channels. This means encouraging employees to pick up the phone and call the IT department directly, rather than relying on contact information within a suspicious email, or to cross-reference urgent requests with colleagues or supervisors through known, secure communication methods.

Beyond email, social engineering takes many other forms. Vishing, or voice phishing, involves attackers using phone calls to impersonate authority figures, IT support, or even colleagues, to extract information or manipulate individuals into granting access. A common vishing scenario might involve an individual calling an employee claiming to be from a bank's fraud department, stating that the employee's account has been compromised and requesting their login details to "secure it." Similarly, pretexting involves creating a fabricated scenario or "pretext" to gain trust and elicit information. An attacker might pose as a researcher conducting a survey on organizational security practices, subtly probing for details about network infrastructure, security policies, or employee roles. Impersonation, whether physical or digital, is another potent tactic.

An individual might attempt to gain physical access to a secure area by wearing a uniform, carrying fake identification, or claiming to be a contractor with an appointment. Training in this area should focus on the importance of strict adherence to identification and access control protocols. This includes verifying badges, questioning unfamiliar individuals in restricted areas, and understanding the procedures for escorting visitors. Role-playing exercises are invaluable here, allowing personnel to practice responding to simulated vishing calls or impersonation attempts in a safe environment. These simulations help build confidence and muscle memory, enabling individuals to react calmly and correctly when faced with a real-world threat.

Influence operations represent a more sophisticated and often prolonged effort to shape perceptions, beliefs, and behaviors. Unlike social engineering, which typically targets immediate gain, influence operations aim to achieve strategic objectives, which can include sowing discord, eroding trust in institutions, or promoting specific narratives that align with an adversary's interests. These operations often leverage propaganda, disinformation, and misinformation. Propaganda involves the systematic dissemination of information, often biased or misleading, to promote a particular political cause or point of view. Disinformation is deliberately false or inaccurate information spread intentionally to deceive. Misinformation, while also false, is spread without malicious intent, often due to misunderstanding or error. Training personnel to identify these tactics requires a critical approach to information consumption. This involves understanding how narratives are constructed, how emotionally charged language is used to bypass rational thought, and how selective use of facts or outright fabrications can distort reality.

Personnel must be trained to critically evaluate information from various sources, particularly social media and less reputable news outlets. This includes cross-referencing information with credible sources, being skeptical of sensationalized headlines, and recognizing common propaganda techniques such as the use of stereotypes, appeals to emotion, and the creation of "us vs. them" narratives. For example, during times of heightened geopolitical tension, an installation might see an increase in online content designed to spread rumors about internal dissent or to foster distrust between different branches or units.

Training modules could analyze historical examples of propaganda and influence campaigns, dissecting their methods and impact. Furthermore, personnel should be educated on the concept of "information hygiene," encouraging them to pause before sharing potentially unverified information, especially within official communication channels, as this can inadvertently amplify disinformation. Understanding the motivations behind influence operations, whether it's to destabilize an organization, demoralize personnel, or gather intelligence through psychological manipulation, is crucial for recognizing and resisting them.

A critical, yet often overlooked, aspect of building resilience is the recognition of insider threats. While many associate threats with external actors, individuals within an organization can pose a significant risk, either intentionally or unintentionally. Intentional insider threats involve individuals who deliberately misuse their authorized access to harm the organization, steal information, or disrupt operations. Unintentional insider threats arise from negligence, errors in judgment, or a lack of security awareness that inadvertently creates vulnerabilities. Training programs must equip personnel to identify subtle behavioral indicators that might suggest an insider threat. These can include signs of financial distress, unusual work hours, expressions of disgruntlement or resentment towards the organization, attempts to access information beyond job requirements, or suspicious interactions with external parties. It is crucial to emphasize that identifying these indicators is not about profiling or suspicion, but about recognizing patterns that warrant further discreet investigation by appropriate security personnel.

Fostering a robust security-conscious culture is the bedrock upon which resilience against social engineering and influence operations is built. This culture should permeate every level of the organization, encouraging individuals to view security not as a set of rules to be followed, but as a shared responsibility. This involves creating an environment where employees feel empowered to speak up about suspicious activities without fear of reprisal. A "see something, say something" ethos must be actively promoted, with clear and accessible reporting mechanisms in place. This might include dedicated hotlines, secure online reporting portals, or designated security points of contact. Training should reinforce the idea that even seemingly minor observations can be crucial pieces of a larger intelligence picture. For example, an employee noticing a colleague repeatedly discussing sensitive project details in a public area, or an individual who seems overly curious about IT infrastructure without a clear need-to-know, should feel comfortable reporting these observations.

A strong security culture involves proactive engagement and continuous reinforcement. This means moving beyond annual security awareness training and incorporating security messaging into daily operations. Regular security briefings, post-exercise debriefs that highlight lessons learned regarding human factors, and leadership that visibly champions security best practices are all vital components. When leaders prioritize security, follow protocols diligently, and openly discuss the importance of vigilance, it sets a powerful example for the entire workforce. Training should also emphasize the interconnectedness of security. A lapse in security by one individual can have cascading effects, compromising the integrity of systems, operations, and the safety of personnel. This understanding fosters a sense of collective ownership and mutual accountability.

The training modules designed to build resilience against social engineering and influence operations should be practical, engaging, and continuously updated. They must move beyond theoretical discussions to incorporate realistic scenarios and hands-on exercises. For instance, a module on phishing could involve participants analyzing real-world phishing emails, identifying the tactics used, and practicing the correct response protocols. A workshop on influence operations might involve analyzing decontextualized news articles or social media posts to identify propaganda techniques and disinformation tactics. Scenarios simulating insider threat indicators should be carefully crafted to be sensitive and focus on observable behaviors rather than assumptions, emphasizing the correct reporting procedures.

Ultimately, the goal is to create an "inoculated" workforce, individuals who are not only aware of the threats posed by social engineering and influence operations but are also equipped with the critical thinking skills, psychological resilience, and ingrained habits necessary to resist manipulation. This requires a sustained investment in training and a commitment to fostering a culture where vigilance, critical analysis, and open communication are not just encouraged, but are integral to the operational ethos. By strengthening the human layer against these pervasive psychological tactics, installations can significantly enhance their overall security posture, ensuring that personnel remain a robust and reliable defense, rather than an exploitable weak point. This requires a constant evolution of training methodologies, mirroring the adaptive nature of adversarial tactics, to ensure that the human element remains a formidable barrier against sophisticated manipulation.

The effectiveness of any security force hinges not only on the quality of its training and the resilience of its personnel but also on the ability to objectively measure and maintain a high state of readiness. This is a dynamic and complex undertaking, requiring a systematic approach to evaluation that moves beyond anecdotal evidence and simple pass/fail criteria. For installation security forces, particularly in an era characterized by multifaceted threats that can emerge from both technological and human vectors, the development and application of robust readiness metrics are paramount. These metrics must provide a clear, actionable picture of the force's capabilities, identifying strengths to be reinforced and weaknesses to be addressed with targeted interventions. The very nature of modern security operations demands a constant state of preparedness, a readiness that is not static but continuously assessed and refined.

At the heart of effective readiness measurement lies the challenge of defining what "ready" truly means. It is not merely the completion of a training course or the satisfactory score on a routine test. Instead, readiness for installation security forces must encompass a spectrum of proficiencies, from the adept operation of sophisticated, integrated defense systems to the swift and decisive execution of complex response plans, all while maintaining an acute and persistent state of situational awareness. The operational environment is rarely static; threats evolve, technologies advance, and the human element, as we have discussed, can be both a vulnerability and a powerful asset. Therefore, readiness metrics must be designed to reflect this inherent dynamism, providing an accurate barometer of the force's ability to adapt and respond effectively to a broad range of contingencies.

One of the most crucial areas for metric development involves the proficiency in operating integrated defense systems. Modern installations are protected by a layered network of technological assets, encompassing surveillance cameras, intrusion detection systems, access control mechanisms, communication networks, and increasingly, cyber defense tools. The effectiveness of these systems is directly proportional to the skill and understanding of the personnel tasked with their operation and maintenance. Readiness metrics in this domain must therefore move beyond basic functionality checks. They should assess the ability of security personnel to not only operate these systems individually but also to integrate their functions in real-time. This means evaluating their capacity to correlate data from disparate sources, for example, linking a sensor alert with visual confirmation from a camera feed, or cross-referencing access logs with communication traffic.

Consider, for instance, the deployment of advanced sensor grids that can detect unauthorized movement or the presence of specific materials. A readiness metric could evaluate a unit's performance not just on identifying an alert, but on its ability to rapidly interpret the sensor data, cross-reference it with other available intelligence (such as known personnel movements or scheduled activities), and initiate the appropriate response sequence, all within a predefined timeframe. This might involve scenarios where multiple sensors are triggered simultaneously, requiring operators to prioritize alerts, differentiate between genuine threats and false positives, and deploy resources effectively. The metrics should quantify the speed of detection, the accuracy of threat assessment, and the efficiency of the initial response actions. This could be measured through timed exercises, simulation software that injects realistic false alarms and genuine threats, and post-exercise critiques focusing on decision-making processes under pressure.

The integration of these technological systems with human responses is a critical facet of readiness. Security forces must be adept at using the information provided by these systems to inform their tactical decisions and physical actions. Metrics can assess the speed and accuracy with which personnel can dispatch patrols based on system alerts, utilize communication systems to coordinate with other units, or employ lockdown procedures triggered by integrated security protocols. The development of realistic training environments, often utilizing advanced simulation and virtual reality technologies, becomes indispensable here. These tools allow for the safe and repeatable testing of personnel's ability to manage complex, multi-system interactions. For example, a simulation could replicate a scenario involving a coordinated cyber and physical intrusion attempt, requiring security personnel to manage network security alerts while simultaneously responding to physical breaches at multiple entry points, all while maintaining communication with command elements. The metrics would track response times, adherence to protocols, and the overall effectiveness of the integrated defense posture.

Beyond technological proficiency, the execution of response plans is a cornerstone of security force readiness. Installations typically have a multitude of pre-defined plans for various contingencies, ranging from active shooter incidents and bomb threats to natural disasters and chemical, biological, radiological, nuclear, and explosive (CBRNE) events. Readiness in this context is measured by the force's ability to transition seamlessly from a state of routine operations to the implementation of these plans, efficiently and effectively. This requires not only familiarity with the plans themselves but also the practical skills and command and control structures necessary for their successful execution.

Scenario-based training and evaluations are the most effective means of assessing this aspect of readiness. These exercises must be designed to be as realistic as possible, reflecting the chaotic and high-pressure nature of actual emergencies. This involves creating complex scenarios that go beyond simple drills. For instance, an active shooter exercise might not only involve responding to the immediate threat but also incorporate secondary challenges such as managing incoming emergency medical services, establishing a perimeter, dealing with panicked civilians, and coordinating with external law enforcement agencies. Readiness metrics would focus on critical decision points: how quickly was the incident command established? Were the correct protocols followed for evacuation and lockdown? How effectively was communication maintained with all relevant parties? What was the timeline for neutralizing the threat and securing the area?

The evaluation of these exercises must be rigorous and objective. This often involves the use of observer-controller teams who are trained to assess performance against established criteria. These criteria should be clearly defined within the response plans themselves, outlining expected actions, timings, and decision-making parameters. Metrics might include measures of initiative taken by personnel on the ground, the effectiveness of leadership at various echelons, the adherence to rules of engagement, and the successful de-escalation of potentially volatile situations. The objective is not simply to see if the plan was followed, but to understand *how* it was followed and whether the outcomes were optimal given the circumstances. Post-exercise debriefings are critical, providing a structured environment for participants and evaluators to discuss what went well, what could have been improved, and what lessons were learned. These lessons then feed back into training and plan revisions, creating a continuous improvement cycle.

Readiness in plan execution extends to the ability to adapt plans when faced with unforeseen circumstances. Real-world incidents rarely unfold precisely as written in a manual. Therefore, metrics should also evaluate a force's capacity for dynamic adaptation and improvisation within the framework of established doctrine and safety guidelines. This might involve assessing how well a team can reroute personnel when an expected access point is blocked, or how effectively they can adjust their search patterns based on evolving intelligence.

Situational awareness, the third critical pillar of readiness, refers to the perception of environmental elements and events with respect to time or space, the comprehension of their meaning, and the projection of their future status. In the context of installation security, it is the ability of every member of the force, from the individual officer on patrol to the commander in the operations center, to understand what is happening around them, why it is happening, and what is likely to happen next. This is perhaps the most intangible, yet arguably the most vital, aspect of readiness, as it underpins effective decision-making in all other areas.

Measuring situational awareness is inherently challenging, but not impossible. It often relies on observing behavior and decision-making processes during realistic scenarios. Metrics can include the speed and accuracy of threat identification, the ability to anticipate adversary actions, and the proactive reporting of anomalies or suspicious activities. For instance, during a simulated patrol, an officer might be evaluated on their ability to notice subtle deviations from normal patterns, an unfamiliar vehicle parked in an unusual location, an individual loitering near a sensitive area, or unusual electronic signals, and to report these observations promptly and accurately.

Training exercises designed to build and test situational awareness often involve information overload, ambiguity, and the introduction of deceptive elements, mirroring the complexities of real-world threat environments. Personnel might be presented with partial or conflicting information and tasked with forming a coherent understanding of the situation. Metrics could assess how effectively they filter noise from signal, identify critical pieces of information, and synthesize disparate data points into a cohesive operational picture. This could involve exercises where security personnel are exposed to a barrage of simulated communications, sensor alerts, and visual cues, and then tasked with accurately describing the overall security posture and potential threats within a given timeframe.

The role of technology in enhancing situational awareness, and consequently its measurement, is also significant. Advanced command and control systems, data fusion platforms, and artificial intelligence-driven analytics can help security forces process vast amounts of information and present it in a more digestible format. Readiness metrics can therefore assess the proficiency with which personnel utilize these tools to achieve and maintain a higher level of situational awareness. This includes their ability to navigate complex dashboards, interpret data visualizations, and leverage analytical tools to identify patterns and predict potential threats.

Fostering a culture of continuous reporting and open communication is essential for building and maintaining situational awareness. Metrics can be developed to track the frequency and quality of information shared between individuals and units. A proactive security force will have personnel who consistently report observations, no matter how minor they may seem, recognizing that these individual pieces of information can contribute to a larger, more complete understanding of the operational environment. This requires establishing clear and accessible channels for reporting and ensuring that personnel feel their contributions are valued and acted upon.

The development of these readiness metrics requires a multidisciplinary approach, drawing on expertise in operational security, intelligence analysis, human factors, and data science. It is not enough to simply invent numbers; the metrics must be meaningful, measurable, achievable, relevant, and time-bound. They must be aligned with the specific threats and operational requirements of the installation. For example, a nuclear facility will have different readiness metrics for its security forces than a research laboratory or a logistics hub. The metrics must also be validated through pilot programs and regularly reviewed and updated to ensure they remain relevant in the face of evolving threats and technologies.

The process of establishing and using readiness metrics must be transparent and communicated effectively to the security forces themselves. Personnel need to understand what is being measured, why it is being measured, and how their performance contributes to the overall readiness of the force. This fosters a sense of ownership and encourages a commitment to continuous improvement. When individuals understand the benchmarks, they are striving for and the impact of their individual performance on collective readiness, they are more likely to engage fully in training and operational activities.

The feedback loop generated by these metrics is crucial. Readiness evaluations are not merely for assessment; they are intended to drive improvement. The data gathered from these metrics should inform training program development, resource allocation, and strategic planning. If metrics consistently reveal a deficiency in a particular area, such as the rapid identification of disguised threats or the coordinated response to a simultaneous cyber and physical attack, then training resources and exercises must be refocused to address that gap. Similarly, if performance in a certain area consistently exceeds expectations, those best practices can be identified, codified, and disseminated across the force.

The measurement and maintenance of readiness for installation security forces are complex but indispensable processes. By developing and rigorously applying metrics that assess proficiency in operating integrated systems, executing response plans, and maintaining situational awareness, organizations can gain a clear and actionable understanding of their security posture. This, in turn, enables the targeted refinement of training, the optimization of resources, and the continuous enhancement of the force's ability to meet the ever-evolving demands of the modern security landscape. The commitment to objective measurement and continuous evaluation ensures that the human layer of defense remains not only trained and resilient but also demonstrably ready to protect critical assets and personnel against a wide spectrum of threats.

The relentless demands of safeguarding sensitive installations place a significant and often underestimated psychological burden on security personnel. Operating within an environment characterized by constant vigilance, the potential for sudden, violent encounters, and the inherent weight of responsibility for protecting lives and critical assets, can exact a profound toll on mental well-being. This subsection delves into the crucial domain of psychological preparedness and mental fortitude, exploring the strategies and practices essential for cultivating a resilient and mentally robust security force. It underscores that while physical readiness and technical proficiency are indispensable, the ability of individuals to maintain peak mental condition under duress is equally, if not more, vital for sustained performance, sound decision-making, and the ultimate effectiveness of installation defense.

Building psychological preparedness is not a singular event but an ongoing process, woven into the fabric of training, daily operations, and the broader organizational culture. It begins with a fundamental understanding that stress is an inherent component of the security profession. Rather than attempting to eliminate stress, the focus shifts to equipping personnel with the tools and coping mechanisms to manage it effectively. This involves proactive measures designed to enhance resilience, the capacity to bounce back from adversity and adapt to challenging circumstances.

Resilience is not an innate trait possessed by a select few; it is a skill that can be cultivated through targeted training and support. This includes fostering a mindset that views challenges not as insurmountable obstacles but as opportunities for learning and growth. Personnel must be encouraged to develop a sense of agency, understanding that their actions and responses can significantly influence outcomes, even in the most stressful situations.

A cornerstone of psychological preparedness is the development of effective stress management techniques. These techniques can range from practical, in-the-moment strategies to longer-term approaches that promote overall mental well-being. Breathing exercises, mindfulness practices, and controlled cognitive reframing techniques can be taught and practiced during training exercises, allowing personnel to internalize these methods for use during actual high-stress events. For instance, a security officer on patrol who experiences a sudden, unexpected alert might employ a brief, controlled breathing sequence to regain composure before reacting. Similarly, mindfulness training can help personnel develop a greater awareness of their internal states, enabling them to recognize the early signs of escalating stress and intervene proactively before it impairs their judgment. Cognitive reframing involves challenging and altering negative or catastrophic thought patterns that can arise during stressful incidents. Instead of dwelling on "what if something terrible happens," personnel can be trained to focus on "what is the immediate threat and what is the best course of action."

Beyond immediate stress reduction, fostering mental fortitude requires a deliberate approach to building emotional regulation and impulse control. Security personnel must be able to process and manage their emotions in a controlled manner, preventing fear, anger, or frustration from dictating their actions. This is particularly critical in scenarios involving potential threats to life, where a measured and rational response is paramount. Training simulations can be invaluable here, creating controlled environments where individuals can practice making critical decisions under simulated duress, receiving immediate feedback on their emotional responses and decision-making processes. These simulations must be designed to replicate the physiological and psychological stressors of real-world incidents, including elevated heart rates, sensory overload, and the pressure of time constraints. Post-simulation debriefings are essential, providing a safe space for personnel to discuss their experiences, identify emotional triggers, and learn from their responses.

The concept of "psychological inoculation" plays a vital role. Similar to how a vaccine introduces a weakened form of a pathogen to build immunity, psychological inoculation involves exposing individuals to simulated stressors in a controlled and supportive manner. This gradual exposure helps them build tolerance and develop effective coping strategies before they face the full impact of real-world crises. For example, initial training might involve simulated scenarios with moderate stress levels, progressing to more complex and demanding situations as personnel demonstrate increasing proficiency in managing their psychological responses. This incremental approach helps to desensitize personnel to the physiological effects of stress and build confidence in their ability to perform under pressure.

The importance of a supportive organizational culture cannot be overstated. When security personnel feel that their mental well-being is genuinely valued by leadership, they are more likely to seek help when needed and to engage in proactive self-care. This involves destigmatizing mental health issues within the force, ensuring that seeking psychological support is seen as a sign of strength, not weakness. Leadership must actively promote open communication, encouraging personnel to discuss their concerns and challenges without fear of reprisal or negative career implications. Establishing access to confidential counseling services, peer support programs, and mental health professionals is crucial. These resources should be readily available and their utilization encouraged. Regular mental health check-ins, similar to physical readiness assessments, can help to identify individuals who may be struggling and require additional support.

Peer support programs can be particularly effective. Security personnel often share unique bonds forged through shared experiences and a common understanding of the challenges they face. Trained peers can provide invaluable support, offering a listening ear, sharing coping strategies, and helping colleagues to navigate difficult emotional experiences. These programs create a network of mutual support, reinforcing the idea that no one is alone in facing the psychological demands of the job. The selection and training of peer support personnel are critical to ensure they are empathetic, discreet, and equipped with the knowledge to guide colleagues towards professional help when necessary.

The nature of the threats that installation security forces face often involves elements of unpredictability and potential for prolonged engagement. This can lead to chronic stress, also known as cumulative stress, which arises from continuous exposure to demanding situations. Chronic stress can have serious long-term consequences for mental and physical health, including burnout, anxiety disorders, depression, and even post-traumatic stress disorder (PTSD). Mitigating chronic stress requires a multifaceted approach. This includes ensuring adequate rest and recovery periods, managing workloads effectively, and providing opportunities for personnel to engage in activities outside of work that promote relaxation and well-being. Leaders must be vigilant in recognizing the signs of chronic stress in their teams, such as decreased motivation, increased irritability, withdrawal, and physical complaints, and intervene promptly to provide support.

The role of sleep hygiene and its impact on mental fortitude is also significant. Sleep deprivation impairs cognitive function, decision-making, and emotional regulation, all of which are critical for effective security operations. Training programs should incorporate education on the importance of sleep and provide practical strategies for improving sleep quality, especially for personnel working irregular shifts or in high-stress environments. This might include guidance on creating conducive sleep environments, managing caffeine intake, and developing pre-sleep relaxation routines. The psychological preparedness of security personnel also extends to their ability to manage the aftermath of critical incidents. Even when a situation is resolved successfully, the emotional and psychological impact on those involved can be profound.

Critical Incident Stress Management (CISM) programs, which involve structured debriefings and psychological first aid, are essential for helping personnel process traumatic events. These interventions, when conducted by trained professionals, can significantly reduce the likelihood of long-term psychological distress. The goal is not to erase the memory of the event but to help individuals integrate the experience in a healthy way, minimizing its debilitating effects.

Moreover, leadership plays a pivotal role in shaping the psychological resilience of their teams. Leaders who demonstrate empathy, provide clear and consistent communication, and actively support their personnel's well-being create an environment where resilience can flourish. They must model healthy coping mechanisms and openly discuss the psychological challenges of the job. This can involve leaders sharing their own experiences (appropriately and within professional boundaries) to normalize the discussion of mental health. A leader's commitment to their personnel's psychological well-being translates directly into the force's overall capacity to withstand and overcome adversity. This includes ensuring that resources for mental health support are not only available but actively promoted and easily accessible.

The development of psychological preparedness must also be integrated into realistic training scenarios. When exercises are designed to simulate the intense pressure and uncertainty of real-world events, personnel have the opportunity to practice and refine their stress management techniques, emotional regulation skills, and decision-making under duress. These scenarios should push personnel to their limits in a controlled manner, allowing them to experience the physiological and psychological effects of stress and learn how to manage them effectively. The feedback provided after these exercises should not only focus on tactical performance but also on the individual's psychological responses and coping strategies.

Ultimately, fostering psychological preparedness and mental fortitude is not merely about mitigating risks; it is about building a force that is not only capable of responding to threats but also capable of thriving in a demanding profession. It is about recognizing that the human element is both the most critical asset and the most vulnerable aspect of any security operation. By prioritizing the mental well-being and psychological resilience of its personnel, installation security forces can ensure that their most valuable resource remains sharp, adaptable, and effective, even in the face of the most challenging circumstances. This commitment to mental fortitude underpins the entire edifice of installation security, ensuring that the individuals tasked with safeguarding vital assets are themselves secure in their mental capacity to perform their duties with unwavering professionalism and efficacy.

Chapter 7: The SMARTIE Architecture:

Building the Foundation

The relentless evolution of security challenges within military installations necessitates a paradigm shift from fragmented, siloed systems to an integrated, intelligent, and adaptable defense posture. This transformation is not merely an operational upgrade; it is a strategic imperative, driven by the need for enhanced situational awareness, proactive threat detection, and agile response capabilities. Traditional security architectures, often characterized by a patchwork of disparate technologies and protocols, struggle to keep pace with the sophistication of modern threats and the sheer volume of data generated by an increasingly complex operational environment. The demand is for a unified, coherent system that can process, analyze, and act upon information from a multitude of sources in near real-time. It is within this critical context that the SMARTIE (SMART Installations Integrated Environment) reference architecture emerges as a foundational element, offering a conceptual blueprint for building such a robust and interconnected security ecosystem.

SMARTIE is not a specific product or a proprietary solution, but rather a guiding framework, a standardized design pattern that defines how various security technologies, data flows, and operational processes can be brought together harmoniously. Its primary objective is to foster interoperability and cohesion, breaking down the artificial barriers that often exist between different security domains—such as physical access control, surveillance, cyber defense, personnel security, and intelligence gathering. By providing a common language and a structured approach to integration, SMARTIE enables these disparate elements to communicate effectively, share data seamlessly, and collaborate towards a unified security objective: the comprehensive protection of military installations. This architectural approach is fundamentally about creating a synergistic effect, where the sum of the integrated parts is significantly greater than the capabilities of each individual component operating in isolation.

The essence of SMARTIE lies in its capacity to serve as a conceptual anchor for the development and deployment of next-generation security systems. It outlines a set of principles, guidelines, and architectural patterns that can be applied across a spectrum of military installations, regardless of their specific size, mission, or geographical location. This reference architecture acknowledges the inherent diversity of security needs and existing infrastructure within the defense sector.

Therefore, it is designed to be flexible and adaptable, allowing for customization and tailoring to meet the unique requirements of each installation while adhering to the overarching principles of integration and interoperability. The goal is to create a robust foundation that can accommodate existing technologies while also providing a clear roadmap for incorporating future innovations.

At its core, SMARTIE emphasizes the concept of a unified security posture. This means moving away from the traditional approach where physical security, cybersecurity, and personnel security, for instance, operate as independent entities. Instead, SMARTIE envisions a scenario where these domains are intrinsically linked, sharing insights and coordinating actions. For example, a physical intrusion detected by perimeter sensors could automatically trigger enhanced cybersecurity monitoring for affected network segments, and simultaneously, intelligence on known threat actors associated with such intrusions could be fed to personnel security vetting systems. This holistic perspective ensures that security measures are not only reactive but also predictive and preventative, leveraging the collective intelligence of the entire security apparatus.

The architecture is structured around key functional domains and the interfaces between them, defining how data is collected, processed, analyzed, and disseminated. This includes establishing standardized protocols for data exchange, ensuring that sensor data from cameras, for instance, can be readily understood and correlated with information from access control systems or network traffic logs. This emphasis on standardization is critical. Without it, the integration of diverse technologies from different vendors would remain a complex and often prohibitively expensive undertaking. SMARTIE provides a common set of specifications that encourage vendors to develop products that are inherently compatible, thus reducing integration challenges and fostering a more competitive and innovative market for defense security solutions.

SMARTIE is designed with scalability and future-proofing in mind. The security landscape is in a perpetual state of flux, with new threats emerging and new technologies constantly being developed. An architecture that cannot adapt to these changes will quickly become obsolete. SMARTIE's modular design allows for the addition of new capabilities and the replacement of outdated components without necessitating a complete overhaul of the system. This ensures that military installations can continuously enhance their security posture, incorporating advancements in areas such as artificial intelligence, machine learning, advanced sensor technology, and autonomous systems, as they become available and mature. The reference architecture acts as a stable framework upon which these dynamic elements can be integrated and leveraged effectively.

The implementation of SMARTIE fosters a significant improvement in situational awareness. By aggregating data from all connected security systems into a centralized or federated platform, it provides security operators with a comprehensive and real-time view of the installation's security status. This consolidated view allows for the rapid identification of anomalies, the assessment of potential threats, and the informed decision-making necessary for effective response. Instead of sifting through disparate alerts from multiple systems, operators are presented with a coherent picture, enabling them to understand the context of events and prioritize actions more efficiently. This enhanced situational awareness is paramount in reducing the time between threat detection and response, a critical factor in mitigating the impact of security incidents.

SMARTIE facilitates a proactive and predictive approach to security management. By analyzing historical data and real-time inputs, the architecture can identify patterns and indicators that may signal an impending threat. Machine learning algorithms, for example, can be trained to recognize subtle anomalies that might be missed by human operators or traditional rule-based systems. This predictive capability allows security forces to move beyond a purely reactive stance and to take preventative measures, thereby disrupting potential attacks before they can occur. This shift from reaction to prediction is a hallmark of advanced security architectures and is a key benefit offered by the SMARTIE framework.

The operational benefits of a SMARTIE-compliant architecture are profound. It enables more efficient resource allocation, as security personnel can be deployed more strategically based on real-time threat assessments. It streamlines investigative processes by providing a unified repository of correlated data from various sources, simplifying the reconstruction of events. It also enhances the overall resilience of the installation's security by reducing dependencies on single points of failure and by enabling graceful degradation of capabilities in the event of localized system failures. The interoperability fostered by SMARTIE means that even if one system is compromised or unavailable, others can often compensate or provide sufficient context to maintain a baseline level of security.

The SMARTIE reference architecture is built upon several fundamental principles that underpin its effectiveness:

First, **Interoperability** is paramount. This principle dictates that all components within the SMARTIE ecosystem must be able to communicate and exchange data seamlessly, regardless of their origin or underlying technology. This is achieved through the adoption of open standards, common data models, and well-defined APIs (Application Programming Interfaces). Interoperability ensures that data from a video surveillance system can be easily ingested by an analytics platform, which in turn can trigger an alert in the access control system, and so on. This interconnectedness is the bedrock upon which the entire integrated environment is built.

Second, **Modularity and Scalability** are essential design considerations. The architecture is envisioned as a collection of independent, yet interconnected, modules that can be easily added, removed, or upgraded. This modularity allows for flexibility in design and deployment, enabling installations to select and implement only the components they need, while also providing the capacity to scale up their security capabilities as requirements evolve or new threats emerge. A small forward operating base, for instance, might deploy a scaled-down version of SMARTIE, while a major continental installation would utilize a far more comprehensive and robust implementation. This inherent scalability ensures the long-term viability and adaptability of the security infrastructure.

Third, **Data Fusion and Analytics** form a critical functional layer within SMARTIE. The architecture is designed to ingest vast amounts of data from diverse sources, ranging from physical sensors and identity management systems to cyber threat intelligence feeds and even open-source information. This raw data is then fused and analyzed, often employing advanced techniques such as artificial intelligence and machine learning, to extract meaningful insights, identify patterns, detect anomalies, and predict potential threats. The value of SMARTIE is not just in collecting data, but in transforming that data into actionable intelligence.

Fourth, **Command and Control (C2) Integration** is a key objective. SMARTIE aims to provide a unified platform for security operations command and control. This means that operators at a central command center have a consolidated view of the entire security landscape, enabling them to monitor events, direct resources, and coordinate responses effectively across all security domains. The architecture facilitates the seamless flow of information to and from C2 systems, ensuring that decisions made at the operational level are based on the most up-to-date and comprehensive situational awareness.

Fifth, **Security and Resilience** are intrinsic to the architecture's design. SMARTIE itself must be secured against cyber threats and physical intrusion. The architecture incorporates robust security measures to protect the integrity, confidentiality, and availability of data and systems. Furthermore, it is designed to be resilient, capable of maintaining essential security functions even in the event of partial system failures or cyberattacks. Redundancy, fault tolerance, and failover mechanisms are integral to ensuring continuous operation and minimizing the impact of disruptions.

Finally, **Standardization and Openness** are guiding principles that promote adoption and innovation. By adhering to open standards and avoiding proprietary lock-in, SMARTIE encourages a broader ecosystem of vendors and technologies to contribute to the defense security landscape. This openness facilitates easier integration of new capabilities, reduces lifecycle costs, and fosters a more competitive environment, ultimately leading to more effective and affordable security solutions for military installations. The reference architecture acts as a common ground, inviting collaboration and shared development.

The practical manifestation of SMARTIE involves establishing standardized interfaces and protocols that enable disparate systems to interact. This could involve defining common data formats for sensor readings, establishing standardized authentication and authorization mechanisms for access control, or creating uniform methods for disseminating alerts and notifications. For example, a network intrusion detection system (NIDS) might publish an alert in a standardized format (e.g., STIX/TAXII for cyber threat intelligence) that can be consumed by a physical security information management (PSIM) system. This PSIM system could then correlate the cyber alert with physical sensor data, such as elevated traffic at a specific gate or unauthorized access attempts within the network perimeter, to provide a more holistic understanding of the potential threat.

Consider a scenario involving unauthorized drone activity detected by radar and optical sensors. In a traditional siloed environment, this detection might trigger an alert within an air defense system, separate from the physical security operations center. Within a SMARTIE framework, however, the drone detection event would be fed into the integrated architecture. This would trigger a cascade of automated actions: the perimeter intrusion detection system might be alerted to potential ingress points; surveillance cameras could be automatically tasked to focus on the drone's projected flight path; cyber security teams would be notified to monitor for potential spoofing or jamming attempts; and the C2 system would provide operators with a unified view of the threat, enabling them to coordinate a multi-layered response involving physical security, electronic warfare, and potentially even air defense assets. The speed and coordination of such a response are exponentially improved by the integrated nature of the SMARTIE architecture.

Another illustrative example involves personnel security. In a SMARTIE-compliant environment, information regarding an individual's clearance status, training records, and any security-related incidents could be securely linked and accessed by authorized systems. If a cyber threat intelligence feed indicates a potential vulnerability associated with a particular individual's online activity (assuming lawful access and data sharing agreements are in place), this information could be flagged to the relevant security personnel. Simultaneously, if that individual attempts to access a restricted physical area and their security profile shows a recent derogatory flag, access could be automatically denied, and a notification sent to security operators. This cross-domain correlation significantly enhances the ability to identify and mitigate insider threats or compromised individuals.

The development and implementation of the SMARTIE reference architecture represent a significant undertaking, requiring collaboration between defense agencies, technology providers, and operational commands. It is a journey towards a more intelligent, resilient, and unified approach to installation security. By establishing this common blueprint, the defense sector can accelerate the transition from fragmented systems to a cohesive security ecosystem, capable of meeting the complex and evolving challenges of the modern era. SMARTIE is more than just an architectural model; it is a strategic enabler, a cornerstone for building the secure, agile, and responsive military installations of the future. It provides the necessary structure to ensure that the vast investments in various security technologies are not wasted in isolation but are leveraged synergistically to create a truly robust and integrated defense. The successful adoption of such a reference architecture is a testament to the commitment to embracing innovation and standardization in safeguarding critical national assets.

The fundamental strength of the SMARTIE reference architecture lies in its inherent modularity, a design principle that underpins its adaptability, scalability, and resilience. Instead of envisioning a monolithic, all-encompassing system, SMARTIE proposes a framework composed of discrete, yet interconnected, functional modules. This decomposition allows for a more agile and manageable approach to building a comprehensive security ecosystem. Each module represents a distinct set of capabilities, such as sensing, data aggregation and processing, advanced analytics, decision support, and response execution. These modules are designed to operate semi-autonomously while maintaining seamless communication and data exchange through standardized interfaces and protocols. This approach liberates installations from the rigid constraints of proprietary, all-in-one solutions, fostering an environment where best-of-breed technologies from various vendors can be integrated effectively. The implications of this modular design are profound, particularly in achieving true interoperability and offering unparalleled flexibility in the face of evolving security landscapes.

Interoperability, the cornerstone of SMARTIE, is directly facilitated by its modular structure. By defining clear, standardized interfaces and data schemas between these functional modules, SMARTIE ensures that systems from different manufacturers can communicate and collaborate effectively. This is not simply about allowing systems to "talk" to each other; it is about enabling them to understand and act upon the information exchanged. For instance, a radar sensor module designed to detect aerial objects can transmit its raw data in a defined format to a data aggregation module.

This module, in turn, processes and normalizes the data before passing it to an analytics module. The analytics module, perhaps employing AI algorithms, might then identify the object as a specific type of drone and generate a threat assessment. This assessment, packaged in a standardized message, is then sent to the decision support module, which might present the information to a human operator or automatically trigger a response protocol within the response execution module. Each step relies on the defined interoperability between modules, ensuring that the flow of information is unimpeded and that the actions taken are informed and coordinated. This significantly reduces the vendor lock-in that has historically plagued defense acquisition, allowing for the selection of components based on merit and mission-specific requirements rather than dictated by a single provider.

The flexibility afforded by modularity is perhaps its most critical advantage in the dynamic world of defense. Military installations are not static entities; their operational requirements, threat environments, and technological landscapes are constantly in flux. A modular architecture allows for the graceful evolution of the security posture without requiring a complete system rip-and-replace. If a new type of sensor technology emerges that offers superior detection capabilities for a specific threat, that sensing module can be integrated into the existing SMARTIE framework by simply adhering to the defined interfaces. Similarly, if a particular analytics algorithm proves highly effective in identifying a novel adversary tactic, that analytics module can be upgraded or replaced without impacting the upstream sensing capabilities or the downstream decision support systems. This capability for "plug-and-play" upgrades and replacements ensures that installations can continuously enhance their security capabilities, incorporating cutting-edge technologies as they mature and become available, thereby maintaining a decisive edge against emerging threats.

Consider the sensing layer, a critical starting point for any security architecture. Within SMARTIE, this layer is conceptualized as a collection of diverse sensing modules. This could include traditional technologies like closed-circuit television (CCTV) cameras, acoustic sensors, seismic detectors, and radar, alongside more advanced capabilities such as lidar, thermal imaging, chemical, biological, radiological, and nuclear (CBRN) sensors, and even social media monitoring tools feeding into an intelligence sensing module. Each of these sensing modules operates with a degree of autonomy, performing its primary function of data acquisition. However, their true power is unlocked when their outputs are standardized and fed into the subsequent layers of the SMARTIE architecture. For example, a perimeter fence sensor module might detect a breach, while a nearby CCTV module automatically identifies the location and begins recording. A thermal imaging module might simultaneously detect an anomaly in heat signatures, providing further corroboration. The modular design ensures that these disparate data streams, each originating from a specialized sensing module, can be ingested by a common data aggregation and processing module, laying the groundwork for correlation and fusion.

Following the sensing modules, the data aggregation and processing layer acts as a vital conduit, bringing together the raw outputs from various sources. This layer is responsible for ingesting, filtering, normalizing, and time-synchronizing the data from the sensing modules. Think of it as a sophisticated data buffet, where information from diverse "dishes" (sensors) is collected, prepared, and presented in a palatable and consistent format for consumption by the analytical engines. The modularity here allows for the selection and configuration of specific aggregation and processing capabilities tailored to the types of sensors deployed. For a facility heavily reliant on video surveillance, this module would be optimized for video streams; for an installation with extensive CBRN monitoring, it would be configured to handle and format chemical and radiological data. Crucially, this layer ensures that data from different origins, be it a physical sensor, a network traffic log, or a human intelligence report, can be represented in a common format, enabling effective cross-domain correlation in subsequent stages.

The analytics module represents the intellectual engine of the SMARTIE architecture, transforming aggregated data into actionable intelligence. This layer is further broken down into specialized sub-modules, each leveraging different analytical techniques. This might include modules for anomaly detection, pattern recognition, predictive modeling, threat assessment, and behavioral analysis. The modular design allows for the integration of various algorithms and AI/ML models, catering to the diverse analytical needs across physical security, cybersecurity, and personnel security domains. For instance, a physical security analytics module might use AI to distinguish between a harmless animal crossing a perimeter and a human intruder. A cybersecurity analytics module could employ machine learning to detect sophisticated phishing attempts or network intrusions. A personnel security analytics module, operating within strict privacy and legal frameworks, might analyze patterns of access and behavior to identify potential insider threats. The ability to swap out, upgrade, or add specialized analytics modules is a direct benefit of the modular approach, ensuring that the architecture remains at the forefront of threat intelligence capabilities.

The decision support module translates the intelligence generated by the analytics layer into actionable options for security personnel. This is where raw insights are refined into clear recommendations and presented in a human-understandable format. This module is designed to augment, not replace, human decision-making. It provides operators with curated information, threat assessments, and potential courses of action, often through sophisticated dashboards and visualization tools. The modularity here allows for customization of the user interface and the decision-making workflows to match the specific operational needs and command structures of an installation. For example, a decision support module for a tactical response team might prioritize real-time threat data and tactical options, while one for a strategic command center might focus on long-term threat trends and resource allocation. The ability to integrate different visualization tools and decision-support frameworks makes SMARTIE highly adaptable to the specific operational tempo and command requirements of any military installation.

The response execution module translates decisions into actions, orchestrating the physical and digital actions required to mitigate threats. This is where the feedback loop is closed, allowing the integrated system to actively manage security. This module can initiate automated responses, such as locking down specific zones, deploying mobile patrols, or rerouting network traffic, or it can issue alerts and directives to human responders. The modularity here allows for a wide range of response mechanisms to be integrated, from automated physical barriers and lighting systems to cyber defense tools and communication channels for personnel. For example, if the decision support module recommends a lockdown of a specific building due to an identified threat, the response execution module would automatically engage the electronic door locks, activate internal surveillance, and dispatch security personnel. Conversely, if a cyber intrusion is detected, it might automatically isolate the affected network segment and trigger a forensic analysis. The flexibility to integrate various automated and manual response mechanisms ensures that the SMARTIE architecture can adapt to the full spectrum of security challenges.

The advantages of this modular, layered approach extend to procurement and lifecycle management. Instead of undergoing lengthy and complex acquisition processes for an entire integrated system, defense organizations can procure and upgrade individual modules as needed. This allows for greater agility in the acquisition cycle, faster adoption of new technologies, and a more cost-effective approach to security modernization. The ability to replace a single, outdated module without disrupting the entire system significantly reduces the total cost of ownership and minimizes operational downtime. This is particularly important in the military context, where budgetary constraints and rapid technological obsolescence are constant challenges. By embracing modularity, SMARTIE enables a more sustainable and adaptable approach to ensuring installation security over the long term.

The modular design inherently promotes redundancy and resilience. If one module experiences a failure or becomes unavailable, the rest of the system can often continue to operate, albeit potentially with degraded capabilities. For instance, if a primary video analytics module fails, the system might revert to a secondary or less sophisticated analytics capability, or it might continue to function by relying more heavily on other sensor inputs and human observation. This fault tolerance is a critical characteristic of robust security architectures, ensuring that the installation remains protected even in the face of component failures or localized disruptions. The interdependencies between modules are carefully managed, and failover mechanisms can be incorporated within each module and between modules to ensure continuity of critical functions.

The practical implementation of this modularity requires a robust framework for defining the interfaces, protocols, and data models that govern communication between modules. This is where the standardization efforts within the SMARTIE architecture become paramount. Open standards and well-defined Application Programming Interfaces (APIs) are essential to ensure that modules developed by different vendors can seamlessly integrate. This might involve adopting industry-standard communication protocols (e.g., MQTT for IoT data, RESTful APIs for web services) and common data formats (e.g., JSON, XML, or specialized formats for specific sensor types). By establishing a comprehensive set of interoperability standards, SMARTIE fosters a competitive marketplace for security solutions, encouraging innovation and driving down costs. It allows military installations to build a heterogeneous security environment, leveraging the best available technologies from across the industry, rather than being confined to a single vendor's ecosystem.

In essence, the modular design of SMARTIE is not merely a technical specification; it is a strategic philosophy. It acknowledges that no single technology or vendor can provide a complete security solution. Instead, it advocates for an integrated ecosystem where specialized capabilities, represented by distinct modules, work in concert to achieve a common security objective. This approach unlocks unprecedented levels of interoperability and flexibility, enabling military installations to build and evolve dynamic, resilient, and highly effective security postures that can adapt to the ever-changing threat landscape and the rapid pace of technological advancement. This inherent adaptability ensures that the SMARTIE architecture remains a relevant and powerful framework for safeguarding critical defense assets well into the future.

The efficacy of any complex, interconnected system hinges on its ability to foster seamless communication and coherent data exchange. Within the SMARTIE architecture, this fundamental requirement is addressed through the rigorous establishment and adherence to common data standards and communication protocols. These are not mere technical niceties; they form the very sinews that bind the diverse modules together, transforming a collection of individual capabilities into a cohesive, intelligent security organism. Without them, even the most advanced sensing, analytical, or response technologies would remain isolated islands of functionality, incapable of contributing to a unified security posture. The core principle is that for disparate systems to work harmoniously, they must speak the same language and agree on the meaning of the words they use.

The journey towards interoperability within SMARTIE begins with defining what information is shared and how it is structured. This involves establishing comprehensive data standards that dictate the format, content, and semantics of the information exchanged between modules. Consider the raw data generated by a network of diverse sensors. A radar system might output target tracks, a thermal camera might provide bounding boxes around heat signatures, and an acoustic sensor might detect specific sound patterns. Each of these data types has its own inherent structure. Data standards within SMARTIE ensure that this raw information is not just passed along, but is translated into a common, machine-readable format.

This might involve defining universal identifiers for objects, standardized units of measurement, consistent timestamp formats (crucially, with agreed-upon time synchronization mechanisms), and common attribute descriptors. For instance, a "threat level" assigned by an early warning radar must be represented in a way that an AI-driven threat assessment module can immediately understand and utilize, rather than requiring a bespoke translation layer for each sensor type. This standardization is critical for enabling data fusion, where information from multiple sources is combined to create a more accurate and comprehensive picture than any single source could provide. Without a common data schema, attempting to fuse data from a radar's azimuth/elevation/range with a camera's pixel coordinates would be akin to trying to merge apples and oranges without a common framework for comparison.

Beyond the structure of the data itself, the communication protocols dictate how this data is transported across the network and between modules. These protocols govern the rules of engagement for data transmission, ensuring reliability, security, and efficiency. In the context of SMARTIE, this means selecting and implementing protocols that can handle a wide variety of data types and traffic patterns, from low-bandwidth sensor alerts to high-volume video streams. For instance, protocols like MQTT (Message Queuing Telemetry Transport) are exceptionally well-suited for telemetry and sensor data due to their lightweight nature and publish-subscribe model, which allows multiple subscribers to receive messages from a single publisher. This is ideal for distributing real-time alerts from perimeter sensors to various analytical and decision-making modules. For more complex interactions or the transfer of larger data payloads, such as image or video feeds destined for deep analysis, RESTful (Representational State Transfer) APIs built over HTTP (Hypertext Transfer Protocol) provide a robust and widely understood framework. These APIs allow modules to request and receive specific resources (data or services) from other modules in a standardized manner. The choice of protocol is not arbitrary; it is dictated by the specific requirements of the data being transmitted and the operational context. SMARTIE anticipates this by allowing for the selection and configuration of appropriate protocols at the interface points between modules.

The implications of robust data standards and communication protocols extend directly to the critical function of integrated decision-making. When threat intelligence, sensor readings, and system status updates are all communicated using a common language and reliable pathways, the analytics and decision support modules can operate with a high degree of confidence. An anomaly detected by a network intrusion detection system, for example, can be relayed using a standardized threat intelligence format. This message, rich with contextual information such as the source IP address, type of anomaly, and potential impact, can then be ingested by a decision support module. This module, in turn, can correlate this cyber threat with physical security alerts, perhaps a suspicious individual accessing a secure server room, and present a unified, multi-domain threat assessment to an operator. This fusion of information, enabled by standardized data and protocols, allows for a more nuanced understanding of the threat landscape, leading to more informed and effective decision-making. The system can move beyond isolated alerts to a holistic view of potential risks.

The ability to standardize command and control messages is paramount for orchestrating responses. When a decision is made, be it by a human operator or an automated process, the command to execute a specific action must be clearly understood by the relevant response module. This involves defining standardized message formats for initiating actions, such as locking down a facility sector, activating specific defensive measures, or dispatching personnel. For example, a command to "initiate lockdown procedure, Sector 4B" must be transmittable in a way that the response execution module can unambiguously interpret and act upon. This command might carry parameters specifying the duration of the lockdown, the specific doors to be secured, and the alert levels to be raised. By adhering to these communication standards, SMARTIE ensures that commands are not misinterpreted, leading to the precise and timely execution of security protocols. This is vital in high-stakes environments where milliseconds can matter, and where miscommunication can have catastrophic consequences.

The commitment to open standards is a cornerstone of the SMARTIE philosophy, fostering an environment of innovation and preventing vendor lock-in. Rather than relying on proprietary communication methods that tie a system to a single manufacturer, SMARTIE advocates for the adoption of widely recognized industry standards and the development of open APIs. This ensures that modules from different vendors can interoperate seamlessly, provided they adhere to the defined SMARTIE standards. This approach democratizes the security ecosystem, allowing defense organizations to select best-of-breed solutions from a competitive marketplace. It also simplifies the integration process, reducing the time and cost associated with bringing new technologies online. When a new sensor or analytics tool is developed, its integration into the SMARTIE framework is significantly streamlined if it can communicate using established protocols and data formats. This agility is crucial in keeping pace with the rapid evolution of threats and technologies.

To achieve this level of interoperability, SMARTIE will likely leverage a multi-layered approach to standardization. At the most fundamental level, this includes the adoption of established network protocols (e.g., TCP/IP, UDP) that provide the underlying transport mechanisms. Building upon this, higher-level protocols and data formats will be defined for specific types of information exchange. This might involve using standards like DDS (Data Distribution Service) for real-time, high-performance data sharing in demanding environments, or leveraging industry-specific standards like STIX (Structured Threat Information Expression) and TAXII (Trusted Automated Exchange of Intelligence Information) for the exchange of cyber threat intelligence. For sensor data, formats like SensorML (Sensor Model Language) could be adapted to describe sensor characteristics and capabilities, while common data models for object detection, classification, and tracking will be essential. The precise suite of standards will evolve, but the commitment to interoperability through commonality will remain constant.

The ongoing maintenance and evolution of these data standards and communication protocols are as critical as their initial definition. As new sensor technologies emerge, or as analytical techniques become more sophisticated, the existing standards may need to be updated or expanded. SMARTIE anticipates this through a governance framework that allows for the formal proposal, review, and adoption of changes to the standards. This ensures that the architecture remains relevant and capable of incorporating future advancements without compromising existing integrations. This iterative process of standardization and refinement is key to the long-term viability and adaptability of the SMARTIE architecture, ensuring it can continuously support the evolving security needs of military installations. It transforms the architecture from a static blueprint into a dynamic, living framework that can adapt and grow with technological progress and emerging threats.

Ultimately, the success of SMARTIE is intrinsically linked to the robust implementation and unwavering adherence to common data standards and communication protocols. These are the invisible threads that weave together the complex tapestry of defense security, enabling information to flow efficiently and accurately across the entire architecture. They empower the system to move beyond the sum of its parts, facilitating integrated decision-making and coordinated response. By embracing standardization, SMARTIE provides the foundational interoperability necessary for military installations to build adaptable, resilient, and highly effective security ecosystems capable of confronting the multifaceted challenges of the modern security landscape. This commitment to a common language ensures that every component, regardless of its origin or specific function, can contribute meaningfully to the overarching mission of safeguarding critical assets.

The SMARTIE architecture is conceived not as a collection of disparate security silos, but as a unified, intelligent organism capable of perceiving, analyzing, and responding to threats across the entire operational spectrum. A critical pillar in achieving this holistic defense capability is the seamless integration of physical, cyber, and air/base defense systems. This integration moves beyond mere co-location of sensors and data feeds; it involves sophisticated fusion, correlation, and synchronized response mechanisms that leverage the unique strengths of each domain to counter increasingly complex, multi-vector attacks. The era of isolated security operations, where perimeter breaches are handled solely by physical security teams and network intrusions by cyber defenders, is rapidly becoming obsolete. Modern adversaries are adept at exploiting the interfaces between these domains, launching coordinated assaults that blur the lines between the physical and digital worlds. SMARTIE's design directly confronts this reality by ensuring that information flowing from every sensor and monitoring point, whether it be a motion detector at a fence line, a network intrusion detection system within the IT infrastructure, or a radar tracking an airborne object, contributes to a single, coherent operational picture.

Consider the foundational element of physical security. This domain typically encompasses a vast array of sensors and systems designed to protect the perimeter and interior of an installation. These include, but are not limited to, CCTV cameras with advanced analytics (such as facial recognition, object detection, and loitering detection), access control systems (card readers, biometric scanners), intrusion detection sensors (motion detectors, seismic sensors, magnetic contacts), perimeter fences with integrated sensors, and even drones for aerial surveillance. The data generated by these systems, while invaluable for monitoring and responding to physical threats, traditionally exists in its own ecosystem.

SMARTIE bridges this gap by ingesting this data in real-time, standardizing it according to the common data schema discussed previously. For instance, an alert from a perimeter intrusion sensor indicating a breach at gate 3 can be enriched with data from nearby CCTV cameras, providing visual confirmation of an individual attempting to bypass the barrier.

Access control logs can be cross-referenced to identify authorized personnel versus unauthorized individuals attempting entry. Thermal imaging cameras might detect a person attempting to conceal themselves in a less-trafficked area. All this physical domain data is fed into the SMARTIE core, where it is contextualized and made available for fusion with other security domains.

Simultaneously, the cyber domain represents the digital heart of any modern military installation. Network monitoring tools, intrusion detection and prevention systems (IDPS), firewalls, security information and event management (SIEM) systems, endpoint detection and response (EDR) solutions, and network traffic analysis (NTA) tools are constantly collecting vast amounts of data about the health, integrity, and activity within the installation's digital infrastructure. This includes logs of network connections, attempts to access sensitive systems, unusual data exfiltration patterns, malware signatures detected on endpoints, and the overall performance of critical network components. In a non-integrated environment, a critical cyber alert might be handled in isolation by the cybersecurity team.

Within SMARTIE, this cyber intelligence becomes a vital input. A detected anomaly, such as a suspicious login attempt from an unusual IP address followed by attempts to access classified databases, can be flagged. This cyber alert, once standardized and contextualized within SMARTIE, can then be fused with physical security data. For example, if the suspicious login attempt from a particular workstation is correlated with an alert from a physical access control system indicating an unauthorized individual in that specific building or office area around the same time, the threat assessment immediately escalates. The system can infer a higher probability of a coordinated physical and cyber intrusion, rather than two unrelated incidents.

The air and base defense domain, crucial for protecting against aerial threats and ensuring airspace security, adds another critical layer. This domain involves radar systems (ground-based surveillance, tracking, and potentially weapon-directing radars), drone detection and counter-drone systems, surface-to-air missile (SAM) systems, anti-aircraft artillery, and potentially air traffic control data. Radar systems provide invaluable information on airborne objects, their altitude, speed, trajectory, and electronic signature. Drone detection systems can identify and track unmanned aerial vehicles, which pose an increasingly significant threat to military installations, from reconnaissance to the delivery of explosives.

SMARTIE integrates the data from these systems, translating radar tracks into standardized object descriptors that can be correlated with other sensor data. For instance, a radar might detect an unidentified aircraft approaching the installation's airspace. In a traditional setting, this might trigger an air defense response protocol. Within SMARTIE, however, this aerial detection can be fused with physical security data. If the trajectory of the airborne object suggests a potential landing or drop-off zone within the installation, physical perimeter sensors in that area can be put on higher alert. If the object is identified as a drone, SMARTIE can initiate both cyber and physical responses, perhaps attempting to jam its control signals (a cyber-physical response) while simultaneously alerting physical security teams to the potential threat on the ground.

The true power of SMARTIE's integration lies in its ability to correlate and fuse data from these seemingly disparate domains to build a comprehensive understanding of a threat and orchestrate a multi-domain response. Imagine a scenario where a sophisticated, multi-vector attack is unfolding. The initial phase might involve a low-observable drone conducting reconnaissance over the installation perimeter. The drone detection system registers its presence, and its flight path is tracked by radar. This data is ingested by SMARTIE. Simultaneously, a series of highly targeted, low-level cyber probes are launched against the installation's network, designed to test firewall resilience and identify potential entry points. These probes might appear as routine network traffic but are flagged by the SIEM and EDR systems as anomalous. In a conventional system, these alerts might be treated separately.

SMARTIE correlates the drone's presence with the timing and location of the cyber probes. It can infer that the cyber activity is not random but is intended to disrupt or distract while the physical threat (the drone) is being deployed, or perhaps to gather intelligence to support a subsequent physical breach. The fusion engine within SMARTIE analyzes these correlated events. The drone's trajectory might be cross-referenced with the physical security sensors. If the drone appears to be heading towards a sensitive area, such as a communication hub or a fuel depot, SMARTIE can alert the physical security forces responsible for that zone and simultaneously task the counter-drone systems to engage. The cyber alerts are analyzed to determine if any probes have been successful. If a particular network segment shows signs of compromise, SMARTIE can recommend or initiate immediate cyber containment measures, such as isolating the affected segment or blocking communication with known malicious IP addresses.

The system can analyze the potential impact of the drone, assessing whether it poses a direct threat or is merely conducting reconnaissance. This comprehensive assessment allows for a more intelligent and proportionate response. Instead of a full-scale air defense activation for a reconnaissance drone, SMARTIE might recommend passive monitoring, enhanced physical patrols in the drone's vicinity, and continued cyber surveillance. If, however, the drone exhibits hostile intent (e.g., it begins a descent into a critical area or deploys a payload), SMARTIE can escalate the response, coordinating the engagement of counter-drone systems while ensuring that physical security forces are in place to secure the landing zone and that any compromised cyber systems are being actively defended.

Another illustrative example involves an attempted insider threat, potentially facilitated by external actors. An employee might attempt to bypass physical security to gain access to a restricted area, perhaps to plant a device or extract sensitive information. Their access card is swiped at a reader near the perimeter, but the system flags it as an unauthorized attempt during non-working hours. This physical alert is immediately ingested by SMARTIE. Simultaneously, network monitoring systems detect an unusual increase in outbound data traffic from the employee's workstation, or perhaps the workstation itself is attempting to communicate with an external, known-malicious server. SMARTIE correlates these events: the unauthorized physical access attempt and the suspicious network activity originating from or related to the individual. This fusion of data points strongly suggests a coordinated effort, where the physical breach is intended to enable or complement a cyber exploit. The system can then trigger a pre-defined response protocol that involves not only physical apprehension of the individual but also immediate cyber lockdown of their workstation and network access, along with a deeper forensic analysis of both their physical and digital footprints. This avoids a scenario where the physical security team apprehends the individual, only for the cyber team to discover later that sensitive data has already been exfiltrated.

The integration is not limited to identifying and tracking threats; it extends to orchestrating coordinated defensive actions. When a complex threat is identified, the response must be swift, precise, and multi-domain. For instance, if a hostile drone is detected approaching the installation, SMARTIE can simultaneously: 1) Alert physical security teams to secure the potential impact zone and prepare for ground response. 2) Task counter-drone systems to intercept or disable the threat. 3) Initiate network segmentation or lockdown protocols for critical IT infrastructure that could be targeted by a follow-on cyber-attack or that might be vulnerable if the drone carries an electronic warfare payload. 4) Provide real-time situational awareness to all relevant command and control nodes, allowing for informed decision-making by human operators. This level of synchronized action is only possible when the underlying systems are integrated at the data and command level, allowing for automated or semi-automated response sequencing. The SMARTIE architecture provides the framework for defining these response playbooks, ensuring that the strengths of each defense domain are leveraged in a complementary fashion. A cyber response might focus on disrupting the drone's communication link, while a physical response focuses on intercepting it, and air defense systems provide broader airspace surveillance and potential engagement.

The underlying technological enablers for this deep integration include advanced data fusion algorithms, machine learning models trained on multi-domain threat patterns, and sophisticated command and control interfaces. Data fusion techniques allow SMARTIE to combine data from different sensor types and formats to produce a more accurate and complete picture. For example, fusing radar data with electro-optical/infrared (EO/IR) sensor data can improve target identification and tracking accuracy, especially in challenging weather conditions. Machine learning plays a crucial role in identifying subtle correlations that human analysts might miss, detecting emergent threat patterns across domains, and predicting potential adversary courses of action. This predictive capability allows for proactive defense, enabling the system to anticipate and prepare for threats before they fully materialize. The command and control interfaces are designed to present this fused, analyzed, and prioritized information to operators in an intuitive and actionable manner, facilitating rapid decision-making and the efficient execution of response protocols, whether they are automated or human-initiated.

The benefits of such a deeply integrated defense architecture are profound. It significantly enhances situational awareness by providing a unified, cross-domain view of threats. This eliminates blind spots and reduces the likelihood of threats slipping through the cracks between traditional security domains. It enables more effective threat detection and attribution, as correlating activity across physical and cyber domains makes it easier to identify coordinated attacks and understand the adversary's full intent. Most importantly, it allows for a more efficient and effective response, enabling the rapid deployment of appropriate countermeasures by leveraging the combined capabilities of physical, cyber, and air defense systems. This multi-layered, coordinated approach is far more resilient and effective against sophisticated adversaries than relying on isolated, single-domain responses. The SMARTIE architecture, by prioritizing the integration of these critical defense layers, provides the foundation for building a truly resilient and adaptive security posture capable of defending against the multifaceted threats of the 21st century. This synergy transforms individual defensive capabilities into a collective strength, where the sum is demonstrably greater than its parts.

The inherent flexibility and adaptability of the SMARTIE architecture are central to its design, ensuring that it can serve as an effective security framework for a wide spectrum of military installations, each possessing unique operational requirements, threat landscapes, and resource constraints. The concept of scalability is not an afterthought but a foundational principle that dictates the modularity and layered approach to its implementation. This allows SMARTIE to be tailored, from its most basic implementation to its most comprehensive deployment, without compromising its core functionality of integrated, intelligent defense.

At its most fundamental level, SMARTIE can be deployed in a lean, highly focused configuration to support the security needs of a small forward operating base (FOB). These austere environments are often characterized by limited personnel, constrained budgets, and a dynamic, immediate threat environment. In such scenarios, the architecture would prioritize the most critical integration points. For a FOB, this might mean fusing data from a limited number of high-resolution perimeter sensors, perhaps a few strategically placed cameras with advanced analytics and acoustic sensors, with basic network intrusion detection systems. The physical security inputs would focus on detecting immediate incursions, while the cyber component would primarily monitor for basic network reconnaissance or exploitation attempts by opportunistic adversaries. The air defense component might be reduced to a simple drone detection system, providing early warning of small unmanned aerial systems that pose a significant risk in such isolated locations. The data fusion engine, while still essential, would be computationally lighter, focusing on correlating these few, high-fidelity data streams to generate actionable alerts. The command and control interface would be streamlined, presenting essential information, such as an alert of an unidentified object approaching the perimeter, or a network anomaly detected on the primary communication link, to a small team of operators responsible for both physical and cyber security.

The response protocols would be pre-defined and automated for the most probable threats, such as triggering localized alarms and illuminating specific sectors when a perimeter breach is detected or automatically isolating a network segment experiencing suspicious traffic. The emphasis here is on providing a crucial layer of integrated awareness and a rapid, albeit limited, response capability that significantly enhances the security posture beyond what individual, disparate systems could offer. The modularity of SMARTIE means that even with a reduced component set, the core principle of correlating data from different domains to inform a unified response remains intact. For example, an acoustic detection of approaching footsteps near the perimeter, combined with an alert from a network sensor indicating unusual outbound data from a nearby workstation, could immediately elevate the alert level and prompt a localized security team to investigate, understanding that this might be a coordinated attempt to probe defenses.

Moving up the scale, a larger, established domestic installation or a significant forward operating base would leverage a more robust implementation of the SMARTIE architecture. These installations typically possess a more extensive physical footprint, a more complex and expansive IT infrastructure, and a wider array of specialized defense systems. For such sites, the SMARTIE framework would encompass a broader spectrum of sensors and data sources. Physical security would involve extensive CCTV networks covering not only the perimeter but also internal areas, sophisticated access control systems across multiple entry points, advanced intrusion detection systems integrated into buildings and infrastructure, and potentially dedicated drone surveillance platforms. The cyber domain integration would extend to comprehensive network traffic analysis, endpoint detection and response across thousands of devices, robust SIEM capabilities for log aggregation and analysis, and active threat hunting operations. Air and base defense would likely include sophisticated radar systems for broader airspace surveillance, dedicated counter-drone systems capable of engaging multiple targets, and integration with higher-level air defense command and control networks.

In this context, the data fusion engine becomes significantly more complex, processing vast volumes of data from hundreds or even thousands of sensors. Machine learning algorithms would be trained on much larger datasets, enabling more nuanced threat identification and predictive analysis. For instance, SMARTIE could correlate patterns of unusual vehicle movement detected by traffic cameras with anomalies in network access logs from a particular facility, suggesting a potential insider threat or a precursor to a physical intrusion. It could fuse data from perimeter sensors with weather data and radar information to better differentiate between natural phenomena and potential aerial threats. The command and control interface would provide a richer, more detailed operational picture, with customizable dashboards, advanced visualization tools, and integrated mission planning capabilities.

Operators would have the ability to drill down into specific events, trace data flows across domains, and conduct sophisticated threat analysis. Response protocols would be more elaborate, incorporating a wider range of automated actions and providing detailed guidance for human intervention. This could include automatically deploying mobile physical security patrols to a high-risk area flagged by fused sensor data, initiating multi-layered cyber containment actions based on detected network intrusion attempts, and coordinating with external air defense assets based on the characteristics of an identified aerial threat. The scalability here is about depth and breadth: more sensors, more data, more complex analysis, and more sophisticated, synchronized responses, all orchestrated through the integrated SMARTIE framework.

At the highest end of the spectrum, critical infrastructure protection sites, such as naval bases, major airfields, or secure research facilities, would utilize the full, enterprise-level implementation of the SMARTIE architecture. These sites represent the apex of security requirements, often facing highly sophisticated adversaries with significant resources. The SMARTIE deployment here would be a comprehensive, deeply integrated system designed for maximum resilience and minimal reaction time. Physical security would be state-of-the-art, incorporating biometrics, advanced acoustic and seismic sensors, automated sentry systems, and potentially directed energy defenses. The cyber domain would be a hardened, resilient network with advanced AI-driven threat detection, active cyber defense capabilities, and sophisticated forensic tools integrated into the core system. Air and base defense would be fully integrated, potentially including advanced missile defense capabilities, dedicated electronic warfare systems, and seamless interoperability with national-level command and control structures.

For these critical sites, SMARTIE would function as a sentient guardian. The data fusion and analysis engine would be at the forefront of technological capability, employing cutting-edge AI and machine learning to not only detect and predict threats but also to generate novel defensive strategies in real-time. It would be capable of identifying highly sophisticated, low-probability-of-intercept threats that might otherwise evade traditional detection methods. For example, SMARTIE could correlate minute changes in electromagnetic spectrum activity with subtle anomalies in network traffic and unusual patterns of physical movement to identify a coordinated electronic warfare and cyber-physical attack in its nascent stages. The command and control system would be an autonomous or semi-autonomous decision-support system, capable of recommending optimal response strategies or even initiating defensive actions based on pre-defined parameters and the system's assessment of threat severity. Human operators would act as strategic overseers, focusing on higher-level decision-making and authorizing more complex or escalatory responses. The response protocols would be highly dynamic and adaptive, capable of reconfiguring defenses in real-time to counter evolving threats.

This might involve seamlessly shifting sensor focus, reallocating cyber defense resources, or coordinating complex multi-domain engagement sequences against advanced adversaries. The system's resilience would be paramount, with built-in redundancy and failover mechanisms ensuring continuous operation even under duress. The modular design allows for specific components to be upgraded or replaced as new technologies emerge, ensuring that the security posture remains cutting-edge and effective against an ever-evolving threat landscape. This level of integration ensures that every sensor, every system, and every defense asset is aware of and contributing to the overall security mission, creating a synergistic effect that far surpasses the sum of individual capabilities.

The underlying principle that enables this scalability is the modular and layered design of the SMARTIE architecture. Each component, whether it be a physical sensor, a cyber defense tool, or an air defense system, is designed to operate independently to a degree, but more importantly, to interface seamlessly with the core SMARTIE platform. This allows for the "plug-and-play" integration of capabilities. For a small FOB, only the essential modules and a scaled-down data processing unit might be deployed. For a large domestic installation, a significantly larger number of modules and more powerful processing capabilities would be utilized. For critical infrastructure sites, the full suite of advanced modules, coupled with high-capacity data analytics and robust network infrastructure, would be implemented.

The data schema and common data standards discussed previously are crucial for this scalability. By ensuring that all data, regardless of its source or domain, is represented in a standardized format, SMARTIE can ingest and process information from a vastly different number of sources and types of sensors without requiring fundamental re-engineering. This common language allows the fusion engine to operate effectively whether it is correlating data from a few sensors or thousands, simplifying the process of adding new capabilities or expanding existing ones. This adaptability means that SMARTIE is not a rigid system but a dynamic framework that can evolve alongside the needs and threats faced by an installation. It can start with a foundational level of integration and grow in sophistication and scope as resources permit or as the threat environment dictates, ensuring that all military installations, regardless of size or mission complexity, can benefit from a unified, intelligent, and adaptive security architecture. The ability to scale SMARTIE also addresses the issue of resource optimization. Smaller installations can achieve a significant security uplift with a minimal investment in core SMARTIE components, while larger and more critical sites can invest in the full spectrum of capabilities without the risk of creating system incompatibilities. This tiered approach ensures that the benefits of integrated defense are accessible across the entire military infrastructure.

Chapter 8: Countering Unmanned Aircraft Systems (C-UAS)

The proliferation of unmanned aircraft systems (UAS), commonly referred to as drones, presents a complex and rapidly evolving threat landscape to military installations globally. No longer confined to niche military applications or the domain of hobbyists, drones have become ubiquitous tools for state and non-state actors alike, capable of sophisticated and devastating operations. The very attributes that make drones attractive for commercial and recreational use, their affordability, accessibility, ease of operation, and low flight profiles, also render them potent weapons and surveillance platforms against fortified military environments. This evolving threat demands a fundamental re-evaluation of traditional security paradigms and necessitates the development of specialized counter-unmanned aircraft systems (C-UAS) capabilities.

Adversaries are leveraging drones in an ever-expanding array of tactics and techniques, each designed to exploit vulnerabilities in established security protocols. The most rudimentary, yet remarkably effective, application is for intelligence, surveillance, and reconnaissance (ISR). Small, inexpensive drones equipped with high-resolution cameras can loiter over military bases for extended periods, gathering invaluable information about force disposition, patrol routes, ingress/egress points, and even the contents of open storage areas. This persistent surveillance allows adversaries to build detailed operational pictures, identify high-value targets, and plan future operations with a reduced element of surprise. The sheer volume of affordable drones available means that even a financially constrained adversary can field persistent ISR capabilities that would have historically required expensive and complex manned aircraft or satellite systems. This data can inform everything from conventional attacks to more insidious forms of disruption.

Beyond passive ISR, drones are increasingly employed for direct harassment and psychological operations. The mere presence of a drone overhead, especially one that cannot be easily identified or countered, can create a climate of unease and disrupt the normal operations of a military installation. For personnel accustomed to dealing with traditional threats from the ground or the air, the constant, low-altitude buzzing of an unknown drone can be a significant source of stress and distraction. This psychological pressure can degrade morale and operational effectiveness.

Adversaries can use drones to deliver propaganda materials, such as leaflets or even small explosive devices, directly into sensitive areas, further amplifying the psychological impact and creating a sense of vulnerability. The psychological toll of an omnipresent, invisible threat cannot be overstated, particularly in forward operating environments where stress levels are already high.

The most alarming development, however, is the weaponization of drones. The integration of explosive payloads, chemical agents, or other hazardous materials onto drones transforms these seemingly innocuous devices into potent aerial munitions. These "suicide drones" or "kamikaze drones" are designed to crash directly into their targets, detonating their payloads upon impact. The variety of payloads can range from small, hand-grenade-sized explosives for disrupting personnel or equipment, to larger, more destructive charges capable of damaging hardened structures. The low flight speed and altitude of many commercial drones make them difficult to detect by radar systems designed to track high-speed aircraft and missiles. Their maneuverability also allows them to navigate complex terrain and exploit unexpected attack vectors, bypassing traditional air defense grids.

The specific threat vectors posed by weaponized drones to military installations can be broadly categorized. The first is direct attack on personnel and facilities. Drones can be employed to target exposed personnel during outdoor activities, airfields during flight operations, or vulnerable points of entry into buildings. The precision with which even small drones can be guided, especially with the advent of GPS and inertial navigation systems, allows for accurate targeting of specific assets or individuals. For instance, a drone laden with explosives could be directed to strike a command center, a fuel depot, or a critical piece of communication equipment, thereby degrading the installation's operational capability. The relative ease with which these drones can be acquired and modified means that an adversary does not need advanced aeronautical engineering expertise to field a significant aerial threat.

Second, drones can be used to deliver chemical, biological, or radiological (CBR) agents. While the payload capacity of most commercially available drones limits the quantity of such agents they can carry, even a small dispersal could have significant consequences in an enclosed or densely populated military environment.

Imagine a drone deliberately dispersing a persistent chemical agent over a barracks, a mess hall, or a command post. The resulting contamination could incapacitate personnel, forcing evacuations, disrupting operations, and necessitating extensive decontamination procedures, all with minimal material cost to the adversary. The psychological impact of such an attack, even if the actual material damage is limited, would also be considerable, fostering fear and distrust.

Third, drones can be employed in swarm tactics, where multiple unmanned aircraft are coordinated to attack simultaneously or in rapid succession. This strategy aims to overwhelm the defensive capabilities of an installation, saturating its sensors and response mechanisms. A swarm of drones, each carrying a small explosive charge, could present a dilemma for C-UAS operators: engaging each drone individually might be resource-intensive, while ignoring them could lead to multiple detonations across the installation. The synergistic effect of a swarm attack can amplify the damage and disruption far beyond what a single drone could achieve. This tactic, once theoretical, has been demonstrated in various conflicts and poses a significant challenge to current defense systems.

The challenges in countering these ubiquitous drone threats are multifaceted and stem from the fundamental design of existing military air defense systems. Traditional air defense relies on radar to detect, track, and engage airborne threats. These systems are typically optimized for detecting larger, faster-moving objects at higher altitudes, such as aircraft, helicopters, and ballistic missiles. Small drones, however, operate at very low altitudes (often below 400 feet, the common regulatory ceiling for drones), have small radar cross-sections due to their size and construction materials (often plastics and composites), and fly at relatively slow speeds. This combination makes them difficult to detect with conventional radar without generating an overwhelming number of false positives from birds, insects, or ground clutter.

The low speed and altitude of drones mean that by the time they are detected by traditional air defense systems, there may be very little time to react. The engagement windows are significantly reduced, and the complex procedures involved in launching and guiding interceptor missiles or engaging with kinetic weapons may not be feasible for such small, agile targets. This temporal constraint is critical; a few seconds can mean the difference between successful interception and a successful attack.

The issue of cost-effectiveness also becomes paramount. Interceptor missiles used in traditional air defense systems are often vastly more expensive than the drones they are designed to destroy. Firing a multi-hundred-thousand-dollar missile to destroy a drone that cost a few thousand dollars, or even less, is an unsustainable economic proposition, particularly if an adversary can field large numbers of cheap drones. This economic asymmetry forces a rethink of engagement strategies, favoring non-kinetic or lower-cost kinetic solutions.

The operational environment of a military installation further complicates detection and neutralization. Bases are often located in or near civilian areas, or in environments with significant natural clutter (trees, hills, buildings) that can mask low-flying drones or interfere with sensor performance. The need to maintain operational readiness and freedom of movement for friendly aircraft, ground vehicles, and personnel also limits the types of defensive measures that can be employed. For example, deploying wide-area jamming systems without careful coordination could inadvertently disrupt friendly communications or navigation systems. Similarly, establishing a rigid exclusion zone around an installation could impede legitimate logistical movements or civilian access.

The threat is amplified by the accessibility of drone technology and the ingenuity of adversaries in adapting it for military purposes. Commercial off-the-shelf (COTS) drones can be purchased by anyone, and their control systems can be modified or bypassed to enable more advanced capabilities, such as autonomous navigation, swarming, and payload deployment. Even individuals with limited technical expertise can often modify drones to carry small explosives or other payloads. This democratization of aerial attack capability means that the threat is not limited to sophisticated state actors but can also be posed by terrorist groups, criminal organizations, or even disgruntled individuals.

The agility and maneuverability of drones, particularly smaller quadcopters, allow them to exploit three-dimensional space in ways that ground-based threats cannot. They can fly over walls, fences, and other physical barriers, bypassing traditional perimeter security measures. They can hover, loiter, and change direction rapidly, making them difficult to track and engage with directed energy weapons or even small arms fire if they are not detected in time. This inherent maneuverability is a significant advantage for attackers, allowing them to probe defenses, find vulnerabilities, and execute attacks from unexpected angles.

The intelligence gathering capabilities of drones also pose a continuous, low-level threat. Even when not weaponized, persistent ISR by drones can compromise the security of sensitive information and operations. The ability to conduct covert surveillance of training exercises, troop movements, or the internal layout of facilities allows adversaries to gain a significant tactical advantage. This threat is ongoing and requires a constant state of vigilance and the ability to detect and deter such activities without unduly impacting operational tempo.

The evolving nature of drone technology itself represents a continuous challenge. As new sensor technologies, propulsion systems, and artificial intelligence capabilities are developed, drones become more capable, more autonomous, and harder to detect. This includes advancements in stealthy drone designs, longer endurance, and the ability to operate in contested electromagnetic environments. The rapid pace of innovation in the commercial drone sector inevitably finds its way into military applications, meaning that C-UAS strategies must be dynamic and adaptable to stay ahead of emerging threats. The challenge is not static; it is a dynamic arms race where new capabilities are constantly being developed by both offense and defense.

The threat posed by drones to military installations is multifaceted, pervasive, and escalating. It encompasses reconnaissance, harassment, psychological operations, and direct kinetic attacks, including the delivery of explosive and chemical payloads. The characteristics of these systems, their low altitude, small size, agility, affordability, and accessibility, render them uniquely challenging for traditional air defense systems. The need to counter this threat effectively requires a comprehensive, integrated approach that combines advanced sensor technologies, sophisticated data fusion and analysis, a range of non-kinetic and kinetic countermeasures, and a robust command and control framework. The ubiquity of the drone threat necessitates a paradigm shift in how military installations conceptualize and implement their security, moving beyond ground-based and high-altitude air defense to encompass the low-altitude, cluttered airspace that drones increasingly dominate.

The initial and arguably most critical phase in any effective counter-unmanned aircraft systems (C-UAS) strategy is the ability to accurately and reliably detect and identify potential threats. This foundational capability acts as the first line of defense, enabling timely and appropriate responses before a drone can achieve its objective, whether it be reconnaissance, harassment, or a kinetic attack. The diverse nature of UAS, ranging from tiny, commercially available quadcopters to larger, more sophisticated military-grade systems, coupled with their operational flexibility, necessitates a multi-layered and technologically advanced approach to detection and identification. Traditional air defense systems, often optimized for larger, faster-moving aerial vehicles, frequently struggle with the unique signature characteristics of drones, such as their low altitude, small radar cross-section, and relatively slow speeds. Consequently, specialized sensor technologies and sophisticated data processing techniques are paramount to overcoming these challenges and establishing a clear understanding of the airspace.

A cornerstone of modern C-UAS detection is the application of multi-mode radar. While conventional radar systems may be ill-suited for low-and-slow targets, advancements in radar technology have yielded specialized variants designed to overcome these limitations. These radars often employ lower frequencies to enhance the detection of smaller objects and are equipped with sophisticated signal processing algorithms to discriminate between genuine UAS and benign clutter such as birds, insects, or even weather phenomena. The 'multi-mode' aspect is crucial, allowing the radar to dynamically adjust its parameters based on the evolving threat environment. For instance, a radar might operate in a wide-area search mode to scan a broad expanse of airspace, then switch to a high-resolution tracking mode once a potential target is identified, providing precise positional data.

Some advanced radars can detect the kinetic energy of a drone's rotors, even if the drone itself has a minimal radar cross-section. Techniques like Doppler processing are essential for distinguishing the subtle movements of drone rotors from the stationary background. The challenge lies not just in detection but in maintaining a stable track as drones maneuver unpredictably, often flying in complex patterns to evade detection or survey specific areas. The ability of these radars to differentiate between various drone types based on their flight characteristics and radar signatures is also an area of active development, moving beyond simple detection to preliminary classification.

Complementing radar, acoustic sensors offer a passive yet highly effective method for detecting drones, particularly those operating at lower altitudes. Drones, especially multi-rotor designs, generate a distinct acoustic signature, the buzzing or whirring sound of their propellers. Arrays of acoustic sensors, strategically deployed around a protected area, can triangulate the source of this sound, providing an independent means of detection and localization. This method is particularly valuable in environments where radar might be hampered by terrain or electronic interference, or where a completely passive detection capability is desired to avoid revealing the presence of defensive systems.

Advanced acoustic processing can even differentiate between various types of drones based on the specific frequencies and patterns of their motor sounds, providing an initial layer of identification. For example, a large, industrial drone will produce a different sound profile than a small, consumer-grade quadcopter. The effectiveness of acoustic sensors can be influenced by ambient noise levels, such as wind, traffic, or other operational sounds within a military installation, necessitating sophisticated noise-filtering algorithms and careful sensor placement.

Electro-optical and infrared (EO/IR) cameras provide another vital layer of detection and identification, leveraging visual and thermal spectrums. High-definition visible light cameras can detect the physical presence of a drone, especially during daylight hours. Their effectiveness is limited by visibility conditions (fog, rain, dust) and the drone's visual signature. Infrared cameras, on the other hand, can detect the heat generated by the drone's motors and electronics, making them effective for both day and night operations and in conditions where visual detection is difficult. Advanced EO/IR systems can employ machine learning algorithms to automatically identify the characteristic shapes and thermal signatures of various drone types. The ability to zoom in on potential targets allows for visual confirmation and identification of markings, payload attachments, or other distinguishing features, providing crucial intelligence for threat assessment and response. The resolution and thermal sensitivity of these cameras are critical, as are their fields of view and pan-tilt-zoom (PTZ) capabilities, which allow for dynamic monitoring of identified threats. Integrating these visual and thermal data streams with other sensor inputs significantly enhances the probability of accurate detection and classification.

Perhaps one of the most underappreciated yet powerful detection methods is radio frequency (RF) scanning. Most commercially available drones, and many military ones, rely on radio communications to receive commands from their operators and to transmit telemetry or video data. RF scanners, also known as spectrum analyzers or SIGINT receivers, can detect these ubiquitous radio signals. By monitoring specific frequency bands commonly used by drones (such as 2.4 GHz and 5.8 GHz), these systems can identify the presence of a drone's control link or data transmission. Advanced RF detection systems can not only detect a signal but also analyze its characteristics, frequency, modulation, bandwidth, and signal strength, to identify the specific type of drone and its potential controller. This can include identifying the drone's make and model by recognizing unique signal patterns or even pinpointing the location of the remote operator.

Direction-finding capabilities are often integrated with RF scanners to provide directional information about the signal source, aiding in localization. The challenge in RF detection lies in the sheer volume of RF signals in any given environment and the ability to distinguish between legitimate, benign signals and those associated with UAS operations. Sophisticated algorithms are required to filter out interference and focus on UAS-specific RF signatures. Some advanced drones employ frequency hopping or encrypted communication protocols to make RF detection more difficult, pushing the boundaries of this technology.

The true power of a robust C-UAS defense lies not in the performance of any single sensor, but in the intelligent fusion of data from multiple sensor modalities. No single sensor is perfect; each has its strengths and weaknesses. Radar excels at long-range detection and tracking, but can struggle with small, low-flying targets in clutter. Acoustic sensors are excellent for low-altitude detection but can be limited by ambient noise. EO/IR cameras provide visual identification but are dependent on line-of-sight and environmental conditions. RF scanners can detect operational links but may miss autonomous or pre-programmed flights. By integrating data from all these diverse sources, a more comprehensive and reliable picture of the airspace emerges. This sensor fusion process involves correlating data points from different sensors, confirming detections, and building a persistent track of a potential UAS. For instance, a radar might detect an object at a certain altitude and speed. An RF scanner simultaneously detects a drone control signal in the same vicinity. An EO/IR camera, slewed to the correlated position, might visually confirm a small aircraft. This confluence of evidence significantly increases confidence in the detection and identification of a UAS, reducing false alarms and enabling a more rapid and accurate assessment of the threat.

The process of sensor fusion typically involves a sophisticated command and control (C2) system. This system ingests raw data from each sensor, preprocesses it to remove noise and extract relevant features, and then employs algorithms to associate correlated data from different sensors. Probabilistic tracking algorithms, such as Kalman filters or particle filters, are often used to maintain a unified track of a target, continuously updating its position, velocity, and trajectory based on incoming sensor data. As more data is fused, the confidence in the track's accuracy increases. This allows for a more informed decision-making process. For example, a single, unconfirmed detection by one sensor might be flagged as a low-confidence event, requiring further observation. A correlated detection across radar, RF, and EO/IR sensors, coupled with a stable track, would immediately elevate the threat level, triggering pre-defined response protocols.

A critical aspect of sensor fusion is the ability to differentiate between benign hobby drones and hostile military or terrorist UAS. This distinction is vital for avoiding unnecessary escalation and resource expenditure. The C2 system, powered by advanced algorithms and potentially artificial intelligence (AI), plays a crucial role here. By analyzing the flight profile (speed, altitude, maneuverability), the RF signature (type of communication, encrypted vs. unencrypted), the visual appearance (size, shape, modifications), and the operational context (location, time of day, activity on base), the system can attempt to classify the detected object. For instance, a drone flying erratically at very low altitudes near a sensitive area might be flagged as a higher threat than a drone observed flying at a regulated altitude in a distant part of the airspace. AI-powered image recognition can identify specific drone models, and behavioral analytics can detect patterns indicative of surveillance or hostile intent.

The ability to query extensive databases of known drone models, their operational characteristics, and their common frequencies further aids in classification. This classification process not only helps in threat assessment but also guides the selection of appropriate countermeasures. A hobby drone detected straying into controlled airspace might be deterred by a warning broadcast, whereas a drone exhibiting characteristics of a weaponized system would necessitate a more robust defensive response. The continuous learning capability of AI systems also allows them to adapt to new drone types and evolving threat tactics, ensuring that the identification process remains effective over time. The goal is to achieve a high degree of certainty regarding the nature and intent of any detected aerial object, enabling commanders to make precise and effective decisions. This requires a sophisticated understanding of drone technology, adversary tactics, and the limitations and capabilities of each sensor system involved in the detection and identification chain.

The preceding discussion has established the critical importance of detection and identification in any robust Counter-Unmanned Aircraft Systems (C-UAS) strategy. However, merely identifying a threat is only the first step. Once a UAS is detected and its potential threat assessed, a decisive response is required. While kinetic measures, such as employing missiles or directed energy weapons, offer a direct and often conclusive method of neutralization, they come with their own set of complexities, including collateral damage risks, cost, and operational limitations. This has led to a significant focus on non-kinetic countermeasures, a category that leverages electronic warfare and other disruptive techniques to neutralize UAS threats without causing physical destruction. Among these non-kinetic approaches, jamming and spoofing stand out as primary tools for electronically disrupting or deceiving unmanned aircraft systems.

At its core, jamming involves the deliberate transmission of radio frequency (RF) signals to interfere with the communication signals of a target UAS. Most drones rely on RF links for several critical functions: receiving commands from their operators (the control link), transmitting telemetry data back to the operator, and often, relaying video or sensor feeds (the data link). By broadcasting powerful RF noise or specific interfering signals on the same frequencies used by the drone's control or data links, a jammer can overwhelm the drone's receivers. This effectively creates an "RF fog" that prevents the drone from receiving commands from its operator or from transmitting vital information. The immediate consequence of a successful jammer is typically a loss of control. The drone may freeze in mid-air, ascend or descend erratically, or, depending on its programming, attempt to execute a pre-programmed safety maneuver.

The effectiveness of jamming is highly dependent on several factors. First, the frequency bands being targeted are crucial. Commercially available drones commonly operate in the 2.4 GHz and 5.8 GHz industrial, scientific, and medical (ISM) bands, which are also used by Wi-Fi and Bluetooth devices. Military or specialized drones might utilize different, often encrypted or frequency-hopping, bands. A jammer must be capable of broadcasting on the specific frequencies used by the target drone. Second, the power and directionality of the jamming signal are paramount. A low-power jammer might only be effective against a drone operating close to the jammer's position, while a more powerful, directional antenna can extend the effective range and ensure the jamming signal is strong enough to overcome the drone's intended signal. The concept of line-of-sight is also relevant, as RF signals are attenuated by physical obstructions.

When a drone loses its control link due to jamming, its response is dictated by its onboard software and fail-safe protocols. Many drones are programmed to initiate a "Return to Home" (RTH) maneuver. This causes the drone to ascend to a pre-set altitude and then fly directly back to its last known takeoff point. If the operator is still within range and able to re-establish a connection, they might regain control.

If the RTH command is also jammed, or if the drone has drifted significantly due to wind or disorientation, this maneuver might not be successful. Alternatively, some drones are programmed to land immediately upon losing their control signal, effectively ending their mission. For more sophisticated drones, losing the primary control link might trigger other behaviors, such as switching to a backup communication channel or continuing a pre-programmed autonomous mission, which can present different challenges for C-UAS operators. The disruption of the data link, even if control is maintained, can be equally effective if the drone's purpose is surveillance or reconnaissance, as the operator will lose the valuable intelligence feed.

The operational environment significantly influences jamming efficacy. In open, unobstructed terrain, a directional jammer can be highly effective at range. However, in complex urban environments with numerous buildings and other RF sources, jamming signals can be reflected, scattered, and attenuated, reducing their effectiveness and potentially leading to unintended interference with other electronic systems. Military installations, with their inherent RF congestion and sensitive electronic equipment, present unique challenges. Deploying a wide-spectrum jammer could inadvertently disrupt friendly communication systems, radar, or other critical infrastructure, necessitating careful spectrum management and targeted jamming approaches. This brings us to the ethical and regulatory considerations. The unauthorized use of jamming equipment is illegal in most jurisdictions due to the potential for interference with public safety communications, air traffic control, and other essential services. Therefore, military and authorized law enforcement agencies operate under strict regulations and require specific authorizations to employ jamming capabilities, particularly outside of designated operational zones.

Beyond simply disrupting communication, spoofing represents a more sophisticated form of electronic attack. Instead of flooding the airwaves with noise, spoofing involves transmitting false or misleading signals designed to deceive the drone's navigation or control systems. The most common application of spoofing targets a drone's Global Navigation Satellite System (GNSS) receiver, such as GPS, GLONASS, Galileo, or BeiDou. GNSS receivers determine a drone's position, velocity, and time by analyzing signals from orbiting satellites. A GNSS spoofer can generate fake satellite signals that are stronger than the authentic ones, convincing the drone that it is located somewhere else entirely.

The impact of GNSS spoofing can be profound. A drone tricked into believing it is in a different location might attempt to navigate towards this false position, leading it off course, into restricted airspace, or even away from its intended target. In extreme cases, a spoofer could create a virtual "safe zone" by making the drone believe it has reached its destination or is in friendly territory, potentially causing it to land prematurely or even return to its operator if the spoofed location is perceived as a designated home point. This can be particularly effective against autonomous drones that rely heavily on GNSS for navigation and may not have sophisticated visual navigation or collision avoidance systems capable of detecting the deception.

Spoofing can also be applied to the drone's control link, though this is generally more complex. Instead of just jamming the control signal, a spoofer could attempt to impersonate the legitimate operator's command station. This would involve capturing or mimicking the drone's communication protocol and then sending fabricated commands, such as "land immediately" or "return to base." Successfully impersonating a drone's legitimate control signal requires a deep understanding of its communication encryption and authentication mechanisms, making it a more advanced attack vector. However, if achieved, it could allow an adversary to take direct control of the drone, essentially hijacking it.

The development of spoofing technology is an ongoing arms race. As GNSS receivers become more sophisticated and incorporate anti-spoofing measures (like signal authentication and multi-constellation reception), spoofer technology evolves to overcome these defenses. Techniques such as "centroid spoofing" or "multi-antenna spoofing" can create more convincing illusions of location, making them harder to detect. The increasing reliance of drones on precise GNSS navigation for tasks like waypoint navigation, precision landing, and formation flying makes them particularly vulnerable to this type of attack.

The effectiveness of both jamming and spoofing is also directly linked to the sophistication of the UAS being targeted. Commercial off-the-shelf (COTS) drones, while increasingly capable, often rely on standard, unencrypted communication protocols and basic GNSS receivers. These systems are generally more susceptible to widely available jamming and spoofing techniques. Military-grade UAS, however, typically incorporate advanced features such as encrypted command and control (C2) links, frequency hopping capabilities, inertial navigation systems (INS) that provide backup navigation when GNSS is unavailable, and sophisticated flight control algorithms designed to detect and reject anomalous sensor inputs, including spoofed GNSS signals. These advanced systems require more specialized and powerful electronic warfare capabilities to defeat.

A key challenge in deploying jamming and spoofing systems is detection and classification of the target. Without accurate identification of the drone's operating frequencies and communication protocols, a jammer or spoofer will be ineffective. This reinforces the necessity of integrated C-UAS systems that combine advanced sensors (radar, EO/IR, RF detection) with intelligent data fusion and electronic warfare capabilities. The C-UAS system must be able to rapidly identify the type of drone, its operational frequencies, and its navigation methods to select the most appropriate and effective electronic countermeasure. For example, if an RF scanner detects a drone operating on a specific frequency band, the C-UAS system can then task a directional jammer to target that particular band, maximizing the probability of success while minimizing the risk of collateral interference.

The concept of "smart jamming" or "adaptive jamming" is an evolving area. Instead of broadcasting a broad spectrum of noise, smart jammers can dynamically analyze the target's signals and emit precisely tailored interference patterns designed to exploit specific vulnerabilities. This can involve techniques like "deception jamming," which not only disrupts but also feeds false information back to the drone, or "follower jamming," which continuously adjusts its frequency and modulation to match the target's evolving signal. Similarly, advanced spoofing can involve creating complex, dynamic false environments to confuse even the most sophisticated navigation systems.

The deployment of non-kinetic C-UAS measures like jamming and spoofing also necessitates careful consideration of the operational context and potential collateral effects. In military operations, the risk of jamming friendly communications or disrupting critical navigation infrastructure is a significant concern. Therefore, these systems are often deployed in a highly controlled and targeted manner. For example, a jammer might be focused only on the specific frequency band used by the suspected threat drone, or it might be activated only when a confirmed hostile UAS is detected within a defined engagement zone. The use of directional antennas is crucial in minimizing the spread of jamming signals.

In civilian law enforcement or security contexts, the legal and regulatory landscape is even more restrictive. The unauthorized use of RF jammers is generally prohibited by telecommunications authorities worldwide. However, in specific, high-risk scenarios, such as protecting critical infrastructure or major public events, governments may grant temporary authorizations for the use of C-UAS systems that include jamming capabilities, often under strict oversight and with defined operational parameters. The balancing act is between enabling effective defense against drone threats and preventing widespread disruption of essential communication services.

The evolution of drone technology is a continuous cycle of innovation. As drones become more autonomous, incorporate enhanced navigation capabilities (like visual navigation systems), and utilize more secure communication protocols, the efficacy of traditional jamming and spoofing techniques may diminish. This drives the need for continuous research and development in electronic warfare to stay ahead of these advancements. Future non-kinetic C-UAS strategies will likely involve even more sophisticated electronic attack and deception techniques, integrated with advanced AI for real-time threat analysis and adaptive response. The ultimate goal is to achieve a decisive electronic advantage, neutralizing drone threats before they can achieve their objectives, all while minimizing collateral impact and adhering to crucial regulatory frameworks. The interplay between detection, identification, and electronic countermeasures forms a dynamic and critical component of modern air defense.

The previous section has thoroughly explored the realm of non-kinetic countermeasures against Unmanned Aircraft Systems (UAS), detailing the mechanisms and implications of jamming and spoofing. While these electronic warfare techniques offer significant advantages in terms of discretion and reduced collateral damage, there are inherent limitations. In scenarios where non-kinetic approaches are insufficient to neutralize a threat, or when a definitive and immediate neutralization is paramount, kinetic solutions become the necessary recourse. These methods employ physical means to directly engage and destroy or disable the offending UAS, offering a conclusive end to the threat. This subsection will delve into the spectrum of kinetic C-UAS technologies, examining both advanced directed energy weapons and more traditional interceptor systems, and critically assessing their efficacy, operational considerations, and inherent trade-offs.

Directed energy weapons represent a significant technological leap in the kinetic C-UAS domain, offering the potential for precise, rapid, and deep magazine engagement. These systems utilize concentrated forms of energy to damage or destroy their targets. Among the most prominent are High-Energy Lasers (HEL) and High-Power Microwave (HPM) weapons. High-Energy Lasers function by focusing a beam of coherent light onto a target. The immense energy concentrated at the focal point causes rapid heating of the target material, leading to structural failure, melting, or ignition. For UAS, this can translate into severing control surfaces, damaging sensors, overheating internal electronics, or even causing the airframe to combust.

The advantages of HEL are considerable. They offer a near-instantaneous speed of light engagement, meaning there is no lead time required for the beam to reach the target, a critical advantage against fast-moving drones. The "magazine" for a laser is essentially the power source; as long as there is electricity, the laser can fire, providing a virtually unlimited number of engagements without the logistical burden of carrying physical ammunition. The precision of a laser beam also allows for highly discriminate targeting, minimizing the risk of collateral damage to surrounding areas or friendly assets, provided the aiming system is accurate. This precision is particularly valuable in complex urban environments or near sensitive infrastructure. However, HEL systems are not without their challenges. Their effectiveness can be significantly degraded by atmospheric conditions such as fog, rain, smoke, or dust, which scatter and absorb the laser energy, reducing its power density at the target.

The range of current HEL systems is also a limiting factor, although ongoing advancements are steadily increasing their effective combat radius. Power requirements for high-energy lasers can be substantial, necessitating robust power generation and cooling systems, which can impact the size, weight, and mobility of the deployed system. The initial cost of procuring and deploying advanced HEL systems remains high, although the cost-per-shot is exceptionally low once operational.

High-Power Microwave (HPM) weapons, conversely, employ directed beams of electromagnetic energy in the microwave spectrum. Unlike lasers that aim to physically destroy a component, HPM weapons typically function by overloading and damaging the sensitive electronic components within the UAS. The intense microwave energy can induce damaging currents in the drone's circuitry, rendering its flight control systems, communication modules, or sensor payloads inoperable. The primary advantage of HPM is its ability to affect multiple targets simultaneously within its beam, and its relative resilience to certain atmospheric obscurants that can hinder laser effectiveness. HPM can penetrate certain materials, allowing it to affect internal electronics without necessarily requiring a direct impact on the drone's exterior.

However, HPM weapons can also have a wider collateral effect radius than lasers, potentially impacting unintended electronic systems in the vicinity. Developing HPM systems with the necessary power, precision, and control to effectively neutralize a diverse range of UAS targets, while simultaneously avoiding interference with friendly electronics, is a complex engineering challenge. The power requirements and cooling needs are also significant considerations for HPM deployment.

Beyond directed energy, traditional kinetic interceptor systems continue to play a vital role in C-UAS operations. These solutions involve launching a physical projectile or another object to physically intercept and destroy or disable the UAS. This category encompasses a broad range of technologies, from specialized munitions to interceptor drones.

One of the most straightforward kinetic approaches involves the use of conventional small arms fire or specialized munitions fired from ground-based weapon systems. For low-flying, slow-moving drones, especially those at close range, engaging them with standard machine guns or rifles can be an effective, albeit often imprecise, method of neutralization. However, this approach carries a significant risk of collateral damage due to the projectiles' trajectory and fragmentation.

For higher-flying or more robust UAS, more specialized munitions are required. This can include proximity-fuzed rounds designed to detonate near the drone, showering it with shrapnel, or guided missiles specifically designed for air-to-air engagements, albeit scaled down for the UAS threat. The primary drawback of employing traditional munitions is the finite magazine capacity; each engagement expends a physical round, and resupply can be a logistical challenge in sustained operations. The cost of employing specialized missiles against inexpensive commercial drones can be prohibitively high, leading to an unfavorable cost-exchange ratio.

A more contemporary kinetic solution involves the use of interceptor drones. These are specialized UAS designed to autonomously or remotely pilot themselves to intercept and neutralize a threat drone. Interceptor drones can employ various methods. Some are equipped with nets or tethers designed to entangle the target drone, bringing it down safely or disabling its rotors. Others may be designed to physically collide with the threat drone, using their own robust construction to damage or destroy the target. Some advanced concepts envision interceptor drones carrying small explosive charges that detonate on contact or in close proximity.

The advantage of interceptor drones lies in their reusability and their ability to operate in complex airspace where traditional ground-based weapons might be too dangerous. They can be deployed from mobile platforms and can be programmed to engage targets at considerable distances. However, developing reliable and effective interceptor drones requires sophisticated navigation, guidance, and control systems, as well as robust airframes capable of withstanding the stresses of interception. The cost of developing, producing, and deploying a fleet of interceptor drones can also be significant, though potentially less than employing numerous specialized missiles.

The operational tempo and cost-effectiveness of kinetic C-UAS solutions are critical considerations. Directed energy weapons, particularly lasers, offer a near-unlimited "magazine" and a very low cost-per-shot, making them attractive for sustained operations against swarms or persistent threats, provided their environmental limitations can be mitigated. HPM weapons also offer the potential for high engagement rates. The initial acquisition cost of these advanced systems is substantial, and their operational deployment requires significant infrastructure, including power and cooling. Traditional munitions, while often more affordable per unit than directed energy systems, are limited by the number of rounds available and the logistics of resupply. The cost-exchange ratio can be particularly unfavorable when using expensive missiles or guided munitions against inexpensive commercial drones. Interceptor drones offer a middle ground, with reusability reducing the per-shot cost over time, but the upfront investment in developing and fielding the drone fleet can be considerable.

Collateral effects remain a paramount concern for all kinetic solutions. While directed energy weapons offer high precision, misfires, beam wander, or targeting errors can still lead to unintended consequences. Atmospheric scattering or absorption can reduce the effectiveness of lasers, requiring operators to maintain engagement for longer periods, increasing the risk of unintended beam exposure. HPM weapons, by their nature, can have a broader area of effect, potentially disrupting friendly electronics if not carefully managed. Conventional munitions inherently pose the greatest risk of collateral damage due to projectile trajectories, fragmentation, and potential for ricochets.

The employment of firearms or explosive ordnance in populated areas or near critical infrastructure requires extremely strict rules of engagement and precise targeting to avoid unacceptable risks to civilian life and property. Interceptor drones, while offering a degree of controlled engagement, can still pose a risk if their interception maneuvers go awry, or if they themselves are downed by countermeasures. The decision to employ any kinetic C-UAS solution must therefore be informed by a thorough risk assessment, carefully weighing the immediate threat posed by the UAS against the potential for unintended harm.

Kinetic countermeasures represent a crucial element of a comprehensive C-UAS strategy, providing decisive means to neutralize airborne threats when non-kinetic methods are insufficient. Directed energy weapons, such as High-Energy

Lasers and High-Power Microwaves, offer the promise of rapid, precise, and deep-magazine engagements, with low cost-per-shot potential but facing challenges related to atmospheric conditions, power requirements, and initial acquisition costs. Traditional interceptor systems, ranging from specialized munitions and interceptor drones to even trained birds of prey, provide a spectrum of physical engagement methods. Each kinetic solution carries its own set of advantages and disadvantages concerning cost, operational tempo, collateral effects, and logistical requirements. The selection and deployment of kinetic C-UAS capabilities must therefore be a carefully considered decision, integrated with robust detection, identification, and non-kinetic systems, to ensure the most effective and responsible defense against the ever-evolving UAS threat landscape.

The preceding discussion has illuminated the diverse array of technologies available for countering Unmanned Aircraft Systems (UAS), spanning both non-kinetic and kinetic domains. However, the mere existence of these tools does not, in itself, guarantee an effective defense. The complexity and evolving nature of the UAS threat landscape necessitate a shift from piecemeal adoption of individual countermeasures to the development and implementation of cohesive, integrated strategies. This subsection pivots to examine the critical elements required to forge such holistic approaches, emphasizing the synergy between detection, identification, and neutralization capabilities, and exploring the operational concepts that underpin their effective deployment. The overarching goal is to move beyond reactive, single-solution responses towards a proactive, layered, and adaptable C-UAS architecture that can contend with the multifaceted challenges posed by modern UAS.

The foundational principle of an integrated C-UAS strategy lies in the establishment of a layered defense architecture. This approach acknowledges that no single sensor or effector system can reliably detect, track, and neutralize every potential UAS threat under all operational conditions. Instead, it advocates for the overlapping and complementary deployment of multiple systems, each designed to address specific aspects of the threat spectrum and operational environment. At the first layer, persistent surveillance is paramount. This involves employing a suite of sensors capable of detecting UAS across various altitudes, speeds, and signatures. Radar systems, particularly those designed for low, slow, small targets (often referred to as "micro-drones"), are essential for initial detection and tracking, providing volumetric coverage and range information. Electro-optical/infrared (EO/IR) cameras offer visual identification and can be highly effective in certain weather conditions, particularly for confirming the presence and type of UAS once detected by other means. Acoustic sensors can sometimes provide early warning, especially for quieter or stealthier drones, by detecting the distinctive sound of their propulsion systems.

Radio frequency (RF) detection systems are crucial for identifying drones that are actively communicating with their operators or using GPS navigation, allowing for the potential detection of their control links and signals. Increasingly, artificial intelligence (AI) and machine learning (ML) algorithms are being integrated into sensor fusion platforms. These algorithms can process data from multiple sensor types simultaneously, correlating disparate pieces of information to build a more accurate and robust picture of the airspace.

This fusion is vital because individual sensors often have blind spots or limitations. For instance, radar can struggle with very small, low-flying targets or discriminate them from clutter, while EO/IR cameras are dependent on visual line-of-sight and can be affected by weather. By combining data from radar, EO/IR, acoustic, and RF sensors, a C-UAS system can achieve a higher probability of detection, more accurate tracking, and a reduced false alarm rate. The AI-powered sensor fusion essentially creates a "digital observer" that can identify patterns and anomalies that a human operator might miss, or that individual sensors cannot reliably detect. This layer of pervasive, multi-spectral sensing forms the eyes and ears of the C-UAS architecture, providing continuous awareness of the protected airspace.

Moving beyond initial detection, the identification, classification, and tracking (ICT) phase is critical. Once a potential UAS is detected, it is imperative to determine what it is, its intended purpose (if discernible), and its precise trajectory. This is where advanced algorithms and potentially human analysis come into play. Classification might involve distinguishing between a commercial off-the-shelf drone, a military-grade system, a swarming formation, or even a balloon or bird that might trigger a false alarm. Tracking involves maintaining a continuous and accurate representation of the UAS's position, velocity, and altitude. The effectiveness of subsequent actions hinges directly on the quality of this ICT data. If a system cannot accurately identify or track a threat, it cannot effectively engage it. This phase often involves integrating data from various sources, including flight path analysis based on telemetry data (if obtainable), visual recognition software, and comparison against known UAS signatures. The precision of the tracking data is paramount, especially when employing kinetic or highly directional non-kinetic effectors, where even slight deviations in aim can lead to missed engagements or unintended consequences.

Advanced C-UAS systems can employ techniques such as Kalman filtering and particle filtering to refine tracking data and predict future trajectories, even in the presence of intermittent sensor readings or evasive maneuvers. AI can be trained on vast datasets of UAS imagery and flight characteristics to rapidly classify detected objects, thereby speeding up the decision-making process and allowing for more timely responses.

The third crucial layer involves the selection and employment of appropriate effector systems. This is where the choice between kinetic and non-kinetic countermeasures, or a combination thereof, becomes critical. An integrated strategy recognizes that different threats may require different responses. For instance, a small, commercially available drone entering a restricted zone might be best dealt with by RF jamming or a targeted RF-directed energy pulse that disrupts its control link. A more sophisticated, autonomous drone or a swarm of drones might necessitate a kinetic response, such as a net-equipped interceptor drone or a directed energy weapon capable of causing physical damage. The concept of "right effector for the right threat" is central to efficiency and cost-effectiveness. Moreover, the effector layer must be dynamically responsive.

The C-UAS command and control (C2) system must be capable of rapidly selecting and tasking the most suitable effector based on the ICT data, the operational environment, and pre-defined rules of engagement. This rapid response capability is vital against fast-moving or swarming threats. The integration of effectors involves not only their technical connectivity but also their seamless activation and deactivation within the C2 framework. This includes managing power requirements for directed energy systems, coordinating flight paths for interceptor drones, and ensuring safe firing arcs for kinetic munitions. The goal is to create a fluid transition from detection to neutralization, minimizing the time window during which a threat can operate unimpeded.

A critical component of any integrated C-UAS strategy is the establishment of robust command and control (C2) structures. Effective C2 ensures that all elements of the C-UAS architecture, sensors, ICT systems, effectors, and human operators, are coordinated and work in concert. This includes developing clear operational doctrines, assigning responsibilities, and defining communication protocols. The C2 system acts as the central nervous system of the C-UAS defense, receiving information from sensors, processing it to generate actionable intelligence, and then directing the appropriate effector to neutralize the threat. This requires sophisticated software platforms that can ingest data from diverse sources, fuse it into a coherent operational picture, and provide intuitive interfaces for human operators to make decisions or to automate decision-making processes within defined parameters.

In a military or security context, the C2 system must also be resilient and interoperable with wider defense networks. It needs to be able to operate in contested electromagnetic environments and share relevant threat data with higher headquarters or allied forces. The development of standardized data links and communication protocols is essential for this interoperability. The C2 architecture must be scalable, capable of expanding or contracting its operational footprint and the number of systems it manages based on the evolving threat and the criticality of the protected asset. The ability to pre-plan responses to anticipated threats, such as setting up specific sensor-effector pairings for known operational areas or times, also falls under the purview of effective C2. This proactive planning can significantly reduce response times and improve the overall effectiveness of the C-UAS defense.

The definition and rigorous application of Rules of Engagement (ROE) are paramount for any C-UAS system, particularly those employing kinetic effectors or operating in complex environments. ROE provide the legal and ethical framework for when and how defensive actions can be taken. They must clearly delineate the conditions under which a UAS constitutes a hostile threat, the escalation pathways for engagement, and the acceptable levels of collateral damage. For instance, ROE might specify that a detected UAS must first be identified and tracked, then potentially warned (if feasible), before an effector is authorized. They must also account for situations where the UAS might be carrying a hazardous payload, or where its failure to respond to warnings might indicate hostile intent. In civilian or quasi-civilian settings, ROE must be exceptionally conservative to minimize the risk to the public. This might mean prioritizing non-kinetic methods or strictly limiting kinetic engagements to situations where there is an immediate and overwhelming threat to life or critical infrastructure.

The integration of ROE into the C-UAS C2 system is crucial, acting as automated checks to prevent unauthorized engagements. This could involve requiring operator authorization for any kinetic action or ensuring that effector systems are only activated within designated safe zones. The dynamic nature of UAS threats and the evolving legal landscape surrounding their use necessitate regular review and updating of ROE. This ensures that they remain relevant, effective, and legally sound.

Seamless integration with the broader installation security framework is another cornerstone of effective C-UAS strategies. A C-UAS system cannot operate in a vacuum. It must be viewed as an integral part of a larger security ecosystem. This means ensuring that C-UAS sensors and alerts are fed into the central security operations center (SOC) alongside other security systems, such as perimeter intrusion detection, access control, and surveillance cameras. This holistic approach allows security personnel to correlate UAS activity with other potential security breaches, providing a more comprehensive understanding of the operational environment. For example, a detected UAS might be attempting to surveil a facility while a ground-based intrusion is simultaneously being attempted. By integrating these feeds, security forces can mount a more coordinated and effective response, recognizing the potential for a multi-faceted attack. This integration also extends to personnel and training. Security guards and response teams must be trained not only in their traditional roles but also in recognizing UAS threats, understanding C-UAS alerts, and knowing the procedures for escalating threats to the C-UAS operators.

The lines of authority and responsibility between general security personnel and specialized C-UAS operators must be clearly defined. Furthermore, the C-UAS system should be considered during the initial design and layout of secure facilities, ensuring that sensor coverage is optimized and that effector systems can be deployed without creating undue risks to friendly personnel or infrastructure. This might involve designating specific zones for C-UAS engagement or ensuring that power and communication infrastructure is available to support C-UAS equipment.

The operational concept of a layered defense architecture necessitates a continuous cycle of "detect, identify, track, decide, act, and assess." This iterative process ensures that the C-UAS system remains adaptive and responsive to evolving threats. The detection phase, as previously discussed, involves broad surveillance. Identification and tracking refine this initial detection into actionable intelligence. The decision phase, guided by ROE and threat assessment, determines the appropriate course of action. The act phase involves the employment of the selected effector. Crucially, the "assess" phase follows every engagement. This involves evaluating the effectiveness of the action taken, was the UAS neutralized? Were there any unintended consequences? This feedback loop is essential for refining future responses, updating threat profiles, and improving the performance of both sensors and effectors. For instance, if a particular jamming frequency proves ineffective against a new type of drone, the system can learn from this and adjust its response profile. Similarly, if a kinetic engagement results in unintended damage, the system can learn to adjust engagement parameters or ROE. This continuous learning and adaptation are vital in staying ahead of adversaries who are constantly upgrading their UAS capabilities.

The implementation of integrated C-UAS strategies also requires a commitment to ongoing training and realistic exercises. Personnel must be proficient in operating the diverse array of sensors and effectors, understanding the C2 system, and executing the defined ROE. Realistic training scenarios, which simulate various UAS threats and operational conditions, are essential for building this proficiency. These exercises should test not only individual system operators but also the entire C-UAS team, including C2 personnel, sensor operators, and effector specialists, to ensure seamless coordination and communication. Exercises should also include joint training with other security and defense elements to validate the integration with the broader security framework.

This might involve simulating a UAS attack during a larger military exercise or a security drill at a sensitive facility. The use of "red teams" or adversary simulation units that can employ actual or simulated UAS against the C-UAS defense provides invaluable opportunities for testing and validation in a controlled, yet realistic, environment. These exercises help identify weaknesses, refine operational procedures, and build confidence in the system's capabilities. Moreover, the dynamic nature of UAS technology and adversary tactics means that training programs must be regularly updated to reflect the latest threats and countermeasures.

The consideration of the electromagnetic spectrum is intrinsically linked to integrated C-UAS strategies. Many C-UAS countermeasures, particularly non-kinetic ones, rely on manipulating or denying RF signals. Therefore, understanding and managing the electromagnetic environment is crucial. This involves not only employing RF detection and jamming capabilities but also protecting friendly communication and navigation systems from disruption. Sophisticated C2 systems can incorporate spectrum management tools that help identify potential interference, allocate frequencies efficiently, and prioritize critical communications. This also extends to the use of directional effects, where RF energy is focused on specific targets to minimize its impact on surrounding systems.

Directed energy weapons, whether laser or microwave, also operate within or interact with the electromagnetic spectrum and require careful consideration of their signatures and potential for interference. The development of C-UAS systems that are "spectrum-aware" and can operate effectively in congested or contested electromagnetic environments is a significant advantage. This may involve employing frequency hopping techniques, using lower-probability-of-intercept/detection (LPI/LPD) communication methods, or developing advanced waveform technologies that are more resilient to jamming.

The strategic integration of C-UAS capabilities also demands foresight and adaptability in anticipating future threats. Adversaries are not static; they continuously evolve their UAS platforms, operational tactics, and countermeasures. An integrated strategy must therefore be designed with future flexibility in mind. This involves choosing C-UAS technologies that are modular and can be upgraded and adopting C2 architectures that can readily incorporate new sensor and effector types as they become available. Continuous research and development, coupled with intelligence gathering on emerging UAS threats, are essential to informing these long-term strategic decisions.

The concept of a "digital twin" or a simulated environment where different C-UAS configurations and responses can be tested and evaluated before physical deployment is also becoming increasingly valuable. This allows for rapid prototyping and adaptation of strategies in response to intelligence about new adversary capabilities. The integration of C-UAS must also consider potential synergistic effects with other defense capabilities. For example, how can C-UAS systems be used in conjunction with electronic warfare (EW) assets, cyber defense teams, or even traditional air defense systems to create a more robust and multi-layered defense against complex aerial threats? The answer to these questions lies in the proactive development of integrated operational concepts that anticipate and leverage these potential synergies.

Ultimately, the development of integrated C-UAS strategies is not merely a technical challenge but a strategic imperative. It requires a fundamental shift in how defense and security forces conceptualize and implement their counter-drone capabilities. By moving towards a layered defense architecture, establishing robust command and control, defining clear rules of engagement, and ensuring seamless integration with existing security frameworks, organizations can build resilient, adaptable, and effective defenses against the pervasive and evolving UAS threat. This holistic approach, underpinned by continuous training, spectrum awareness, and a forward-looking perspective, is the only viable path to achieving comprehensive protection in an increasingly drone-enabled world.

The focus must remain on creating a dynamic, intelligent, and coordinated system that can not only react to threats but also anticipate and deter them, thereby ensuring the safety and security of critical assets and personnel.

Chapter 9: Addressing Directed Energy and Cyber Threats

The landscape of modern warfare and security is being dramatically reshaped by the rapid evolution and proliferation of advanced technologies. Among these, Directed Energy (DE) weapons represent a particularly potent and growing threat, transitioning from the realm of science fiction to tangible operational capabilities.

These systems, which include lasers and High-Power Microwave (HPM) devices, offer a distinct set of advantages and present a unique set of challenges to conventional defense strategies. Unlike kinetic weapons that rely on the physical impact of projectiles, DE weapons deliver their effects using concentrated beams of electromagnetic energy. This fundamental difference enables them to achieve effects at the speed of light, bypassing many of the limitations associated with traditional ordnance, such as ballistic trajectories, ammunition logistics, and the need for precise physical targeting of moving components.

The increasing sophistication and decreasing cost of DE technology mean that capabilities once exclusive to major military powers are becoming more accessible to a wider range of state and non-state actors. This democratization of advanced weaponry significantly broadens the potential threat spectrum that security forces must contend with. For critical infrastructure, military installations, and sensitive government facilities, the implications are profound. DE weapons are not merely theoretical future threats; they are emerging as credible tools for disrupting, disabling, or destroying vital assets. Their ability to operate with precision and speed makes them particularly effective against targets that are vulnerable to rapid incapacitation or destruction, and for which traditional responses might be too slow or too resource-intensive.

One of the primary vulnerabilities that DE weapons exploit is the reliance of modern systems on sophisticated sensors and communication networks. Lasers, for instance, can be designed to incapacitate or destroy optical sensors – the eyes of many surveillance and targeting systems. A precisely aimed laser beam, even one of relatively low power, can permanently damage or blind sensitive imaging equipment, rendering an otherwise advanced system useless. Think of sophisticated radar arrays, thermal imagers, or day/night optical cameras. These are critical for situational awareness, early warning, and target acquisition.

A directed energy attack on these assets can effectively create blind spots, leaving a facility vulnerable to subsequent attacks or infiltration. The speed of light delivery means that by the time an optical sensor detects an incoming threat (if it can even detect a laser), it may already be too late to avoid the damage. This speed advantage, coupled with the ability to precisely target delicate components without necessarily destroying the entire platform, offers a significant tactical edge to an adversary.

High-Power Microwave (HPM) weapons offer a different, yet equally disruptive, mode of attack. Instead of physically damaging components, HPM weapons deliver intense bursts of microwave energy designed to overload and disrupt sensitive electronic systems. This energy can induce damaging currents and voltages within circuits, causing them to malfunction, reset, or suffer permanent damage. The effects can be widespread, impacting not just a single piece of equipment but potentially an entire network of interconnected systems. Communications equipment, command and control nodes, navigation systems, and even the electronic control units within vehicles and unmanned systems are all susceptible to HPM effects. An HPM attack could effectively create an electronic blackout, severing communication links, disrupting GPS navigation, and rendering automated defense systems inoperable. The challenge with HPM is that the damage may not always be immediately apparent as a physical breach. Electronics might appear intact but be rendered non-functional, leading to a period of uncertainty and confusion for defenders. The range and power of HPM weapons are increasing, and their potential to disable large areas or multiple systems simultaneously makes them a significant concern for the resilience of any technologically dependent defense posture.

The implications of DE weapons extend beyond just disabling equipment; they can also pose a direct threat to personnel. While higher-power lasers capable of rapidly incapacitating humans are still largely in the realm of development and are subject to international agreements concerning blinding laser weapons, lower-power lasers can be used for harassment and disorientation. Imagine a scenario where personnel operating critical systems, or even those on perimeter duty, are momentarily blinded or disoriented by a laser flash. This brief incapacitation could be enough to facilitate an intrusion, disable a guard's ability to respond to a threat, or create chaos. Similarly, while HPM weapons are primarily designed to affect electronics, extremely high-power concentrations could potentially have non-lethal effects on biological systems, though this is a more speculative and less developed area of DE application compared to anti-materiel effects. The primary concern remains the disabling of the systems that personnel rely upon for their protection and mission execution.

The DE threat is further amplified by the potential for DE weapons to be integrated into unmanned platforms, including drones. Small, commercially available drones can be modified to carry relatively low-power lasers for nuisance purposes or even to deliver small HPM emitters. More sophisticated military drones can be equipped with more potent DE payloads, allowing for standoff attacks against critical assets. This combination of DE technology with the mobility and accessibility of unmanned systems creates a highly flexible and potentially persistent threat. An adversary could deploy drones equipped with DE payloads to continuously probe defenses, disrupt sensor networks, or provide targeting information for subsequent kinetic attacks, all while remaining at a safe distance from physical counterattacks. The ability to rapidly deploy and redeploy DE-equipped drones means that defenses must be not only robust but also highly dynamic and responsive to threats emerging from multiple vectors.

The non-traditional nature of DE attacks complicates traditional detection and attribution. Unlike a projectile or missile, a laser beam or an HPM pulse can be difficult to detect as it travels through the air. By the time its effect is observed, a damaged sensor, a disrupted communication link, the source of the attack may have already moved or ceased its operations. This makes the attribution of DE attacks challenging, potentially leading to delayed or misdirected responses. Developing effective early warning systems that can detect the subtle signatures of DE weapon deployment, such as the optical distortions caused by high-power lasers or the electromagnetic emissions associated with HPM systems, is therefore a critical area of research and development. Without robust detection and tracking capabilities specifically tailored to DE phenomena, defenders will remain largely reactive, dealing with the consequences of an attack rather than preventing it.

The psychological and operational impact of DE weapons should not be underestimated. The knowledge that key systems are vulnerable to instantaneous, invisible attack can sow uncertainty and erode confidence in technological defenses. This psychological dimension can be as debilitating as the physical damage inflicted. In a high-stakes operational environment, the fear of a sudden, inexplicable system failure due to a DE attack could lead to hesitation, indecision, and a breakdown in coordinated defense.

This makes the development of comprehensive countermeasures, which not only mitigate the physical effects but also address the psychological impact, a strategic imperative. Building resilience through redundancy, hardening of critical electronic systems against EMP effects (which share some principles with HPM), and developing operational doctrines that account for the potential of DE attacks are all vital steps in this direction. The growing accessibility and diverse applications of Directed Energy weapons demand a proactive and sophisticated approach to defense, one that moves beyond conventional understandings of threat and response to embrace the unique challenges posed by energy-based weaponry.

The escalating threat posed by directed energy (DE) weapons, specifically lasers and High-Power Microwave (HPM) systems, necessitates a paradigm shift in how we approach defense strategies. The speed-of-light engagement capability and the potential for widespread electronic disruption offered by these technologies render many traditional defensive measures insufficient. Consequently, a robust and multi-layered defense architecture is paramount to safeguarding critical infrastructure, military assets, and sensitive operational capabilities. This involves not only understanding the fundamental characteristics of laser and HPM attacks but also proactively implementing specialized countermeasures and hardening protocols. The objective is to render our most vital assets resilient to these novel forms of attack, ensuring operational continuity and mission success in an increasingly complex threat environment.

One of the foundational pillars of defending against laser and HPM attacks is the concept of asset hardening. This involves a proactive approach to making vulnerable systems more resistant to the specific effects of directed energy. For laser threats, which primarily target optical and sensor systems, hardening can involve the application of specialized coatings or materials designed to absorb or diffuse laser energy, preventing it from reaching and damaging sensitive optical components.

These coatings might be spectrally selective, designed to counter specific laser wavelengths commonly employed by adversaries. Furthermore, physical barriers and enclosures can be engineered with materials that possess high reflectivity or ablative properties, designed to vaporize or deflect incoming laser energy before it can compromise the protected system. For instance, optical apertures on sensors, which are often the most vulnerable points, can be protected by deployable shutters or intricate labyrinthine structures that scatter light. The design considerations for these hardened enclosures must balance survivability with operational functionality, ensuring that the protective measures do not unduly impede the intended performance of the sensor or system during normal operations. The development of smart shutters, which can automatically deploy upon detection of a laser threat, further enhances this capability, providing a dynamic layer of defense.

Beyond passive hardening, active optical countermeasures play a crucial role in deceiving or defeating laser-guided systems. These countermeasures aim to mislead the targeting sensors of laser-armed platforms or to mask the signature of the protected asset. Techniques can range from employing advanced camouflage and signature management to deploying decoys and obscurants. Electro-optic countermeasures, for example, can actively generate false targets or alter the perceived spectral characteristics of an asset, making it difficult for a laser designator or seeker to lock on or track accurately. The use of aerosolized obscurants, such as smoke or chaff, can create a temporary visual screen that diffuses or scatters laser energy, disrupting the beam path. The effectiveness of obscurants is often dependent on environmental conditions and the specific wavelength of the laser.

More sophisticated countermeasures involve the generation of dazzling or blinding effects, not to incapacitate personnel, but to overload and saturate the optical sensors of attacking systems, rendering them temporarily ineffective. This can be achieved through the deployment of high-intensity strobes or directed light sources. The strategic deployment of decoys, which mimic the thermal or optical signatures of high-value assets, can also divert incoming laser energy and thus protect the actual target.

For HPM threats, the challenge shifts from the direct destruction of optical components to the disruption and damage of electronic systems. Hardening against HPM attacks typically involves electromagnetic shielding and filtering. Critical electronic components, circuit boards, and entire systems can be enclosed within Faraday cages or shielded enclosures constructed from conductive materials that block or attenuate electromagnetic radiation. The effectiveness of such shielding depends on the frequency range of the HPM pulse, the conductivity of the shielding material, and the integrity of the enclosure, including any apertures or penetrations. The design of these shielded environments must account for power, data, and ventilation needs, ensuring that these essential connections are also filtered to prevent the ingress of damaging electromagnetic energy. Specialized filters, such as electromagnetic interference (EMI) filters, are incorporated into power and data lines to prevent induced currents from propagating into sensitive electronics. The concept of "EMP hardening," developed to protect against nuclear electromagnetic pulses, provides a valuable foundation for HPM defense, as many of the principles of shielding and filtering are transferable.

The concept of "circuit hardening" is vital for HPM resilience. This involves designing electronic circuits with inherent robustness against overvoltage and overcurrent conditions. Techniques such as the use of transient voltage suppressors (TVS diodes), metal-oxide-varistors (MOVs), and fast-acting fuses can help to clamp or divert damaging surges of current and voltage, protecting more sensitive semiconductor components. The selection and placement of these protection devices are critical, and their effectiveness is often optimized for specific threat profiles. Designing redundant systems and critical redundancies within electrical pathways can also provide a degree of resilience. If one component or pathway is damaged by an HPM attack, a secondary system can take over, maintaining operational functionality. This is particularly important for command and control systems, communication networks, and vital sensor suites.

In addition to hardening and shielding, specialized materials offer advanced protective capabilities. For laser defense, materials with high thermal conductivity can help dissipate the heat generated by absorbed laser energy, preventing localized overheating and damage. Ablative materials, designed to vaporize in a controlled manner when struck by high-energy laser beams, can absorb significant amounts of energy by undergoing a phase change, effectively sacrificing a thin layer of material to protect the underlying structure.

These materials can be integrated into protective coatings or laminates. For HPM defense, the development of novel electromagnetic shielding materials, such as conductive nanocomposites or metamaterials, offers the potential for lighter, more flexible, and more effective shielding solutions. Metamaterials, in particular, can be engineered to exhibit unique electromagnetic properties, allowing for the manipulation of electromagnetic waves in ways not possible with conventional materials, potentially enabling more efficient and targeted shielding.

The development of Directed Energy Counter-Weapon Systems represents the next frontier in actively combating laser and HPM threats. These systems are designed not merely to defend, but to neutralize the DE threat itself. For laser attacks, this can involve High-Energy Laser (HEL) systems designed to intercept and destroy incoming laser threats or to dazzle and disable enemy laser-targeting systems. A defensive HEL could be employed to track an incoming laser beam and project a counter-beam of sufficient power to disrupt the enemy beam or damage the enemy's emitter. The speed of light engagement of laser weapons means that defensive systems must also operate at or near the speed of light, requiring highly responsive tracking and firing mechanisms. Similarly, HPM counter-weapon systems are being developed to generate targeted HPM pulses that can disrupt or disable enemy DE emitters or electronic systems. These offensive HPM systems are designed to be precise and focused, capable of disabling specific enemy assets without causing collateral damage to friendly forces or civilian infrastructure.

The operationalization of these counter-DE systems requires sophisticated tracking, targeting, and fire control systems. Advanced radar, electro-optical sensors, and signal intelligence (SIGINT) capabilities are needed to detect, identify, and track incoming DE threats. Once a threat is identified, the defensive system must be able to slew rapidly and accurately engage the target. This demands high-speed actuators, robust computational power, and integrated battle management systems. The effectiveness of counter-DE systems is also dependent on understanding the characteristics of the adversary's DE weapons – their power, wavelength, pulse duration, beam divergence, and operational doctrine. This intelligence is crucial for tailoring the countermeasure response.

The integration of DE counter-weapon systems into existing defense architectures presents significant challenges and opportunities. These systems can be deployed on fixed sites, mobile platforms, or even unmanned aerial vehicles (UAVs), providing a flexible and adaptable defense capability. The synergy between kinetic defense systems and DE counter-weapon systems is also a critical area of development. A layered defense might involve using DE systems for early detection and disruption of threats, followed by kinetic weapons for final neutralization if necessary. This combined approach leverages the strengths of both types of weaponry to create a more robust and resilient defense posture.

A comprehensive understanding of DE weapon characteristics is fundamental to developing effective countermeasures. This includes detailed knowledge of the power levels, beam quality, pulse repetition frequencies, and wavelengths of laser systems, as well as the frequency bands, pulse widths, peak powers, and spatial profiles of HPM devices. For instance, knowing the specific wavelengths used by adversary lasers allows for the development of spectrally tuned optical coatings and filters. Understanding the operating frequencies of enemy HPM systems informs the design of appropriate shielding and filtering materials. Intelligence gathering on adversary DE capabilities, including their deployment patterns, technological advancements, and intended uses, is therefore a critical enabler for defense planning. This intelligence should inform the selection and implementation of specific hardening techniques, countermeasures, and counter-weapon systems.

Response protocols for DE attacks must also be developed and rehearsed. These protocols should outline the steps to be taken upon detection of a DE threat, including the immediate activation of countermeasures, the assessment of damage, the implementation of redundant systems, and the potential deployment of counter-

DE assets. Clear lines of command and control are essential, as is the ability to rapidly adapt response strategies based on the evolving nature of the threat. Training personnel to recognize the signatures of DE attacks and to respond appropriately is equally important. The psychological impact of DE attacks, characterized by their instantaneous and often invisible nature, can lead to confusion and hesitation. Therefore, training must also address the psychological resilience of personnel operating under such conditions.

The survivability of critical infrastructure hinges on a proactive and adaptive approach to defense against DE threats. This involves a continuous cycle of threat assessment, vulnerability analysis, technology development, and operational integration. As DE technology continues to advance, so too must our defensive capabilities. This necessitates sustained investment in research and development, fostering collaboration between government, industry, and academia, and ensuring that defense strategies evolve in lockstep with the evolving threat landscape. The challenges are significant, but the imperative to protect vital assets and ensure national security demands nothing less than a dedicated and forward-looking approach to directed energy defense.

The digital domain, once considered a secondary theater of operations, has unequivocally become a primary battleground. The persistent and evolving nature of cyber threats targeting military installations presents a complex and insidious challenge, demanding a continuous adaptation of defensive strategies. Adversaries, whether state-sponsored actors, sophisticated criminal organizations, or even ideologically motivated groups, relentlessly probe for weaknesses in the intricate web of networks, operational technology (OT), and critical infrastructure control systems that underpin modern military operations. These incursions are not random acts of digital vandalism; they are often meticulously planned campaigns designed to achieve specific strategic objectives, ranging from crippling command and control (C2) capabilities to exfiltrating sensitive intelligence or even subtly manipulating operational parameters to induce catastrophic failures.

Among the most concerning of these digital assailants are Advanced Persistent Threats (APTs). These are not your typical opportunistic malware infections. APTs are characterized by their sustained, stealthy, and highly targeted nature. An APT actor will dedicate significant resources and time to infiltrate a specific network, establish a foothold, and then remain undetected for extended periods, meticulously mapping the network, identifying critical assets, and awaiting the opportune moment to strike.

Their objective is rarely immediate destruction; instead, it is often to conduct long-term espionage, pilfering classified data, technological blueprints, or strategic plans. This patient approach allows them to evade conventional security measures that are often designed to detect rapid, high-volume intrusions. The methodology of an APT typically involves a multi-stage attack: initial reconnaissance to identify vulnerabilities, a carefully crafted exploit to gain access (often through spear-phishing campaigns targeting specific individuals with high-level access), the establishment of a persistent presence through backdoors or compromised credentials, lateral movement across the network to reach high-value targets, and finally, data exfiltration or preparation for a later disruptive action. The sheer persistence and the adaptive nature of these actors mean that defenses must be equally persistent and dynamic, employing continuous monitoring, threat hunting, and rapid incident response.

Ransomware, while often associated with commercial enterprises, poses a significant and growing threat to military operations. Unlike APTs, which focus on stealth and long-term intelligence gathering, ransomware actors aim to disrupt operations and extort financial gain. By encrypting critical data, disabling essential systems, or locking down operational technology, these attacks can bring military bases, logistics networks, or even weapon systems to a grinding halt. The impact of such an attack can be profound, not only in terms of operational paralysis but also in the potential compromise of sensitive mission-critical information that may be rendered inaccessible.

The rapid proliferation of ransomware-as-a-service (RaaS) models has lowered the barrier to entry for cybercriminals, leading to an increase in the sophistication and frequency of these attacks. Military organizations, with their vast digital footprints and reliance on interconnected systems, present highly attractive targets for ransomware gangs who understand that the cost of downtime can be astronomically high. The challenge lies not just in preventing initial infection, but in ensuring robust data backup and recovery capabilities that are themselves isolated from the primary network to prevent them from being compromised alongside the main systems.

The vulnerability of the modern military supply chain represents another critical vector for cyberattack. From the microchips embedded in complex weapon systems to the software that manages logistics and communications, military hardware and software often rely on a global network of suppliers. Each link in this chain, if not adequately secured, can become a point of entry for adversaries. Supply chain attacks can manifest in various forms. Attackers might compromise a software vendor and inject malicious code into legitimate updates that are then distributed to military users. They could tamper with hardware during the manufacturing process, embedding backdoors or listening devices. Or they could target the logistics providers responsible for transporting sensitive equipment, intercepting and altering components. The SolarWinds incident, while primarily impacting civilian entities, starkly illustrated the potential for supply chain compromise to have far-reaching national security implications. For military organizations, the reliance on a complex and often opaque global supply chain creates a persistent blind spot that adversaries can exploit to gain access to sensitive systems and data without ever directly engaging the military's primary defenses. This necessitates a rigorous vetting of all suppliers, continuous monitoring of the supply chain for anomalies, and the implementation of stringent security controls for all third-party software and hardware.

Espionage campaigns, conducted through cyber means, remain a cornerstone of intelligence gathering for many nation-states. These campaigns are designed to systematically collect information that provides strategic, operational, and tactical advantages. This can include sensitive technological research and development, details of future military deployments, troop movements, diplomatic negotiations, or intelligence assessments. The methods employed are diverse, ranging from sophisticated phishing attacks designed to steal credentials, to the deployment of custom malware to siphon data from air-gapped systems through covert channels, and the exploitation of zero-day vulnerabilities in widely used software.

The goal is to build a comprehensive picture of an adversary's capabilities, intentions, and weaknesses. The sheer volume of data generated by military operations, coupled with the interconnectedness of systems, provides fertile ground for these espionage efforts. Protecting against such campaigns requires not only strong technical defenses but also robust counter-intelligence measures, user awareness training, and a deep understanding of the information that is most valuable to potential adversaries.

The increasing convergence of Information Technology (IT) and Operational Technology (OT) systems presents a particularly acute challenge. OT encompasses the hardware and software that control industrial processes, such as those found in power grids, manufacturing plants, and, crucially, military command and control systems, weapon platforms, and base infrastructure. Historically, OT systems were often air-gapped and isolated, making them less vulnerable to traditional IT-based cyberattacks. However, the drive for efficiency, data integration, and remote management has led to the increasing interconnection of IT and OT networks.

This convergence, while offering benefits, creates new pathways for attackers. A compromise in the IT network, which may have more robust but also more familiar security controls, can now serve as a gateway to the OT environment, where systems may be older, less patched, and more critical to physical operations. The consequences of an OT compromise can be devastating, leading to physical destruction, loss of life, or widespread disruption. For example, an attack on a base's power management system could disable essential services, or an intrusion into a missile defense system's control logic could render it inoperable or even, in a worst-case scenario, cause it to misfire. Defending this converged environment requires a holistic security approach that understands the unique characteristics and vulnerabilities of OT systems, implementing specialized security controls and monitoring mechanisms that can detect anomalous behavior within these critical operational environments.

The very nature of military operations introduces unique vulnerabilities. The need for rapid deployment, the use of mobile and often remote command posts, and the operation in contested electromagnetic environments can all create windows of opportunity for cyber adversaries. Maintaining secure communication channels in austere or hostile conditions is a significant challenge. Adversaries may attempt to intercept, jam, or spoof communications, thereby disrupting command and control.

The proliferation of Internet of Things (IoT) devices within military installations, from smart sensors to networked surveillance cameras, also expands the attack surface. These devices, often deployed for convenience or enhanced situational awareness, may have weak default security settings and may not be regularly patched, making them easy targets for initial network compromise or for use as pivot points into more sensitive networks. The sheer scale and complexity of military networks, spanning global bases, deployed forces, and cloud environments, create a vast and constantly shifting landscape that defenders must secure.

The evolving tactics employed by adversaries also necessitate a proactive and intelligence-driven defense. Beyond the well-established threats, new attack vectors are constantly emerging, often leveraging emerging technologies. The weaponization of artificial intelligence (AI) for automated vulnerability discovery, sophisticated social engineering, or the generation of hyper-realistic phishing content is a growing concern. Similarly, the use of quantum computing, while still in its nascent stages, poses a future threat to current encryption standards, requiring the development and implementation of quantum-resistant cryptography.

The adversary is not static; they are continuously learning, innovating, and adapting their methods to exploit the latest technological advancements and the inherent complexities of military systems. This demands a defense that is not only robust but also agile, capable of anticipating future threats and rapidly integrating new defensive capabilities. The cyber battlefield is a dynamic and unforgiving arena where vigilance, continuous adaptation, and a deep understanding of adversary motivations and methodologies are paramount to maintaining operational security and national security.

The digital domain, once considered a secondary theater of operations, has unequivocally become a primary battleground. The persistent and evolving nature of cyber threats targeting military installations presents a complex and insidious challenge, demanding a continuous adaptation of defensive strategies. Adversaries, whether state-sponsored actors, sophisticated criminal organizations, or even ideologically motivated groups, relentlessly probe for weaknesses in the intricate web of networks, operational technology (OT), and critical infrastructure control systems that underpin modern military operations. These incursions are not random acts of digital vandalism; they are often meticulously planned campaigns designed to achieve specific strategic objectives, ranging from crippling command and control (C2) capabilities to exfiltrating sensitive intelligence or even subtly manipulating operational parameters to induce catastrophic failures.

Among the most concerning of these digital assailants are Advanced Persistent Threats (APTs). These are not your typical opportunistic malware infections. APTs are characterized by their sustained, stealthy, and highly targeted nature. An APT actor will dedicate significant resources and time to infiltrate a specific network, establish a foothold, and then remain undetected for extended periods, meticulously mapping the network, identifying critical assets, and awaiting the opportune moment to strike. Their objective is rarely immediate destruction; instead, it is often to conduct long-term espionage, pilfering classified data, technological blueprints, or strategic plans. This patient approach allows them to evade conventional security measures that are often designed to detect rapid, high-volume intrusions.

The methodology of an APT typically involves a multi-stage attack: initial reconnaissance to identify vulnerabilities, a carefully crafted exploit to gain access (often through spear-phishing campaigns targeting specific individuals with high-level access), the establishment of a persistent presence through backdoors or compromised credentials, lateral movement across the network to reach high-value targets, and finally, data exfiltration or preparation for a later disruptive action. The sheer persistence and the adaptive nature of these actors mean that defenses must be equally persistent and dynamic, employing continuous monitoring, threat hunting, and rapid incident response.

Ransomware, while often associated with commercial enterprises, poses a significant and growing threat to military operations. Unlike APTs, which focus on stealth and long-term intelligence gathering, ransomware actors aim to disrupt operations and extort financial gain. By encrypting critical data, disabling essential systems, or locking down operational technology, these attacks can bring military bases, logistics networks, or even weapon systems to a grinding halt. The impact of such an attack can be profound, not only in terms of operational paralysis but also in the potential compromise of sensitive mission-critical information that may be rendered inaccessible.

The rapid proliferation of ransomware-as-a-service (RaaS) models has lowered the barrier to entry for cybercriminals, leading to an increase in the sophistication and frequency of these attacks. Military organizations, with their vast digital footprints and reliance on interconnected systems, present highly attractive targets for ransomware gangs who understand that the cost of downtime can be astronomically high. The challenge lies not just in preventing initial infection, but in ensuring robust data backup and recovery capabilities that are themselves isolated from the primary network to prevent them from being compromised alongside the main systems.

The vulnerability of the modern military supply chain represents another critical vector for cyberattack. From the microchips embedded in complex weapon systems to the software that manages logistics and communications, military hardware and software often rely on a global network of suppliers. Each link in this chain, if not adequately secured, can become a point of entry for adversaries. Supply chain attacks can manifest in various forms. Attackers might compromise a software vendor and inject malicious code into legitimate updates that are then distributed to military users. They could tamper with hardware during the manufacturing process, embedding backdoors or listening devices. Or they could target the logistics providers responsible for transporting sensitive equipment, intercepting and altering components.

The SolarWinds incident, while primarily impacting civilian entities, starkly illustrated the potential for supply chain compromise to have far-reaching national security implications. For military organizations, the reliance on a complex and often opaque global supply chain creates a persistent blind spot that adversaries can exploit to gain access to sensitive systems and data without ever directly engaging the military's primary defenses. This necessitates a rigorous vetting of all suppliers, continuous monitoring of the supply chain for anomalies, and the implementation of stringent security controls for all third-party software and hardware.

Espionage campaigns, conducted through cyber means, remain a cornerstone of intelligence gathering for many nation-states. These campaigns are designed to systematically collect information that provides strategic, operational, and tactical advantages. This can include sensitive technological research and development, details of future military deployments, troop movements, diplomatic negotiations, or intelligence assessments. The methods employed are diverse, ranging from sophisticated phishing attacks designed to steal credentials, to the deployment of custom malware to siphon data from air-gapped systems through covert channels, and the exploitation of zero-day vulnerabilities in widely used software. The goal is to build a comprehensive picture of an adversary's capabilities, intentions, and weaknesses. The sheer volume of data generated by military operations, coupled with the interconnectedness of systems, provides fertile ground for these espionage efforts. Protecting against such campaigns requires not only strong technical defenses but also robust counter-intelligence measures, user awareness training, and a deep understanding of the information that is most valuable to potential adversaries.

The increasing convergence of Information Technology (IT) and Operational Technology (OT) systems presents a particularly acute challenge. OT encompasses the hardware and software that control industrial processes, such as those found in power grids, manufacturing plants, and, crucially, military command and control systems, weapon platforms, and base infrastructure. Historically, OT systems were often air-gapped and isolated, making them less vulnerable to traditional IT-based cyberattacks. However, the drive for efficiency, data integration, and remote management has led to the increasing interconnection of IT and OT networks. This convergence, while offering benefits, creates new pathways for attackers. A compromise in the IT network, which may have more robust but also more familiar security controls, can now serve as a gateway to the OT environment, where systems may be older, less patched, and more critical to physical operations. The consequences of an OT compromise can be devastating, leading to physical destruction, loss of life, or widespread disruption. For example, an attack on a base's power management system could disable essential services, or an intrusion into a missile defense system's control logic could render it inoperable or even, in a worst-case scenario, cause it to misfire. Defending this converged environment requires a holistic security approach that understands the unique characteristics and vulnerabilities of OT systems, implementing specialized security controls and monitoring mechanisms that can detect anomalous behavior within these critical operational environments.

The very nature of military operations introduces unique vulnerabilities. The need for rapid deployment, the use of mobile and often remote command posts, and the operation in contested electromagnetic environments can all create windows of opportunity for cyber adversaries. Maintaining secure communication channels in austere or hostile conditions is a significant challenge. Adversaries may attempt to intercept, jam, or spoof communications, thereby disrupting command and control. The proliferation of Internet of Things (IoT) devices within military installations, from smart sensors to networked surveillance cameras, also expands the attack surface. These devices, often deployed for convenience or enhanced situational awareness, may have weak default security settings and may not be regularly patched, making them easy targets for initial network compromise or for use as pivot points into more sensitive networks. The sheer scale and complexity of military networks, spanning global bases, deployed forces, and cloud environments, create a vast and constantly shifting landscape that defenders must secure.

The evolving tactics employed by adversaries also necessitate a proactive and intelligence-driven defense. Beyond the well-established threats, new attack vectors are constantly emerging, often leveraging emerging technologies. The weaponization of artificial intelligence (AI) for automated vulnerability discovery, sophisticated social engineering, or the generation of hyper-realistic phishing content is a growing concern. Similarly, the use of quantum computing, while still in its nascent stages, poses a future threat to current encryption standards, requiring the development and implementation of quantum-resistant cryptography. The adversary is not static; they are continuously learning, innovating, and adapting their methods to exploit the latest technological advancements and the inherent complexities of military systems. This demands a defense that is not only robust but also agile, capable of anticipating future threats and rapidly integrating new defensive capabilities. The cyber battlefield is a dynamic and unforgiving arena where vigilance, continuous adaptation, and a deep understanding of adversary motivations and methodologies are paramount to maintaining operational security and national security.

Building resilient cyber defenses and response capabilities is no longer an option, but a fundamental imperative for military installations operating in today's complex threat landscape. This necessitates a multi-layered, proactive, and adaptive security posture that moves beyond traditional perimeter-based defenses to embrace a more comprehensive and integrated approach. At the core of this strategy lies the principle of Zero Trust Architecture (ZTA). This security model operates on the fundamental assumption that no user, device, or network segment can be implicitly trusted, regardless of its location or previous verification. Every access request must be rigorously authenticated, authorized, and continuously validated. In a military context, this translates to strict identity management for all personnel, rigorous device posture assessment before granting network access, and the principle of least privilege, ensuring that users and systems only have the permissions absolutely necessary to perform their designated functions. Implementing ZTA means treating every connection, internal or external, as potentially hostile, thereby significantly reducing the attack surface and limiting the lateral movement of adversaries should an initial compromise occur. This is a paradigm shift from the old "trust but verify" model to a "never trust, always verify" approach, which is critical for protecting sensitive military data and operational systems.

Complementary to Zero Trust is the strategic deployment of network segmentation. Instead of maintaining a flat, undifferentiated network, military installations must logically divide their networks into smaller, isolated zones based on function, sensitivity, and trust levels. This means creating distinct segments for critical infrastructure control systems (OT), sensitive research and development environments, administrative networks, and general user access. By segmenting the network, a breach in one segment is contained and prevented from easily spreading to other, more critical areas. For instance, if an adversary manages to compromise a less sensitive administrative segment, the robust security controls and isolation mechanisms between this segment and the OT network would act as a significant barrier, preventing them from reaching systems that control power, water, or weapon platforms. This segmentation can be achieved through various technologies, including firewalls, virtual local area networks (VLANs), and micro-segmentation solutions that allow for granular control down to individual workloads. The design and maintenance of these segments require a deep understanding of data flows and interdependencies within the installation, ensuring that legitimate operations are not unduly hindered while maximizing defensive effectiveness.

A cornerstone of proactive defense is continuous monitoring and logging. In a Zero Trust environment, every interaction, connection, and data access must be meticulously recorded and analyzed. This generates a wealth of telemetry data that, when effectively processed, can reveal subtle anomalies indicative of malicious activity. Advanced Security Information and Event Management (SIEM) systems, coupled with Endpoint Detection and Response (EDR) and Network Detection and Response (NDR) solutions, are essential for collecting, correlating, and analyzing this vast amount of data in near real-time. Continuous monitoring allows for the detection of deviations from normal behavior, such as unusual login patterns, unauthorized access attempts to sensitive resources, unexpected data transfers, or the execution of suspicious processes. This constant vigilance is crucial for identifying low-and-slow attacks that might otherwise go unnoticed by traditional signature-based antivirus solutions. The ability to retain and analyze historical logs is also vital for forensic investigations and for understanding the evolution of an attack campaign.

Crucially, these monitoring efforts must be informed by integrated threat intelligence. Passive monitoring is insufficient; defenses must be actively informed by the latest information on adversary tactics, techniques, and procedures (TTPs), indicators of compromise (IOCs), and emerging vulnerabilities. This threat intelligence can be sourced from a variety of channels, including government intelligence agencies, industry-specific sharing groups, commercial threat intelligence providers, and open-source information. Integrating this intelligence into security tools and operational workflows allows for the proactive identification of threats that are actively targeting similar organizations or that are known to be in use by specific adversary groups. For example, if intelligence indicates that a particular APT group is using a new exploit for a widely used software, security teams can prioritize patching that vulnerability and deploying specific detection rules to look for signs of that exploit being used within their network. This fusion of internal monitoring data with external threat intelligence creates a dynamic defense that can anticipate and counter threats before they can inflict significant damage.

Beyond prevention and detection, the ability to mount a swift and effective incident response is paramount. Even the most robust defenses can be breached, making a well-rehearsed and comprehensive incident response plan indispensable. This plan should clearly define roles and responsibilities, establish communication protocols, outline procedures for containment, eradication, and recovery, and include mechanisms for post-incident analysis and lessons learned. When an incident is detected, the primary objectives are to quickly contain the spread of the compromise, minimize damage to critical systems and data, and restore normal operations as swiftly and safely as possible. This involves isolating affected systems, blocking malicious IP addresses, revoking compromised credentials, and initiating recovery procedures from secure, verified backups. The incident response team must be skilled in digital forensics, malware analysis, and system recovery. Regular tabletop exercises and simulations are crucial to test the efficacy of the incident response plan, identify gaps, and ensure that personnel are familiar with their roles and the procedures to be followed. The speed and effectiveness of incident response can be the difference between a minor disruption and a catastrophic failure.

Robust backup and disaster recovery strategies are critical components of resilience. Data backups are not merely about restoring lost files; they are about ensuring operational continuity in the face of catastrophic cyber events. Military organizations must maintain multiple, geographically dispersed, and physically isolated backup copies of critical data and system configurations. These backups must be regularly tested to ensure their integrity and the ability to restore systems from them. The principle of air-gapping backups, meaning they are not directly connected to the operational network, is vital to prevent them from being compromised alongside the primary systems, as seen with some ransomware attacks. A well-defined disaster recovery plan outlines the steps necessary to restore critical functions and operations at an alternate site or using alternative infrastructure if the primary facility becomes unavailable due to a cyber-attack or other disruptive event. This comprehensive approach to data protection and operational continuity significantly reduces the potential impact of a successful cyber intrusion.

The human element remains a critical, yet often vulnerable, component of cyber defense. Comprehensive security awareness training for all personnel, from senior leadership to frontline operators, is non-negotiable. This training must go beyond basic phishing awareness and delve into the evolving tactics of social engineering, the importance of strong password hygiene, the secure handling of sensitive information, and the procedures for reporting suspicious activity. For personnel with elevated access privileges or those working with sensitive systems, more specialized training on secure coding practices, secure configuration management, and threat hunting methodologies may be necessary. Regular, engaging, and context-specific training helps to create a security-conscious culture where individuals understand their role in protecting the installation's cyber assets and are empowered to identify and report potential threats. The adversary will always seek to exploit the weakest link, and a well-trained workforce significantly strengthens the defensive posture by making them less susceptible to manipulation.

Resilience is not a static state but an ongoing process of adaptation and improvement. This requires a commitment to continuous vulnerability management and patching. Regular scanning of networks and systems for known vulnerabilities, followed by timely and effective patching of software and firmware, is essential. In complex military environments with legacy systems and strict testing requirements, a pure "patch-as-soon-as-available" approach might not always be feasible. Therefore, a risk-based approach is necessary, prioritizing the patching of the most critical vulnerabilities on the most sensitive systems. For systems that cannot be immediately patched, compensating controls, such as enhanced monitoring, network segmentation, or intrusion prevention systems, must be implemented. This ongoing cycle of vulnerability identification, assessment, remediation, and verification ensures that the defensive posture remains current and effective against evolving threats. The integration of automated vulnerability assessment tools with manual penetration testing and red team exercises provides a comprehensive view of the security posture and helps to identify weaknesses before adversaries can exploit them. This continuous cycle of assessment and improvement is what truly builds and sustains cyber resilience.

The convergence of directed energy (DE) and cyber warfare represents a paradigm shift in adversarial capabilities, moving beyond isolated attacks to a sophisticated, multi-domain approach. This synergy, where the capabilities of one domain amplify the vulnerabilities of the other, creates novel and deeply concerning threat vectors for military installations and critical infrastructure. Understanding this combined-arms strategy is not merely an academic exercise; it is a strategic imperative for developing robust defenses that can anticipate and neutralize threats that leverage both the physical and digital realms simultaneously. This interplay can manifest in numerous ways, each presenting a unique challenge to traditional, siloed defensive architectures.

One of the most direct forms of synergy involves using directed energy weapons to create an opening for subsequent cyber intrusion. Imagine a scenario where an adversary employs a pulsed energy weapon (PEW) or a high-power microwave (HPM) system to temporarily disrupt or permanently disable critical physical sensors on the perimeter of a military facility. These sensors might include radar arrays, electro-optical/infrared (EO/IR) cameras, acoustic sensors, or even the communication links that relay data from these sensors back to the command center. By effectively blinding these physical detection systems, the adversary significantly degrades the installation's ability to detect an approaching physical threat, such as an infiltration team or a drone carrying cyber-payloads. With the physical sensors rendered inoperable, the adversary can then exploit this temporary or permanent blind spot.

Cyber intrusion tools, perhaps delivered via a compromised drone that now operates with reduced risk of detection, or even through physically introduced malware during the chaos of the DE attack, can be deployed. The compromised communication links, if not fully destroyed, could become conduits for unauthorized data injection or exfiltration. Without the real-time situational awareness provided by the now-disabled physical sensors, defenders may be slow to detect the cyber intrusion, mistaking the initial sensor failure as a technical malfunction rather than a deliberate preparatory step for a digital assault. This allows attackers to gain a foothold within the network, move laterally, and achieve their objectives, be it data theft, system sabotage, or the disabling of internal defenses, with a significantly reduced risk of early detection and interdiction.

Conversely, the synergy can also flow in the opposite direction: a cyber attack paving the way for a directed energy engagement. Consider a scenario where an adversary first launches a sophisticated cyber offensive aimed at degrading or disabling the defensive systems that protect against DE threats. This could involve targeting the command and control systems responsible for operating counter-DE systems, such as electronic warfare suites or directed energy countermeasures. Alternatively, the cyber attack might focus on disabling the very power grids or cooling systems that are essential for the operation of an installation's own DE defensive assets. In more advanced scenarios, an adversary might launch a cyber attack that specifically targets the software or firmware of an installation's radar or sensor networks. By subtly manipulating the data streams or introducing false positives, the cyber attack could effectively 'trick' the defensive systems into misidentifying threats, ignoring real ones, or even misdirecting valuable defensive assets. For instance, a cyber attack could cause a facility's sophisticated missile defense radar to report phantom targets in a specific sector, compelling the operators to divert their most potent DE defensive systems to that area.

While these defensive systems are thus occupied and potentially even overloaded with false data, the adversary can then launch a physical DE attack from a different, undefended direction. The physical DE weapon, whether a laser designed to blind optical sensors or an HPM device intended to fry electronics, can then strike with much greater efficacy against a target that is either unaware of the incoming threat or has had its ability to respond crippled by the preceding cyber operation.

The complexity of this synergy is further amplified by the potential for cascading effects. A successful DE attack that permanently damages a critical piece of network hardware, such as a router, switch, or server, can have far-reaching implications that extend beyond the immediate physical loss. If this hardware is part of a vital network backbone, its destruction can not only disrupt communications but also isolate entire segments of the network. This isolation, while intended to protect remaining systems, can paradoxically make them more vulnerable to subsequent cyber attacks. For example, if a critical data center becomes isolated due to the destruction of its network uplink by a DE weapon, and its internal security systems rely on external threat intelligence feeds for real-time updates, that isolated data center may no longer be receiving critical security patches or updated threat signatures. This makes its systems, once thought to be protected by isolation, susceptible to older, known vulnerabilities that would have been mitigated by timely updates in a connected environment. Adversaries are acutely aware of such vulnerabilities and can exploit this post-DE-attack state of isolation and potential security drift.

The psychological and operational impact of a combined DE and cyber attack should not be underestimated. The sudden disabling of physical sensors or communication lines by a DE weapon can induce confusion and panic. In such a heightened state of stress, personnel are more susceptible to social engineering tactics, making them more likely to fall for phishing attempts or other forms of manipulation that can lead to a cyber breach. The disruption caused by a DE attack can also degrade the effectiveness of human-in-the-loop decision-making processes. If operators are struggling with faulty displays, unreliable sensor data, or communication blackouts, their ability to accurately assess threats and authorize defensive actions is compromised. This degraded human performance creates an exploitative window for cyber attackers who can then operate with greater impunity within the network.

The development of effective countermeasures against such synergistic attacks requires a fundamental rethinking of defensive architectures. Instead of treating cyber and physical defenses as separate domains, a truly integrated and resilient defense posture must view them as interconnected components of a single defensive ecosystem. This means that cyber defenses must be designed with an awareness of the potential physical impacts of DE weapons, and conversely, physical defenses must be hardened against cyber intrusion. For instance, critical network infrastructure should be housed in physically hardened facilities that are also protected against electromagnetic interference. Communication lines should be redundant and diverse, with some pathways physically protected or using resilient technologies that are less susceptible to DE effects.

The concept of "cyber hardening" for physical systems becomes paramount. This involves applying robust cybersecurity principles to the control systems and embedded software that manage physical assets, including those that might be targeted by DE weapons. For example, the firmware of radar systems, optical sensors, and communication arrays must be regularly updated, access controls must be rigorously enforced, and anomalous behavior must be continuously monitored for any indication of cyber compromise that could precede or accompany a DE attack. Similarly, DE defensive systems themselves must be subjected to the same rigorous cybersecurity standards as any other critical IT or OT system. This includes ensuring that their command and control software is secure, that their communication links are encrypted and authenticated, and that they are protected from unauthorized access or manipulation.

The intelligence gathering and analysis processes must also be integrated. Threat intelligence that identifies potential DE capabilities of adversaries should be correlated with intelligence on their known cyber intrusion tools and techniques. This allows for the proactive identification of potential synergistic attack scenarios. For example, if intelligence indicates that a specific adversary possesses advanced HPM capabilities and has a known history of using sophisticated spear-phishing campaigns, defense planners can anticipate a scenario where the HPM is used to disable sensors, creating an environment conducive to a subsequent cyber intrusion facilitated by a successful phishing attack on key personnel. This integrated threat picture enables the development of more targeted and effective defensive strategies.

The principle of operational resilience in the face of multi-domain attacks is also crucial. This involves designing systems and operational procedures that can withstand or rapidly recover from a combined DE and cyber assault. This might include maintaining backup physical sensors that are shielded or located in different areas, employing resilient communication technologies like mesh networks that can reroute traffic around damaged nodes, and developing pre-defined response protocols that account for simultaneous physical and digital disruptions. For example, if a DE attack disables primary communication links, pre-established procedures might direct personnel to switch to secondary, more secure, or less susceptible communication methods.

The ongoing evolution of both DE technologies and cyber warfare tactics necessitates a continuous and adaptive approach to defense. As DE weapons become more precise, more portable, and capable of targeting a wider range of electronic systems, and as cyber attackers develop increasingly sophisticated methods to bypass defenses, the synergy between these domains will only become more pronounced. Future conflicts may see adversaries employing synchronized attacks where DE weapons disable physical defenses and communications, while a concurrent cyber offensive exploits the resulting confusion and disruption to achieve strategic objectives. This could range from crippling a nation's power grid by targeting its control systems with a combination of HPM and cyber intrusion, to neutralizing a military outpost by disabling its radar and communication infrastructure with DE while simultaneously infiltrating its network to disable internal security systems and gain control of critical assets.

The synergy between directed energy and cyber attacks represents a significant escalation in the complexity and effectiveness of adversarial capabilities. It moves beyond single-domain engagements to a coordinated, multi-faceted assault that leverages the inherent vulnerabilities of interconnected physical and digital systems. Recognizing and understanding this dangerous interplay is the foundational step towards developing comprehensive defensive strategies. This requires a paradigm shift in how military installations and critical infrastructure are secured, moving towards integrated, resilient architectures that harden both physical assets against cyber threats and cyber systems against DE effects. Only by embracing this holistic, multi-domain approach can we hope to effectively defend against the increasingly sophisticated threats of the future, where the lines between the physical and digital battlefields are not just blurred, but intentionally interwoven by a determined adversary. The proactive integration of cyber and DE defense planning, coupled with continuous intelligence sharing and adaptive technological development, will be crucial in maintaining a decisive advantage in this evolving landscape.

Chapter 10: The Human Factor: Insider Threats and Social Engineering

The human element, often touted as the strongest link in any security chain, can just as readily become its most vulnerable point. This is particularly true when considering the persistent and insidious threat posed by insiders. These are not external adversaries attempting to breach perimeter defenses; rather, they are individuals who already possess authorized access to sensitive systems, data, or physical locations. Their trusted status, earned through employment, contracts, or privileged roles, grants them a unique vantage point and an inherent advantage that external attackers can only dream of. The damage an insider can inflict, whether through deliberate malice, negligence, or unwitting compromise, can be profound and far-reaching, often exceeding the impact of many external cyberattacks. The very fact that they are already within the trusted domain means that traditional security measures, focused on keeping the 'out' out, are fundamentally challenged. Detection becomes exponentially more difficult, as their actions may initially appear as legitimate use of their granted privileges, masking malicious intent or dangerous carelessness.

Insider threats can broadly be categorized into a few distinct, though sometimes overlapping, groups. The first and perhaps most concerning is the malicious insider. This individual acts with deliberate intent to cause harm, steal information, disrupt operations, or gain some form of personal or financial benefit through illicit means. Their motivations can vary widely: disgruntlement over perceived unfair treatment, ideological opposition to the organization's mission, financial desperation, or even coercion by external actors. A malicious insider often possesses intimate knowledge of the organization's security protocols, its operational procedures, and its critical assets. They understand where the vulnerabilities lie and how to exploit them without immediately triggering alarms. For instance, a disgruntled IT administrator might systematically exfiltrate sensitive intellectual property over several months, disguising the data transfers as routine backups or system updates. Or, a security guard might intentionally disable surveillance systems in specific areas for a set period, facilitating the unauthorized entry of accomplices or the removal of physical assets. The sheer audacity and often calculated nature of these actions underscore the difficulty in anticipating and preventing them, as they are carried out by individuals who are, by definition, part of the trusted community. Their actions are not random acts of vandalism but often precise, targeted operations designed for maximum impact or stealth.

A second significant category is the negligent insider. Unlike the malicious actor, this individual does not intend to cause harm. Instead, their actions stem from a lack of awareness, carelessness, or a failure to adhere to established security policies and procedures. While their intent is not malicious, the consequences of their negligence can be equally devastating. A common example involves the mishandling of sensitive information, such as an employee accidentally emailing confidential documents to an external party, losing a company-issued laptop containing classified data, or falling prey to a sophisticated phishing scam that compromises their credentials.

The proliferation of personal devices and remote work further exacerbates this risk. An employee who casually shares login credentials with a colleague, bypasses multi-factor authentication prompts without understanding the implications, or uses unsecured Wi-Fi networks for accessing sensitive company data can inadvertently open a gaping security hole. Their actions, born out of convenience or a lack of training, can provide a direct pathway for external attackers to penetrate the network or gain access to critical information. The challenge with negligent insiders is that they are often unaware of the severity of their actions until significant damage has occurred. Rectifying this requires not only robust security technologies but also a pervasive culture of security awareness and continuous training that emphasizes the 'why' behind security protocols, not just the 'what'.

The third crucial category is the compromised insider. This individual is not necessarily acting maliciously or negligently, but their access has been gained or exploited by an external entity. This compromise can occur through various means, most notably through social engineering. An adversary might target an employee through a phishing email, a pretexting phone call, or even a direct personal interaction, tricking them into revealing their credentials or performing actions that benefit the attacker. Once compromised, the insider effectively becomes an unwitting pawn, their authorized access now serving the agenda of a hostile party. For example, an employee might be tricked into downloading malware disguised as a legitimate work document, or they might be coerced into granting remote access to their workstation under false pretenses. In some cases, the compromise can be more   direct, involving the use of advanced techniques like malware that subtly alters an insider's behavior or even implants false information into their systems. The danger here lies in the fact that the compromised insider may not even be aware that they have been targeted or that their actions are aiding an adversary. This makes detection exceptionally difficult, as their activities might appear normal to casual observation, while in reality, they are systematically undermining the organization's security. The reliance on external actors to compromise insiders highlights the interconnected nature of threats, where sophisticated external capabilities are leveraged to bypass internal trust structures.

The inherent difficulty in addressing insider threats lies in their very nature: they originate from within. Unlike external attacks that can be thwarted by firewalls, intrusion detection systems, and perimeter security measures, insider threats operate in a domain where access is already granted. This significantly complicates detection and prevention strategies, demanding a more nuanced and multi-layered approach. A key aspect of this is vigilance and robust vetting processes. From the initial hiring stages, thorough background checks are crucial. This involves not only verifying professional credentials and employment history but also assessing an individual's character, identifying any potential red flags, and understanding their motivations. For positions of significant trust or access to highly sensitive information, more in-depth investigations, including psychological assessments and continuous monitoring, may be warranted. This isn't about creating a surveillance state, but about ensuring that individuals entrusted with critical responsibilities are indeed trustworthy and have the integrity to uphold their duties.

Beyond initial vetting, continuous monitoring and behavioral analysis are essential. While traditional security tools focus on network traffic and system logs, an effective insider threat program must also analyze user behavior. This involves establishing baselines of normal activity for individuals and roles and then flagging deviations that could indicate malicious intent or negligence. For instance, an employee who suddenly starts accessing sensitive files outside their usual work hours downloads an unusually large volume of data, or attempts to access systems they have never interacted with before might trigger an alert. Similarly, unusual login patterns, such as attempts to access systems from atypical locations or at odd times, can be indicative of a compromised account or malicious activity. Modern security information and event management (SIEM) systems, coupled with user and entity behavior analytics (UEBA) solutions, are critical in this regard. These tools can correlate data from various sources – logs, network activity, application usage – to identify anomalous patterns that might escape human observation. However, it is crucial that these systems are not solely reliant on automated alerts; they must be supported by skilled analysts who can investigate these anomalies, distinguish between genuine threats and false positives, and take appropriate action. The goal is to detect suspicious activity early, before significant damage can be done.

Another critical layer of defense involves access control and the principle of least privilege. This means that individuals should only be granted the minimum level of access necessary to perform their job functions. Overly broad access permissions are a significant risk, as they provide potential attackers, whether internal or external, with a wider attack surface and more opportunities for misuse. Regularly reviewing and revoking access privileges, especially when an employee changes roles, leaves the organization, or their access is no longer required, is a fundamental security practice. Implementing robust authentication mechanisms, such as multi-factor authentication (MFA), significantly reduces the risk of unauthorized access, even if credentials are compromised. MFA adds an extra layer of security by requiring users to provide two or more verification factors to gain access, making it much harder for an attacker to impersonate a legitimate user.

Data loss prevention (DLP) systems also play a vital role in mitigating insider threats. These systems are designed to detect and block potential data breaches by monitoring and controlling data in use, in motion, and at rest. DLP solutions can identify sensitive information, such as personally identifiable information (PII), financial data, or intellectual property, and prevent it from being exfiltrated through unauthorized channels, such as email, web uploads, or USB drives. By setting policies that define what constitutes sensitive data and how it can be handled, organizations can significantly reduce the risk of accidental disclosure or deliberate theft by insiders. The effectiveness of DLP, however, relies on accurate data classification and well-defined policies that reflect the organization's risk appetite and operational realities.

Beyond technological solutions, fostering a strong security culture is paramount. This involves clear communication of security policies, comprehensive and ongoing security awareness training, and encouraging employees to report suspicious activity without fear of reprisal. When employees understand the importance of security, the potential consequences of breaches, and their role in protecting the organization, they are more likely to be vigilant and to act responsibly. This culture should permeate all levels of the organization, from senior leadership to entry-level staff.

Regular training sessions, phishing simulations, and clear communication channels for reporting security concerns can help to reinforce this culture. Establishing a clear reporting mechanism for security incidents and encouraging a non-punitive approach to accidental disclosures (where appropriate) can encourage greater transparency and quicker response times. The aim is to create an environment where security is seen as a shared responsibility, not just an IT department's concern.

Offboarding procedures must be robust and rigorously executed. When an employee leaves an organization, their access to all systems, data, and physical locations must be immediately and completely revoked. Failure to do so creates a significant window of opportunity for a departing employee, especially one who may be disgruntled, to cause harm or exfiltrate sensitive information. This includes deactivating all user accounts, disabling key cards, retrieving all company assets, and ensuring that no residual access or data remains accessible. The offboarding process should be a well-defined, automated workflow where possible, to minimize the risk of human error or oversight. This diligent attention to detail during transitions is critical in preventing a former trusted individual from becoming a lingering threat.

The insider threat is a complex and multifaceted challenge that demands a holistic approach, integrating technology, processes, and human factors. It requires organizations to move beyond traditional perimeter-based security and embrace strategies that acknowledge the inherent risks posed by those who are already within the trusted environment. By implementing robust vetting, continuous monitoring, stringent access controls, effective data protection measures, fostering a strong security culture, and executing diligent offboarding procedures, organizations can significantly mitigate the persistent and potent threat of the insider. The commitment to addressing this vulnerability is not just a matter of compliance; it is a strategic imperative for safeguarding national security interests and ensuring operational continuity in an increasingly complex threat landscape.

Social engineering represents a pervasive and often underestimated threat to organizational security. Unlike technical exploits that target system vulnerabilities, social engineering preys upon human psychology, exploiting our innate trust, desire to be helpful, or susceptibility to authority and urgency. Adversaries employing these tactics aim to manipulate individuals into divulging sensitive information, granting unauthorized access, or performing actions that compromise security. Recognizing and effectively mitigating these techniques is therefore a crucial component of a robust defense strategy, particularly when dealing with the human factor in security.

One of the most prevalent and insidious social engineering tactics is phishing. Phishing attacks typically manifest as deceptive electronic communications, most commonly emails, but also text messages (smishing) and voice calls (vishing). The objective is to trick the recipient into believing the message is from a legitimate source, such as a trusted colleague, a vendor, a government agency, or a well-known online service. These messages are crafted to elicit an urgent response. They might warn of a security breach, an account problem, or an unpaid invoice, demanding immediate action. This action often involves clicking a malicious link that directs the user to a fake login page designed to steal their credentials, or downloading an infected attachment that installs malware on their system. For instance, an employee might receive an email that appears to be from the IT department, stating their password has expired and providing a link to reset it. Upon clicking the link, they are taken to a spoofed website that looks identical to the company's legitimate portal.

When they enter their old and new passwords, the attacker captures this information, gaining access to their account. Another common phishing lure involves urgent requests for financial information, such as credit card numbers or bank account details, often under the guise of a prize, a refund, or a charitable donation. The sheer volume and sophistication of phishing attempts mean that even security-aware individuals can sometimes fall victim. The key to recognizing phishing lies in scrutinizing the sender's email address (which is often subtly different from the legitimate one), checking for grammatical errors and awkward phrasing, and being wary of any message that demands immediate personal information or threatens negative consequences for inaction.

Closely related to phishing is spear-phishing, a more targeted form of the attack. Instead of casting a wide net, spear-phishing campaigns are meticulously researched and personalized to specific individuals or groups within an organization. Attackers will gather intelligence about their targets through social media, company websites, or previous breaches to craft highly convincing messages. For example, an attacker might impersonate a CEO or a senior executive and send an email to an employee in the finance department, requesting an urgent wire transfer to a particular account, citing a confidential business deal. The message would likely include details that only someone familiar with the company's operations would know, making it appear legitimate and increasing the likelihood of compliance. The use of personalized greetings, references to specific projects, or even intimate knowledge of internal communication styles can make spear-phishing incredibly effective, bypassing the skepticism that general phishing emails might elicit.

Another significant social engineering tactic is pretexting. This involves creating a fabricated scenario or "pretext" to gain the victim's trust and persuade them to provide access or information. The attacker assumes a false identity and invents a story that justifies their need for the information or action they are requesting. This often involves impersonating someone in a position of authority or someone who has a legitimate reason to ask for the information. For example, an attacker might call an employee claiming to be from the HR department, conducting a routine audit of employee records, and asking for personal details like social security numbers or dates of birth. Or they might pose as a vendor who needs to verify billing information. The effectiveness of pretexting relies heavily on the attacker's ability to appear credible and confident. They may have already gathered information through reconnaissance to make their story more believable. A common scenario involves an attacker calling an employee, claiming to be from the IT help desk, stating they have detected a security issue with the employee's computer and need remote access to fix it. The employee, concerned about their system's security, grants the attacker access, unknowingly allowing them to install malicious software or steal data.

Baiting is a tactic that plays on greed or curiosity. Attackers offer something enticing in exchange for the victim's cooperation or information. This could be a free download of a popular movie or software, a giveaway, or access to exclusive content. The "bait" is often presented in a way that seems too good to be true, but its allure can override caution. In the digital realm, baiting often involves offering free software or media that is loaded with malware. Users who download and install it become infected. The principle is simple: create an attractive lure, and people will often take the bait without fully considering the risks.

Quid pro quo, meaning "something for something," is another manipulative technique. In this scenario, the attacker offers a supposed benefit or service in exchange for information or access. This is distinct from baiting as it often involves a direct exchange. For instance, an attacker might call employees in a company claiming to be conducting a survey on IT services. They offer a small gift or a chance to win a prize in return for answering questions about their system usage or login procedures. In other instances, an attacker might pose as a colleague from another department who is struggling with a particular software and asks for assistance, using the opportunity to extract information about system configurations or password policies. The perceived exchange of value, whether it's a promised gift, assistance, or simply the act of helping a colleague, makes the victim more likely to comply with the attacker's requests.

Beyond these common tactics, several other social engineering techniques warrant attention. Tailgating or piggybacking refers to the act of an unauthorized person following an authorized individual into a restricted area. This often relies on the politeness or inattentiveness of the authorized person, who might hold the door open for the follower without verifying their identity or access privileges. This is particularly a risk in physical security settings where access is controlled by keycards or security personnel. An attacker might simply loiter near a secure entrance and wait for an employee to badge in, then walk in behind them. Shoulder surfing involves an attacker discreetly observing a person's screen or keyboard to obtain sensitive information, such as passwords or PINs, as they are entered. This can happen in public places, office environments, or even through the use of surveillance equipment. Last, water-testing involves an attacker making seemingly innocent or minor requests for information, gradually building a rapport and gathering details bit by bit, which can then be used for more significant attacks.

Recognizing these diverse social engineering tactics is the first critical step in mitigating their impact. This recognition is best fostered through comprehensive and ongoing security awareness training. Such programs should educate employees on the various methods attackers use, provide clear examples of malicious communications, and emphasize the importance of critical thinking and skepticism. Training should not be a one-time event but a continuous process, as social engineering techniques constantly evolve. Regular refreshers, interactive modules, and real-world simulations can keep employees engaged and vigilant.

Establishing clear protocols for verifying information and requests is equally vital. Employees should be trained to question unusual or urgent requests, especially those involving the transfer of funds, the sharing of sensitive data, or the granting of system access. Organizations should implement a "two-person rule" or a confirmation process for significant actions, such as large financial transactions or changes to critical system configurations. This might involve requiring verbal confirmation from a supervisor or a designated security officer before proceeding. For instance, if an email from a senior executive requests an immediate contract transfer, the employee in finance should be trained to verify the request through a separate communication channel, such as a direct phone call to the executive's known number, rather than relying solely on the email.

Fostering a culture where employees feel comfortable and empowered to report suspicious activity is paramount. This includes creating clear channels for reporting such incidents and ensuring that employees are not penalized for reporting potential threats, even if they turn out to be false alarms. A "see something, say something" mentality, coupled with a non-punitive reporting system, encourages proactive engagement with security. The human firewall is only as strong as its weakest link, and social engineering exploits precisely those vulnerabilities. By equipping individuals with the knowledge to identify these manipulative tactics and establishing robust procedural safeguards, organizations can significantly enhance their resilience against these pervasive threats. This involves a sustained commitment to education, clear communication, and the promotion of a security-conscious mindset throughout the entire organization. The goal is to cultivate a workforce that is not just aware of social engineering, but actively prepared to resist it, thereby forming a formidable barrier against adversaries who seek to exploit human trust and fallibility.

The evolving landscape of security threats necessitates a paradigm shift from solely external defenses to a more nuanced understanding and mitigation of internal vulnerabilities. While social engineering and external attacks often grab headlines, the silent, often overlooked threat comes from within an organization. These are the insider threats – individuals who have legitimate access to sensitive information, systems, or facilities, but who, for various reasons, exploit that access to cause harm, steal data, or disrupt operations. Identifying these potential threats before they manifest into damaging incidents is a critical challenge, and a significant part of the solution lies in the sophisticated application of behavioral analysis and anomaly detection.

The core principle behind behavioral analysis in this context is the understanding that individuals, when operating within their normal routines, exhibit predictable patterns of behavior. These patterns encompass a wide range of activities: the times they log in and access specific systems, the types and volume of data they download or upload, the frequency and nature of their communications, the physical locations they frequent within organizational premises, and the sequences of actions they typically perform. Anomalies, by definition, are deviations from these established norms. By meticulously monitoring and analyzing these behavioral footprints, organizations can establish a baseline of "normal" activity for each employee or for groups of employees with similar roles. Any significant departure from this baseline can then be flagged as a potential indicator of malicious intent, a compromised account, or a lapse in security protocols.

One of the foundational aspects of behavioral analysis is the examination of access patterns. This involves tracking who accesses what, when, and from where. For instance, a typical employee in the accounting department might log in between 8:00 AM and 5:00 PM on weekdays, primarily accessing financial databases and accounting software. If this employee suddenly begins accessing highly sensitive human resources data late at night, or attempts to log in from an unusual geographic location outside of their usual travel patterns, these actions would represent significant anomalies. Similarly, an increase in failed login attempts followed by a successful login from a new device could indicate a compromised credential. Advanced systems can correlate these access events with other data points, such as network traffic, to paint a more comprehensive picture. For example, if an employee who usually transfers only small amounts of data suddenly initiates a massive download of proprietary design documents to an external storage device, this would be a clear red flag.

Beyond just system access, communication habits also offer valuable insights. Analyzing communication logs, while respecting privacy, can reveal unusual patterns. This might include an employee suddenly initiating a high volume of communication with external parties they have never interacted with before, or an unusual frequency of sensitive keywords appearing in internal or external communications. For instance, if an employee who typically communicates only with their team members suddenly starts sending encrypted emails to unknown external addresses or frequently searches for information related to data exfiltration techniques, these could be indicators of preparatory actions for malicious intent. The detection of such anomalies often requires sophisticated natural language processing (NLP) tools that can analyze the content and context of communications, identifying deviations from normal conversational styles and topics.

The way individuals handle data is another critical area for behavioral analysis. This encompasses not only what data they access but also how they interact with it. For example, an employee who normally only views documents might suddenly start copying, pasting, or attempting to move large amounts of data. The timing of these actions is also crucial. Actions taken outside of normal working hours or attempts to access data immediately before an employee resigns or is terminated, can be particularly suspicious. Furthermore, the use of unauthorized devices, such as personal USB drives or cloud storage services to transfer company data, can be flagged by data loss prevention (DLP) systems that monitor endpoint activity. Detecting these anomalies can help prevent data breaches before they occur, safeguarding intellectual property and confidential information.

The technologies underpinning behavioral analysis and anomaly detection are diverse and rapidly evolving. User and Entity Behavior Analytics (UEBA) platforms are at the forefront of this field. UEBA systems collect data from various sources, including network logs, endpoint activity, application usage, and identity and access management systems. They then employ machine learning algorithms and statistical models to establish baseline behaviors and identify deviations. These systems are designed to move beyond simple rule-based alerts, which can generate a high number of false positives, and instead focus on identifying sequences of unusual events that, when taken together, form a strong indicator of compromise or insider threat. For instance, a UEBA might detect a user logging in from two geographically impossible locations within a short period, followed by an attempt to access a highly restricted database, and then an unusual data transfer. Individually, these events might be explainable, but in combination, they trigger a high-priority alert.

Another crucial technology is Security Information and Event Management (SIEM) systems, which aggregate and analyze security-related data from across an organization's IT infrastructure. While SIEMs have historically focused on correlating known threat patterns, their capabilities are increasingly being enhanced with UEBA functionalities. By integrating behavioral analytics into SIEM platforms, organizations can gain a more holistic view of their security posture, identifying both known threats and novel, behavior-driven anomalies. This integrated approach allows for more efficient threat hunting and incident response, as security teams can quickly sift through vast amounts of data to pinpoint suspicious activities.

Data Loss Prevention (DLP) solutions play a vital role in monitoring and controlling the flow of sensitive data. DLP systems can be configured to detect and block unauthorized attempts to transfer, copy, or print confidential information. By analyzing the content of data and the context of its transfer, DLP can identify when an employee is trying to exfiltrate information, even if they are using seemingly legitimate channels. For example, a DLP system could flag an employee attempting to email a large spreadsheet containing customer financial details to a personal email address, or to upload it to a personal cloud storage account. These systems act as a critical line of defense against intentional or unintentional data leakage.

The implementation of behavioral analysis and anomaly detection is not without its challenges. A primary concern is the potential for privacy violations and the impact on employee morale. Constantly monitoring employee activities can lead to a feeling of being surveilled, which can erode trust and negatively affect productivity. Therefore, it is imperative that organizations strike a delicate balance between security needs and employee privacy rights. This involves clear communication about what is being monitored, why it is being monitored, and how the data is being used. Transparency is key to fostering a positive work environment while still maintaining robust security. Policies should clearly define the scope of monitoring, ensuring that it is focused on detecting security risks rather than general employee performance.

The risk of false positives remains a significant hurdle. Machine learning algorithms, while powerful, are not infallible. They can sometimes misinterpret legitimate, albeit unusual, employee behavior as malicious. This can lead to unnecessary investigations, wasted resources, and frustration for employees who are wrongly flagged. Organizations must therefore invest in fine-tuning their anomaly detection models, regularly reviewing and refining the thresholds for alerts. Establishing clear protocols for investigating flagged anomalies, including human oversight and the opportunity for employees to explain their actions, is essential to mitigate the impact of false positives. A multi-layered approach, where an initial anomaly detection alert triggers further contextual analysis and verification steps, can significantly reduce the rate of false alarms.

The definition of "normal" behavior is also not static. Employee roles and responsibilities can change, leading to shifts in their access patterns and data handling habits. New technologies and workflows are constantly being introduced, altering how employees interact with systems. Therefore, continuous adaptation and refinement of behavioral baselines are crucial. UEBA systems need to be continuously updated and retrained to reflect these changes. This might involve periodic recalibration of algorithms or the implementation of automated processes that detect significant shifts in aggregate behavior, prompting a review and potential update of individual baselines.

The effectiveness of behavioral analysis is directly tied to the quality and comprehensiveness of the data collected. Incomplete or inaccurate data logs can lead to flawed baselines and missed anomalies. Organizations need to ensure that their logging infrastructure is robust, covering all relevant systems and endpoints, and that logs are retained for a sufficient period to allow for meaningful historical analysis. This requires a strategic investment in logging tools and infrastructure, as well as clear policies on data retention.

Despite these challenges, the strategic implementation of behavioral analysis and anomaly detection offers a powerful means of proactively identifying and mitigating insider threats. By understanding that malicious actions, even by trusted individuals, often manifest as deviations from established patterns, organizations can build more resilient security postures. This approach complements traditional security measures by focusing on the human element, which often remains the most vulnerable aspect of any security framework.

The process typically begins with establishing robust data collection mechanisms. This involves ensuring that all relevant systems, from network devices and servers to endpoint computers and cloud applications, are configured to generate detailed audit logs. These logs should capture information such as login attempts, access to files and databases, application usage, data transfers, and system configuration changes. The granularity of these logs is critical; the more detailed the information, the more precise the behavioral baseline can be.

Once the data is collected, it is fed into a UEBA or advanced SIEM platform. Here, machine learning algorithms come into play. These algorithms analyze the historical data to identify typical user behaviors. This includes understanding normal working hours, common access times, frequently used applications, typical data access volumes, and communication patterns. For example, the system might learn that an employee in the marketing department typically accesses customer relationship management (CRM) data and marketing analytics platforms between 9 AM and 6 PM on weekdays, downloading reports that are usually a few megabytes in size.

When a deviation occurs, the system flags it. This could be an employee suddenly accessing financial records outside of their departmental purview, or an attempt to download several gigabytes of data at 3 AM. The UEBA system assigns a risk score to these anomalies, based on factors such as the severity of the deviation, the sensitivity of the accessed data, and the user's role and history. A single, minor anomaly might trigger a low-priority alert, perhaps requiring simple verification. However, a series of high-risk anomalies, such as accessing sensitive HR files, followed by attempts to copy data to a USB drive, and then unusual network traffic to an unknown external IP address, would trigger a critical alert requiring immediate investigation.

This investigative phase is crucial and requires a human element. Security analysts review the triggered alerts, correlating the flagged anomalies with other security events and contextual information. They might interview the employee in question, review company policies, and assess the overall risk. The goal is to determine whether the anomaly represents a genuine security threat or a legitimate, albeit unusual, activity.

Effective behavioral analysis also extends to recognizing patterns that might indicate a compromised account rather than a malicious insider. For instance, a sudden surge in login failures from a particular account, followed by a successful login from an unusual IP address and geographic location, strongly suggests that the account credentials have been stolen. The UEBA system can detect this sequence of events and alert the security team to investigate the compromise and take immediate steps to secure the account, such as resetting the password and blocking the suspicious IP address.

The analysis of communication patterns, when conducted with strict adherence to privacy regulations, can uncover subtle indicators. For example, an employee who suddenly starts using encrypted messaging applications for work-related communications, or who frequently communicates with individuals outside the organization who have no clear business relationship, might be engaged in activities that could lead to information leakage or social engineering vulnerabilities. Advanced NLP tools can help analyze the sentiment and topic of communications to detect unusual deviations from professional norms.

The success of these techniques also relies on a strong security culture within the organization. Employees must understand the importance of security protocols and be encouraged to report suspicious activities without fear of reprisal. When anomalies are investigated, employees should be given the opportunity to provide context. This collaborative approach not only helps in accurately identifying threats but also reinforces trust and transparency.

In essence, behavioral analysis and anomaly detection shift the focus from simply reacting to known threats to proactively identifying unknown or developing risks. By understanding the normal rhythms of an organization's digital life, and by vigilantly watching for deviations, security teams can detect the subtle, often clandestine, activities that characterize insider threats and compromised accounts. This proactive stance, empowered by sophisticated technology and a commitment to privacy, is an indispensable component of a comprehensive modern security strategy, helping to protect valuable assets from those who have been granted privileged access.

The most effective defense against insider threats begins long before an individual gains access to an organization's sensitive data and systems. It commences with a rigorous and comprehensive vetting process designed to identify potential risks at the earliest possible stage. This initial screening is not merely a bureaucratic hurdle; it is a critical security measure that forms the bedrock of an organization's human-centric defense strategy.

The objective is to assess not only an individual's skills and qualifications but, more importantly, their trustworthiness, loyalty, and potential susceptibility to coercion or manipulation. By implementing stringent best practices for personnel screening and background checks, organizations can significantly reduce the likelihood of entrusting sensitive responsibilities to individuals who might pose a future risk.

Second, a criminal record check is indispensable. This should not be limited to a single jurisdiction but should encompass all relevant geographical areas where the candidate has resided or worked. Modern background check services can access extensive databases, including federal, state, and local records. The nature of any offenses is paramount; while minor infractions may not be disqualifying, convictions related to theft, fraud, data breaches, or espionage would raise significant red flags. Organizations must have clear policies regarding the adjudication of criminal records, ensuring that decisions are made consistently and fairly, taking into account the nature of the offense, the time elapsed, and its relevance to the position being offered.

Third, credit history and financial stability checks can also provide valuable insights. While seemingly unrelated to cybersecurity, financial difficulties can create vulnerabilities. An individual facing significant debt or financial hardship might be more susceptible to bribery, extortion, or the temptation to engage in illicit activities for financial gain. These checks are particularly important for positions involving financial responsibilities, access to sensitive financial data, or significant decision-making authority. Again, clear policies are needed to ensure these checks are conducted ethically and in compliance with all relevant privacy regulations. A history of responsible financial management can indicate a level of maturity and reliability. Beyond these standard checks, organizations should also consider education and professional license verification. This ensures that the candidate possesses the claimed qualifications and that their credentials are legitimate. Fraudulent academic credentials or misrepresented professional licenses can be indicators of a willingness to deceive, which is a concerning trait in any employee, especially those in security-sensitive roles.

Reference checks are a crucial, albeit sometimes challenging, component of the vetting process. Beyond the typically provided professional references, organizations should consider seeking references from individuals who can speak to the candidate's character and integrity from different perspectives. This might include former supervisors who are not typically provided as references, or even, where appropriate and with the candidate's consent, personal references who can attest to their honesty and reliability. It is important to ask specific, behavioral-based questions designed to elicit concrete examples of integrity and trustworthiness. For instance, instead of asking "Is this person honest?", a more effective question would be "Can you describe a situation where this individual demonstrated exceptional integrity under pressure?"

The vetting process should also extend to social media and online presence checks. In today's digital age, an individual's online footprint can reveal a great deal about their character, affiliations, and attitudes. This involves reviewing publicly available social media profiles, personal websites, and online forums. While intrusive surveillance is inappropriate, a review of publicly accessible information can highlight concerning content, such as affiliations with extremist groups, expressions of extreme dissatisfaction with previous employers, or discussions that indicate a disregard for security or ethical conduct. It is vital that these checks are conducted in a manner that is consistent, objective, and avoids discriminatory practices based on protected characteristics.

A critical element of the initial vetting is the integrity interview. This is a structured interview conducted by trained security or HR personnel specifically designed to assess a candidate's honesty, ethical reasoning, and understanding of security responsibilities. Candidates can be presented with hypothetical scenarios involving ethical dilemmas, data security breaches, or conflicts of interest, and their responses can provide valuable insights into their decision-making processes and their commitment to organizational values. This interview also provides an opportunity for the candidate to ask questions about the organization's security policies and expectations, further gauging their level of engagement and understanding.

Once an individual is employed, the need for vigilance does not cease. Continuous monitoring throughout an individual's tenure is equally crucial in mitigating insider risks. The dynamics of an individual's life can change, introducing new vulnerabilities or shifting their motivations. Therefore, a static vetting process is insufficient; organizations must implement ongoing screening mechanisms to adapt to these evolving circumstances.

One of the primary forms of continuous monitoring is through regular re-vetting and periodic background checks. For employees in highly sensitive positions, these checks should be conducted at regular intervals, perhaps annually or biennially. The scope of these re-vetting processes may vary depending on the individual's role and access level, but they can include updated criminal record checks, financial reviews, and verifications of ongoing professional licenses. These periodic checks serve to identify any significant changes in an individual's circumstances that might have occurred since their initial screening.

Beyond formal re-vetting, ongoing behavioral monitoring and anomaly detection, as discussed in the preceding sections, plays a vital role in continuous screening. By establishing baselines of normal behavior and identifying deviations, organizations can detect early warning signs of potential insider threats, compromised accounts, or disgruntlement that might lead to malicious actions. This includes monitoring access logs, data handling patterns, and communication activities for unusual trends. For example, a sudden increase in access requests to highly sensitive data outside of an employee's normal duties, or an unusual pattern of late-night system access, could indicate a developing risk that requires further investigation.

Management observation and awareness are also critical components of ongoing screening. Supervisors and managers are often in the best position to observe changes in an employee's behavior, attitude, or circumstances. These changes might include signs of increased stress, unusual secrecy, increased financial discussions, or expressions of disgruntlement. Organizations should foster a culture where managers are trained to recognize these potential indicators and are provided with clear channels to report their concerns to the appropriate security or HR personnel. This is not about encouraging constant surveillance of employees by their peers or managers, but rather about cultivating a heightened awareness of interpersonal dynamics and potential risk factors within the team. Exit interviews serve as an important part of the continuous screening cycle, even at the point of an employee's departure. A well-conducted exit interview can uncover valuable information about an employee's experience, any grievances they may have harbored, and their future plans. This information can help identify systemic issues within the organization that might have contributed to disgruntlement, and it can also provide insights into potential security risks if an employee is leaving under adversarial circumstances. It is an opportunity to ensure that all company assets, including data and access credentials, are returned or revoked, and to remind departing employees of their ongoing obligations regarding confidentiality agreements.

The security awareness training that employees receive throughout their tenure is also a form of continuous screening. By regularly educating employees about current threats, including social engineering tactics and the importance of data security, organizations reinforce the desired security behaviors and make employees more vigilant. Training sessions also provide opportunities for employees to ask questions and raise concerns, which can sometimes uncover latent issues or misunderstandings that could pose a security risk. This continuous reinforcement of security principles helps to maintain a strong security culture and makes employees less susceptible to manipulation.

Organizations must consider the loyalty and trustworthiness assessment throughout an individual's career. This is not a single event but an ongoing process that is influenced by the individual's performance, adherence to policies, and overall conduct. Evidence of strong ethical behavior, commitment to the organization's mission, and a willingness to uphold security protocols should be recognized and reinforced. Conversely, any pattern of policy violations, unethical conduct, or a perceived lack of commitment to the organization can, over time, contribute to a reassessment of an individual's trustworthiness. This assessment should be integrated into performance reviews and overall employee evaluations, ensuring that a holistic view of the individual is maintained.

Developing robust vetting and screening processes is a multi-faceted endeavor that spans the entire lifecycle of an employee's engagement with an organization. It begins with stringent initial background checks, encompassing employment verification, criminal history, financial stability, and educational credentials, supplemented by thorough reference and social media checks, and a critical integrity interview. This foundation is then reinforced through continuous monitoring mechanisms, including periodic re-vetting, ongoing behavioral analysis, managerial awareness, insightful exit interviews, and consistent security awareness training. By integrating these practices, organizations can build a resilient defense against insider threats, ensuring that individuals entrusted with sensitive access and information consistently meet the highest standards of trustworthiness, loyalty, and security adherence throughout their service. This proactive and persistent approach is not merely about preventing breaches; it is about cultivating an environment where trust is earned and continuously validated, forming an indispensable layer of an organization's overall security posture.

The preceding discussion has underscored the critical importance of stringent vetting and continuous monitoring in mitigating insider threats and the vulnerabilities exploited by social engineering. However, these technical and procedural safeguards, while essential, operate most effectively when underpinned by a robust and pervasive security-conscious culture. This is not an incidental outcome; it is a deliberate and ongoing endeavor that transforms security from a set of rules to be followed into an intrinsic value system embraced by every member of the organization. It shifts the paradigm from external enforcement to internal commitment, where individuals proactively contribute to the collective security posture.

Cultivating such a culture requires a multi-pronged approach, centered on education, empowerment, and accountability. At its core, it necessitates that every individual, regardless of their role or seniority, understands that security is not solely the purview of a dedicated department or IT specialists. It is a shared responsibility, deeply woven into the fabric of daily operations. This understanding must be built upon clear, consistent, and accessible communication. Employees need to comprehend the 'why' behind security policies and procedures, how their actions, or inactions, can directly impact the organization's integrity, the confidentiality of its data, and the safety of its operations. This involves moving beyond rote memorization of rules to fostering a genuine appreciation for the threats that exist and the potential consequences of security lapses.

Regular, engaging, and context-specific training plays a pivotal role here. This training should not be a one-off event but an evolving program that addresses new threats, adapts to technological advancements, and reinforces fundamental security principles. It should incorporate real-world examples, case studies, and interactive elements to make the information relatable and memorable. For instance, simulations of phishing attacks or discussions about the methods used in social engineering can be far more impactful than abstract warnings. The goal is to equip employees with the knowledge and critical thinking skills to recognize and respond to potential security risks in their day-to-day work.

Empowerment is the next crucial pillar in building a security-conscious culture. This means creating an environment where employees feel confident and encouraged to report suspicious activities or security concerns without fear of reprisal or ridicule. Many potential security incidents are averted because an observant employee notices something out of the ordinary and speaks up. If employees believe that reporting a minor anomaly will lead to unnecessary scrutiny of their own actions, or if they perceive their concerns will be dismissed, they are less likely to escalate.

Therefore, organizations must establish clear, well-defined, and accessible channels for reporting security incidents. These channels should be confidential and allow for anonymous reporting if an individual prefers. Crucially, when a report is made, it must be taken seriously, investigated promptly and thoroughly, and feedback should be provided to the reporting individual, even if it's just to acknowledge the report and confirm that it has been addressed. This demonstrates that their vigilance is valued and reinforces the importance of their role in security. This process builds trust and encourages a proactive mindset, transforming employees from passive observers into active participants in the organization's defense. The feedback loop is particularly important; even if a reported incident turns out to be a false alarm, informing the employee about the outcome helps them understand the process and reinforces that their contribution is appreciated. This can involve a simple email from the security team acknowledging the report and stating that it was investigated and found to be benign, or a more detailed explanation if appropriate and feasible.

Transparency and trust are inextricably linked to empowerment. A culture of security thrives when there is open communication about security challenges and successes. This doesn't imply revealing sensitive operational details, but rather being transparent about the overall security strategy, the types of threats the organization faces, and the rationale behind certain security measures. When employees understand the 'why' behind restrictions or protocols, they are more likely to accept and adhere to them. For example, explaining the risks associated with using personal USB drives, rather than simply banning them, helps employees understand the potential for malware or data exfiltration. Similarly, sharing anonymized case studies of successful social engineering attacks and how they were thwarted can be a powerful educational tool.

Trust is a two-way street; the organization must trust its employees to act responsibly, and employees must trust that the organization has their best interests at heart and will support them when they make good-faith efforts to uphold security. This trust is built over time through consistent actions that align with stated values. It involves leadership consistently modeling the desired security behaviors. If leaders are seen to bypass security protocols or treat security as an afterthought, it sends a powerful negative message throughout the organization. Conversely, when leaders visibly champion security initiatives, adhere strictly to policies, and publicly acknowledge the contributions of employees to security efforts, it sets a strong positive example.

Accountability is the final critical element. While fostering a supportive environment is essential, there must also be clear understanding that security is a non-negotiable aspect of employment. This means that breaches of security policy, whether accidental or intentional, will have consequences. These consequences should be fair, consistent, and proportionate to the severity of the infraction. This does not advocate for a punitive, zero-tolerance approach that discourages reporting, but rather for a system where responsibility is assigned and acknowledged.

Accountability ensures that security policies are not treated as optional guidelines but as fundamental requirements for all personnel. It reinforces the understanding that everyone's actions contribute to the overall security of the organization, and therefore, everyone is accountable for those actions. This might involve disciplinary actions for negligence, but it also includes recognizing and rewarding individuals who demonstrate exceptional commitment to security. Performance reviews can incorporate security awareness and adherence as a metric, recognizing individuals who actively contribute to a secure environment. This could include proactively identifying vulnerabilities, reporting suspicious activities that lead to a positive outcome, or consistently demonstrating best practices in data handling and access control. Such recognition can serve as a powerful motivator, further embedding security consciousness into the organizational culture.

Integrating security into the onboarding process for new employees is paramount. From day one, new hires should be immersed in the organization's security ethos. This includes comprehensive initial training that clearly outlines security policies, acceptable use of technology, data handling procedures, and the channels for reporting concerns. This sets the expectation from the outset that security is a fundamental aspect of their role. It also provides an opportunity to address the human element of security, explaining how social engineering tactics can be employed and how to recognize and resist them. The onboarding process is a critical juncture to establish the foundations of a security-conscious mindset, ensuring that new team members understand their responsibilities and feel empowered to contribute to the organization's safety from the very beginning of their tenure. This initial immersion is more effective than trying to correct ingrained habits or misunderstandings later.

The physical environment also plays a role in reinforcing a security-conscious culture. Clear signage indicating security protocols, designated areas for sensitive work, and visible security measures can serve as constant reminders of the importance of security. Even seemingly small details, like ensuring that sensitive documents are not left unattended on desks, or that meeting rooms are secured when not in use, contribute to a pervasive security awareness. These environmental cues, when consistently applied, reinforce the message that security is an integral part of the workplace, not an abstract concept.

The organization's leadership bears the ultimate responsibility for championing and sustaining a security-conscious culture. Their commitment must be visible and unwavering. This means not only allocating resources for security initiatives but also actively participating in security awareness programs, communicating security expectations regularly, and holding themselves and others accountable for security breaches. When leadership prioritizes security, it signals its importance to the entire organization, creating a ripple effect that influences attitudes and behaviors at all levels. Leaders must consistently demonstrate that security is not a trade-off for efficiency or productivity but a fundamental enabler of both. They must articulate a clear vision where security is integrated into strategic planning and decision-making, rather than being an afterthought or a reactive measure.

This proactive approach, driven by leadership commitment, is essential for embedding security consciousness deep within the organizational DNA. It fosters an environment where individuals are not only aware of security risks but are actively motivated to mitigate them, transforming the human factor from a potential vulnerability into the organization's most formidable defense. This continuous reinforcement, from onboarding to daily operations and leadership communication, is the bedrock upon which a truly resilient security posture is built. The ongoing dialogue about security, the celebration of security successes, and the lessons learned from security incidents all contribute to a dynamic and evolving security culture that remains adaptive and effective in the face of ever-changing threats.

Chapter 11: Implementation Playbooks: Pathways to SMART Installations

The successful integration of the Secure, Modular, Agile, Resilient, and Trusted (SMART) Installation framework is not an overnight endeavor. It is a strategic undertaking that requires careful planning, a deliberate sequence of actions, and a commitment to iterative improvement. Recognizing the inherent complexity and the diverse nature of existing infrastructures, a phased implementation strategy provides a structured and manageable roadmap for this transformation. This approach allows organizations to transition incrementally, building capabilities, demonstrating value, and adapting to challenges along the way, thereby minimizing disruption and maximizing the likelihood of successful adoption.

The initial phase of any SMART Installation rollout is invariably the Assessment and Planning stage. This is the foundational step, where a comprehensive understanding of the current state is established. It involves a deep dive into existing infrastructure, operational workflows, security protocols, and the technological architecture. This assessment must be thorough, identifying not only immediate vulnerabilities and inefficiencies but also potential integration points and existing strengths that can be leveraged. Key considerations during this phase include a detailed inventory of all physical and digital assets, an analysis of current cybersecurity postures, an evaluation of existing data management practices, and an assessment of personnel training and awareness levels regarding security.

Understanding the organizational culture, stakeholder buy-in, and resource availability is critical. This phase requires multidisciplinary input, involving IT, security, operations, facilities management, and potentially legal and compliance departments. The output of this stage is a detailed report that maps the current landscape, highlights areas requiring improvement in alignment with SMART principles, and forms the basis for developing a strategic implementation plan. This plan should clearly define the scope of the initial rollout, prioritize key functionalities, establish realistic timelines, allocate necessary resources, and identify key performance indicators (KPIs) for measuring progress and success. It's also crucial to define what "SMART" means in the context of the specific installation, what specific improvements are we aiming for in terms of security, modularity, agility, resilience, and trustworthiness? For instance, a military base might prioritize enhanced perimeter security and interoperability with allied systems, while a critical infrastructure facility might focus on reducing single points of failure and improving operational continuity in the face of cyberattacks.

Following a thorough assessment and the development of a strategic plan, the next logical step is the Pilot Program phase. This phase is designed to test the SMART framework in a controlled environment, allowing for the validation of assumptions, identification of unforeseen challenges, and refinement of the implementation approach before a full-scale deployment. The pilot should focus on a specific, well-defined segment of the installation or a particular set of functionalities. This could involve implementing a modular network architecture in a single building, deploying a new identity and access management system for a select group of users, or testing an agile operational procedure for a specific task.

The key is to select a pilot scope that is representative enough to yield meaningful insights but small enough to be managed effectively and contain any potential issues. During the pilot, meticulous data collection is paramount. This includes tracking implementation timelines, monitoring system performance, assessing security effectiveness, evaluating user adoption and feedback, and documenting any technical glitches or operational disruptions. The insights gained from the pilot program are invaluable. They provide concrete data on the efficacy of the chosen technologies, the effectiveness of training materials, and the practicality of the proposed workflows. This information allows for adjustments to the overall strategy, technical configurations, and operational procedures. It's an opportunity to learn from mistakes in a low-risk setting, ensuring that the broader rollout is more efficient and effective. For example, a pilot might reveal that the user interface for a new security monitoring tool is not intuitive, leading to a decision to invest in user experience redesign before wider deployment. Or, it might demonstrate that the chosen modular hardware requires more complex integration than initially anticipated, prompting a re-evaluation of procurement strategies.

Once the pilot program has successfully demonstrated the viability and benefits of the SMART framework, the implementation transitions into the Phased Rollout and Core Capability Scaling phase. This is where the scope of the SMART integration begins to expand, moving beyond the controlled environment of the pilot to encompass broader segments of the installation. This phase is characterized by a structured, iterative deployment of core SMART capabilities across different areas or functions.

It's crucial to break down the full implementation into manageable stages, prioritizing based on risk, operational impact, and strategic importance. For instance, foundational security enhancements might be deployed first, followed by advancements in modularity and agility. Each phase of the rollout should build upon the lessons learned from the pilot and previous deployment stages. This involves the systematic implementation of selected SMART technologies and methodologies. This might include deploying standardized, modular hardware across multiple facilities to enhance flexibility and reduce lifecycle costs. It could involve the integration of advanced identity and access management systems to strengthen security and streamline user provisioning. The rollout would also encompass the adoption of agile operational practices, enabling faster adaptation to changing mission requirements or threat landscapes.

Throughout this scaling phase, robust project management is essential. This includes maintaining clear communication channels with all stakeholders, providing ongoing training and support to personnel, and rigorously monitoring progress against predefined milestones and KPIs. The focus remains on incremental delivery of value, ensuring that each stage of the rollout yields tangible improvements in security, efficiency, or resilience. For example, a phased rollout might begin with upgrading network infrastructure in critical operational hubs, followed by the deployment of enhanced endpoint security solutions across the entire installation, and then the implementation of a new, secure data analytics platform. This approach allows teams to focus their efforts and resources effectively, gradually building the desired SMART capabilities.

It also provides opportunities for continuous feedback and refinement, enabling the implementation team to adapt to evolving needs and challenges. The concept of modularity is particularly critical here. Instead of attempting a complete overhaul, the phased approach leverages modular components that can be integrated and scaled independently. This minimizes dependencies between different parts of the infrastructure and allows for flexibility in adapting to future technological advancements or changing operational requirements. This iterative expansion ensures that the organization doesn't bite off more than it can chew, making the journey towards a fully SMART installation both achievable and sustainable.

The final, and arguably most critical, phase is Continuous Optimization and Evolution. The successful implementation of a SMART framework is not a terminal point; it is an ongoing process of refinement and adaptation. This phase recognizes that the threat landscape, technological advancements, and organizational needs are in constant flux. Therefore, the installation must be designed and managed to continuously evolve. This involves establishing mechanisms for ongoing monitoring, performance analysis, and proactive adaptation. Regular reviews of security metrics, operational efficiency, and system resilience are essential. This data-driven approach allows for the identification of emerging vulnerabilities, areas where performance can be improved, and opportunities to enhance agility and trustworthiness.

Key activities within this phase include regular security audits, penetration testing, and vulnerability assessments to ensure that the security posture remains robust against evolving threats. It also involves analyzing operational data to identify bottlenecks, inefficiencies, or areas where greater agility can be achieved. This might lead to the reconfiguration of modular components, the adoption of new software updates, or the refinement of operational procedures. Furthermore, this phase emphasizes a culture of continuous learning and improvement. Feedback loops from users, incident reports, and performance data should be actively utilized to inform future development and enhancements.

The organization must remain agile in its approach, willing to re-evaluate and adapt its strategies and technologies as needed. This could involve incorporating new cybersecurity tools, embracing advancements in artificial intelligence for threat detection, or adopting emerging best practices in data governance and privacy. The goal is to ensure that the SMART installation not only meets current requirements but is also future-proofed, capable of adapting to unforeseen challenges and opportunities. This perpetual cycle of assessment, adaptation, and enhancement is what truly distinguishes a SMART installation, it is a dynamic, living ecosystem rather than a static, fixed deployment. A regular review might uncover that a specific type of social engineering attack is becoming more prevalent, prompting an update to user training modules and the implementation of new detection mechanisms within the network. Similarly, analysis of system uptime might reveal that certain hardware components are nearing the end of their optimal lifespan, triggering a planned upgrade cycle based on the modular architecture.

This proactive and adaptive mindset is the hallmark of a truly resilient and secure operation, ensuring that the investment in the SMART framework continues to deliver maximum value over the long term. It transforms the implementation from a project with a defined end date into a continuous journey of improvement, fostering a culture of vigilance and innovation that is paramount in today's complex security environment.

This foundational step, the detailed assessment of current capabilities, is the bedrock upon which any successful SMART Installation is built. It transcends a mere inventory of existing assets; it is a deep, analytical dive into the current state of security across all relevant domains, physical, cyber, air defense, and crucially, the human element. Without this rigorous evaluation, any subsequent implementation plan would be akin to building on shifting sands, prone to failure and incapable of delivering the promised resilience, agility, and trustworthiness. The objective is not simply to document what exists but to critically appraise its efficacy, identify its shortcomings when measured against the demanding standards of a SMART Installation, and establish a clear, data-driven baseline from which progress can be measured and the return on investment in future enhancements can be justified.

Evaluating current physical security measures requires a systematic review of the installation's perimeter defenses, access control points, surveillance systems, and internal security protocols. This involves scrutinizing the integrity of fencing, walls, and other physical barriers, assessing the effectiveness of intrusion detection systems, and analyzing the operational readiness and coverage of closed-circuit television (CCTV) networks. The functionality and adequacy of access control mechanisms, including card readers, biometric scanners, and manned guard posts, must be examined.

The effectiveness of lighting, the presence and visibility of security personnel, and the procedures for managing entry and exit of personnel and vehicles are critical components of this assessment. An installation might have robust perimeter fencing but inadequate lighting in certain sectors, creating blind spots for surveillance and potential ingress points for adversaries. Similarly, an access control system might be technically advanced but rendered less effective by lax adherence to established protocols by personnel or a lack of real-time monitoring and response capabilities. The assessment should also consider the physical security of critical infrastructure and sensitive areas within the installation, such as data centers, power substations, and command and control facilities, ensuring they are adequately protected from unauthorized physical access, sabotage, or environmental hazards. This necessitates understanding the physical layout, the interdependencies between different physical security assets, and the current maintenance schedules and operational status of all components.

The cyber security assessment delves into the digital heart of the installation, examining its network architecture, data protection mechanisms, and the effectiveness of its cyber defense strategies. This includes a thorough review of network segmentation, firewall configurations, intrusion prevention and detection systems (IPS/IDS), and endpoint security solutions. The strength of authentication and authorization protocols, including multi-factor authentication (MFA) deployment and the rigor of identity and access management (IAM) policies, is paramount. An evaluation of data encryption practices, both in transit and at rest, is essential, as is an understanding of current backup and disaster recovery procedures. The assessment must also consider the vulnerability of operational technology (OT) and industrial control systems (ICS) if they are present, as these often present unique challenges due to legacy systems and specialized protocols. Identifying the extent of known vulnerabilities within the existing software and hardware stack, along with the process for patch management and vulnerability remediation, is a critical exercise.

For example, an installation might possess advanced intrusion detection systems but fail to adequately update its firewall rules in response to emerging threats, leaving critical network segments exposed. Another common gap is the lack of robust logging and monitoring across the entire cyber infrastructure, making it difficult to detect sophisticated, low-and-slow attacks or to perform effective forensic analysis after an incident. The assessment should also consider the organization's overall cyber hygiene practices, including policies on password management, acceptable use of IT resources, and the procedures for reporting suspected cyber incidents.

Air defense capabilities, particularly relevant for installations with strategic or operational significance, require a distinct evaluation. This involves assessing the existing sensor network for detecting airborne threats, including radar systems, electro-optical/infrared (EO/IR) sensors, and other surveillance assets. The integration and effectiveness of command and control (C2) systems responsible for processing sensor data, identifying threats, and coordinating responses are crucial.

The assessment should examine the readiness and capability of any deployed interceptor systems, including surface-to-air missiles (SAMs) and close-in weapon systems (CIWS), as well as the training and proficiency of the personnel operating these systems. The effectiveness of electronic warfare (EW) capabilities designed to disrupt or deceive enemy air and missile systems also falls under this purview. For an installation reliant on air superiority, a gap might exist in the early warning detection range of its radar systems, or in the speed at which its C2 system can process and disseminate threat information to engagement platforms. The interoperability of air defense systems with national or allied air defense networks is also a critical factor, ensuring seamless information sharing and coordinated responses. A thorough assessment would map the "kill chain" for potential airborne threats, identifying where each stage of detection, tracking, identification, decision, and engagement is most vulnerable.

Perhaps the most critical and often overlooked domain is the human element. The assessment of human security capabilities must evaluate the awareness, training, and behavioral patterns of all personnel operating within or interacting with the installation. This includes assessing the effectiveness of security awareness training programs, focusing on topics such as insider threat detection, social engineering defense, phishing awareness, and proper handling of sensitive information. The clarity and adherence to security policies and procedures by staff are vital. This involves understanding how personnel are vetted, the robustness of background checks, and the ongoing monitoring processes.

The assessment should also consider the psychological readiness and resilience of personnel, particularly those in critical roles, and the support mechanisms in place to address stress and burnout, which can impair decision-making and increase vulnerability. For instance, an installation might have state-of-the-art cyber defenses, but if personnel are not adequately trained to recognize phishing attempts or report suspicious activities, these sophisticated systems can be bypassed through human error or malicious intent. A gap might also exist in the reporting culture, where individuals are hesitant to report unusual observations due to fear of reprisal or a lack of clear reporting channels. Evaluating the effectiveness of insider threat programs, including the tools and processes used to identify and mitigate potential insider risks, is also a significant component. This requires understanding how behavioral analytics, anomaly detection, and human intelligence gathering are integrated.

Identifying critical gaps and vulnerabilities requires a structured approach that synthesizes the findings from each of these domains. This involves comparing the current capabilities against the defined requirements of a SMART Installation. For a SMART Installation, this means evaluating against specific criteria for enhanced security (e.g., zero-trust architecture, multi-layered defenses), modularity (e.g., ease of component replacement, scalability), agility (e.g., rapid adaptation to new threats or mission changes), resilience (e.g., ability to withstand and recover from disruptions), and trustworthiness (e.g., verifiable integrity of systems and data). For example, a gap in physical security might be the reliance on a single, redundant power source for critical surveillance systems, impacting resilience.

In the cyber domain, a gap could be the lack of micro-segmentation in the network, allowing a breach in one area to rapidly spread. For air defense, a gap might be the absence of a redundant radar system, creating a blind spot if the primary system fails. Within human security, a gap could be the absence of regular, scenario-based training for responding to active threats, impacting agility and resilience.

Prioritization of these identified gaps is paramount and must be guided by a comprehensive threat assessment and an understanding of the installation's mission criticality. Threats should be analyzed in terms of their likelihood and potential impact. Mission criticality involves understanding which functions or assets are indispensable for the installation's core purpose. Gaps that pose the greatest risk to the most critical functions are typically assigned the highest priority. For instance, a gap that directly enables a high-probability, high-impact cyberattack against a mission-critical command and control system would likely be prioritized above a minor inefficiency in a non-critical administrative system. This prioritization framework ensures that resources are allocated effectively and that the most significant vulnerabilities are addressed first, maximizing the impact of security investments. This process often involves risk matrices, where the likelihood of a threat exploiting a vulnerability is plotted against the severity of the consequences, allowing for a quantitative or qualitative ranking of risks. The output of this phase is a prioritized list of identified vulnerabilities and a clear articulation of the risks associated with each.

Establishing a baseline for measuring progress and return on investment (ROI) is the final, yet essential, step in this assessment phase. This baseline is a snapshot of the installation's security posture before any SMART implementation begins. It provides the reference point against which all future improvements will be measured. Key performance indicators (KPIs) should be defined for each domain of security, aligned with SMART principles. For physical security, KPIs might include the number of successful perimeter breaches per quarter, response times to detected intrusions, or the percentage of critical areas under constant surveillance.

For cyber security, KPIs could encompass the mean time to detect (MTTD) and mean time to respond (MTTR) to cyber incidents, the number of critical vulnerabilities patched within a defined timeframe, or the percentage of network traffic encrypted. Air defense KPIs might include the probability of detecting an incoming threat within a specified range and timeframe, or the success rate of engagement against simulated targets. Human security KPIs could involve the results of phishing simulation exercises, the percentage of personnel completing mandatory security training, or the number of reported suspicious activities that led to the prevention of an incident. The baseline data for these KPIs provides the starting point. Subsequently, as new technologies and processes are implemented, ongoing measurement against these KPIs will demonstrate the effectiveness of the SMART framework, quantify the improvements achieved, and provide the data necessary to justify continued investment and to calculate the tangible ROI of the transformation. This data-driven approach is fundamental to demonstrating the value of the SMART Installation initiative and ensuring its long-term sustainability and success.

The journey toward a SMART Installation is not a sterile, theoretical exercise; it is a complex, real-world endeavor fraught with the practical challenges of integrating cutting-edge technologies with established, often aging, infrastructure. This section delves into the critical aspect of Technology Integration and Interoperability Challenges, recognizing that the mere acquisition of advanced systems is insufficient. True advancement lies in their seamless fusion, enabling a cohesive and responsive security posture. The foundational principle guiding this integration must be adherence to robust architectural frameworks, such as the proposed SMARTIE (Secure, Modular, Agile, Resilient, Trustworthy, Integrated, and Enduring) architecture. SMARTIE is not merely a buzzword; it represents a strategic imperative. It provides a blueprint for ensuring that new technological components do not become isolated islands of capability but rather integral, communicating nodes within a larger, intelligent network. Without such a guiding framework, the risk of creating a collection of disparate, expensive, and ultimately ineffectual systems is exceedingly high. Each new system, from advanced AI-driven surveillance analytics to sophisticated cyber threat intelligence platforms, must be evaluated not only for its standalone efficacy but for its potential to connect, share data, and collaborate with existing security layers, physical, cyber, and human.

One of the most pervasive hurdles is the inherent complexity arising from the coexistence of legacy systems and modern technological advancements. Military installations, by their very nature, are long-lived entities. Their infrastructure, built over decades, often comprises a patchwork of technologies with varying lifecycles, communication protocols, and data formats. Introducing a new, state-of-the-art sensor array designed to communicate via high-bandwidth, IP-based protocols into an environment where critical command and control systems still rely on serial interfaces or proprietary communication buses presents an immediate and significant integration challenge. This is not a hypothetical scenario; it is a daily reality for defense IT and security professionals.

The goal must be to achieve a "fused security environment," a concept that transcends simply layering new technologies on top of old. It implies a dynamic, interconnected ecosystem where information flows freely and intelligently between components, enabling a holistic understanding of the operational environment. Consider the challenge of integrating a new drone detection system that utilizes advanced radar and acoustic sensors with an existing physical security perimeter. If the new system's output, perhaps a real-time threat alert with precise geolocation, cannot be automatically ingested and displayed on the security operations center's (SOC) common operating picture (COP) platform, itself potentially a legacy system, then its value is significantly diminished.

The security operator might receive an alert, but then must manually correlate this with visual feeds from CCTV, access control logs, and potentially even radio communications, all of which consume precious time during a critical event. This manual intervention introduces delays, increases the cognitive load on operators, and elevates the risk of human error, fundamentally undermining the "agile" and "responsive" tenets of a SMART Installation. Overcoming these interoperability issues necessitates a proactive and strategic approach, beginning with a deep understanding of the existing technological landscape. This involves detailed inventories not just of hardware and software, but of their underlying communication protocols, data schemas, and APIs (Application Programming Interfaces). Where direct integration is not feasible due to proprietary systems or outdated standards, middleware solutions become indispensable.

These software layers act as translators, bridging the communication gap between disparate systems. For example, an open-source middleware platform could be configured to poll a legacy alarm panel for status updates, translate the data into a standardized format (like XML or JSON), and then push that information to a modern cloud-based security management system. Similarly, the development and adoption of industry-standard communication protocols and data models are crucial. Initiatives promoting open standards, such as those within the Internet of Things (IoT) or specific defense interoperability frameworks, can significantly ease integration efforts. The SMARTIE architecture itself should champion the use of such open standards, making it clear that future technology procurements will prioritize systems designed for seamless integration.

The management of vendor relationships is another critical, yet often underestimated, aspect of technology integration. Defense installations frequently procure technologies from a diverse range of suppliers, each with their own proprietary systems, support structures, and development roadmaps. Ensuring that these diverse systems can coexist and cooperate requires careful planning and a strategic approach to procurement. Contracts must explicitly include clauses demanding adherence to established interoperability standards and the provision of open APIs.

A collaborative approach with vendors is often more productive than an adversarial one. Establishing joint working groups or technical exchange meetings early in the procurement cycle can help identify potential integration challenges before they become costly roadblocks. This also allows vendors to understand the installation's overall SMART vision and to align their product roadmaps accordingly. For instance, a vendor providing a new biometric access control system should be engaged not just on its standalone performance but on how its data can be shared with the installation's personnel management system, the physical security information management (PSIM) platform, and potentially even the cyber threat intelligence fusion cell. This requires vendors to be transparent about their system's data output capabilities and their willingness to work with third-party integration partners. The aim is to move away from a model where each system is a black box and towards one where all components are transparent, configurable, and designed to interoperate.

The challenge extends beyond mere data exchange to the fusion of operational contexts. A physical security system might detect an unauthorized individual attempting to breach a perimeter. A cyber system might simultaneously detect an anomalous login attempt from an unusual IP address. A truly fused environment would correlate these events in near real-time. The individual at the perimeter might be attempting to gain physical access to a server room, or the anomalous login might be a precursor to a cyberattack targeting the same area. Without sophisticated integration, these events might be flagged independently, with human operators struggling to connect the dots under pressure.

The SMARTIE architecture, with its emphasis on integration, mandates the development of platforms capable of ingesting data from disparate sources, applying analytics to identify correlations, and presenting these insights in a unified, actionable format. This might involve a sophisticated PSIM platform acting as the central nervous system, or it could be a more distributed intelligence model where AI agents embedded within individual systems can communicate and share threat assessments. For example, a perimeter intrusion detection system, upon detecting an anomaly, could automatically query the cyber intrusion detection system for any related network traffic patterns emanating from or directed towards the compromised physical zone. The results of this query would then be appended to the initial alert, providing security personnel with a richer, more comprehensive understanding of the threat.

Ensuring the trustworthiness of integrated systems is paramount. As systems become more interconnected, the attack surface expands, and the potential for cascading failures increases. Therefore, the integration process must be underpinned by rigorous cybersecurity principles. Zero-trust architectures, where no device or user is implicitly trusted, regardless of their location within the network, are essential. This means that even when a new system is integrated, it must be subject to continuous monitoring, authentication, and authorization checks.

The data it shares must be verified for integrity, and its access to other systems must be strictly controlled based on the principle of least privilege. The SMARTIE framework's emphasis on "Trustworthy" directly addresses this, requiring that all integrated components and their communications are auditable, verifiable, and resilient to tampering. This often involves the use of cryptographic techniques to secure data in transit and at rest, robust identity and access management for all system components, and continuous security validation processes. For instance, before allowing a newly integrated sensor network to feed data into the air defense command and control system, its data streams would be continuously monitored for anomalies, and its firmware would be periodically verified against known-good hashes to ensure it hasn't been compromised.

The sheer volume and velocity of data generated by modern, integrated security systems also present a significant challenge. As more sensors, cameras, and analytical tools are brought online, the data streams can become overwhelming. Effective integration requires not only the ability to connect systems but also to process, filter, and analyze this deluge of information intelligently. This is where Artificial Intelligence (AI) and Machine Learning (ML) play a transformative role. AI/ML algorithms can sift through vast datasets to identify patterns, detect anomalies, and flag potential threats that might be missed by human operators or simpler rule-based systems.

The effective deployment of AI/ML for integration purposes requires careful consideration of data quality, model training, and bias mitigation. The integration strategy must account for how AI/ML capabilities will be applied across the fused security environment, not just within individual systems. For example, a central analytics platform might be tasked with correlating video analytics from multiple CCTV cameras with acoustic sensor data from perimeter sensors and network traffic logs from internal servers. This platform would learn normal operational patterns and flag deviations, such as unusual movement patterns near a critical facility coinciding with elevated network activity directed towards that facility's control systems. The output from this central AI would then be prioritized and presented to security personnel, enabling a more efficient and effective response.

The modularity aspect of the SMARTIE architecture is also crucial in addressing integration challenges. A modular design allows for individual components or subsystems to be upgraded or replaced without necessitating a complete overhaul of the entire system. This inherent flexibility simplifies the integration of new technologies over time and makes it easier to address interoperability issues as they arise. If a particular communication protocol becomes obsolete or a vendor discontinues support for a legacy interface, a modular system allows for the targeted replacement of that specific module, rather than requiring the entire security infrastructure to be re-engineered.

This also facilitates a phased implementation strategy, where integration efforts can be prioritized and rolled out incrementally, reducing the risk and disruption associated with a "big bang" approach. For example, an installation might decide to first integrate its new smart grid power management system with its existing building management system, focusing on energy consumption and fault detection. Later, it can integrate this with the physical security system to ensure critical power is maintained for essential security functions during grid instability, and further integrate with cyber monitoring to detect any malicious attempts to manipulate the power grid. Each of these integrations can be approached as a distinct, manageable project, building upon the foundation of modularity.

Ultimately, successful technology integration for SMART Installations hinges on a paradigm shift from managing individual systems to orchestrating a cohesive security ecosystem. This requires a blend of technical expertise, strategic foresight, and a commitment to open standards and collaborative vendor engagement. The challenges are significant, spanning legacy system constraints, proprietary technologies, data management complexities, and the imperative of maintaining trust and security in an increasingly interconnected environment. By embracing architectural principles like SMARTIE, focusing on deliberate interoperability, and fostering strong partnerships, installations can navigate these complexities to build truly fused security environments that are greater than the sum of their parts, providing enhanced resilience, agility, and trustworthiness in the face of evolving threats. The investment in robust integration planning and execution is not an optional add-on; it is a fundamental prerequisite for realizing the transformative potential of SMART Installations.

The transition to a SMART Installation is an undertaking that demands not only technological acumen and strategic vision but also a rigorous and disciplined approach to financial management. Resource allocation and budgeting are, therefore, not secondary considerations but fundamental pillars upon which the entire SMART framework rests. Without a clear, well-defined, and adequately funded plan, even the most theoretically sound security architecture risks remaining an aspiration rather than a tangible reality. This subsection is dedicated to illuminating the pathways for effective resource allocation and budgeting, ensuring that the investment in SMART security is both strategic and sustainable.

At the heart of any successful financial commitment lies a compelling business case. For SMART Installations, this case must articulate not just the need for enhanced security but the tangible benefits and return on investment (ROI) that these advanced capabilities will deliver. This requires moving beyond a purely defensive posture and framing security as a critical enabler of operational effectiveness, mission assurance, and force protection. The business case should meticulously detail the current security vulnerabilities, the projected threats, and how the proposed SMART solutions will directly mitigate these risks. Quantifying these benefits is paramount.

This might involve estimating the reduction in potential financial losses due to cyber breaches or physical intrusions, calculating the improved efficiency of security operations through automation and AI, or even assessing the intangible but critical benefits of enhanced personnel safety and confidence. For example, an installation might present data showing the average downtime and associated costs incurred by previous security incidents, then project the potential savings from a new, integrated early warning system that reduces response times and minimizes operational disruption. Similarly, the increased operational tempo enabled by enhanced cyber resilience – allowing for more secure and rapid data exchange critical for modern warfare – can be translated into mission-readiness metrics that resonate with higher echelons of command.

Identifying and securing the necessary funding is a multi-faceted challenge that often requires navigating complex organizational structures and diverse funding streams. Within the Department of Defense (DoD) and similar security-focused organizations, resources are typically allocated through various channels. These can include specific appropriations for research, development, testing, and evaluation (RDT&E;), as well as funds designated for procurement of new systems and infrastructure modernization.

Installations may have access to dedicated programs focused on enhancing physical security, cybersecurity, or critical infrastructure protection. Understanding these existing programs and aligning SMART Installation initiatives with their objectives is crucial. For instance, the DoD's efforts to bolster cybersecurity resilience or its investments in next-generation surveillance technologies might offer direct avenues for funding. Beyond these specific programs, installations might also leverage broader infrastructure improvement funds. These funds, often allocated for general upgrades and modernization, can be utilized to incorporate SMART security components as part of larger capital projects, such as upgrading network infrastructure or modernizing building systems. The key is to be proactive in identifying these opportunities and tailoring proposals to meet the eligibility criteria and strategic priorities of each funding source. Developing strong relationships with budget and finance offices, as well as with program managers responsible for relevant funding streams, is indispensable for this process.

Prioritization of investments is a critical component of effective resource allocation, especially when faced with finite budgets. Not all SMART security capabilities can or should be implemented simultaneously. A phased approach, guided by a comprehensive risk assessment and a clear understanding of mission-critical requirements, is essential. The SMARTIE (Secure, Modular, Agile, Resilient, Trustworthy, Integrated, and Enduring) architecture, with its emphasis on modularity and integration, provides a valuable framework for this. Prioritization should focus on foundational elements that enable subsequent enhancements. For example, investing in a robust, secure network infrastructure is often a prerequisite for deploying advanced AI-driven analytics or sophisticated data fusion platforms.

Similarly, establishing a strong baseline of cybersecurity for critical command and control systems might take precedence over deploying the latest in advanced biometric access control. This prioritization should be data-driven, informed by threat intelligence, vulnerability assessments, and a thorough cost-benefit analysis of each potential investment. High-impact, high-priority initiatives that address the most significant risks or offer the greatest operational advantages should be championed first. For example, if an installation faces a persistent and evolving cyber threat to its logistical networks, prioritizing the deployment of advanced cyber threat intelligence platforms and Zero Trust architecture principles would be a logical and necessary step. This layered approach ensures that resources are directed towards areas where they will yield the most significant improvements in overall security posture.

A cornerstone of sustainable security investment is the meticulous application of cost-benefit analyses (CBAs). A CBA goes beyond simply comparing the upfront acquisition cost of a technology with its projected security benefits. It encompasses a holistic evaluation of all costs and benefits over the entire lifecycle of the system. This includes not only the initial purchase price but also the costs associated with installation, training, operation, maintenance, upgrades, and eventual decommissioning.

On the benefits side, it must consider not only the direct reduction in security incidents but also the indirect advantages, such as improved operational efficiency, enhanced mission assurance, and potentially reduced insurance premiums or regulatory penalties. For instance, when evaluating the implementation of an AI-powered video surveillance system, a CBA would compare the cost of the cameras, analytics software, servers, and operator training against the projected reduction in manual monitoring effort, the improved accuracy of threat detection leading to faster response times, and the potential for reduced theft or vandalism. The analysis should also account for the cost of *not* investing, the potential financial losses, reputational damage, and mission degradation that could result from maintaining the status quo in the face of evolving threats. This comprehensive approach helps to justify the investment and demonstrate its long-term value.

Lifecycle cost considerations are inextricably linked to the CBA and are vital for ensuring that SMART Installations are not only implemented but also maintained and evolved effectively over time. A system that appears cost-effective initially might become prohibitively expensive to operate or maintain in the long run if its lifecycle costs were not adequately considered during the procurement phase. This means looking beyond the initial acquisition and delving into the ongoing expenses. For example, a highly sophisticated sensor system might require specialized, expensive maintenance contracts or proprietary spare parts that are difficult to source.

Conversely, a more open, modular system that adheres to industry standards might offer lower long-term operational costs due to easier maintenance, wider availability of parts, and competitive upgrade pathways. The budgeting process must therefore include provisions for ongoing maintenance, software updates, cybersecurity patching, and future technology refreshes. This proactive financial planning prevents a scenario where critical security systems become obsolete or fall into disrepair due to a lack of allocated operational and maintenance funds. It also supports the "Enduring" aspect of the SMARTIE architecture, ensuring that the security posture remains robust and relevant throughout the lifespan of the installation.

The budgeting process for SMART security must be agile and adaptive. The threat landscape is constantly evolving, and technological advancements emerge at a rapid pace. A rigid, multi-year budget that cannot accommodate unforeseen threats or new opportunities can quickly render security investments inadequate. Therefore, installations should strive to incorporate flexibility into their financial planning. This might involve establishing contingency funds for emergent threats, dedicating a portion of the budget for research and pilot programs to explore emerging technologies, or adopting more flexible procurement models that allow for phased deployments and iterative upgrades. The "Agile" tenet of the SMARTIE architecture is as relevant to financial planning as it is to technological implementation. It implies a willingness to re-evaluate priorities and reallocate resources as circumstances change. For example, if a new type of cyber threat emerges that poses an immediate risk to a particular system, the installation should have the financial mechanisms in place to quickly procure and deploy countermeasures without waiting for the next annual budget cycle. This agility is crucial for maintaining a proactive and responsive security posture in a dynamic environment.

The development of compelling business cases, the identification of diverse funding sources, the strategic prioritization of investments, and the diligent application of cost-benefit and lifecycle cost analyses are all critical components of effective resource allocation and budgeting for SMART Installations. This financial discipline is not a bureaucratic impediment but an essential enabler, transforming the vision of enhanced security into a realizable and sustainable reality. By embracing these principles, installations can ensure that their investments in advanced security are not only strategically sound but also financially prudent, providing enduring protection and enhancing mission effectiveness in an increasingly complex world. The financial roadmap for a SMART Installation must be as meticulously crafted as its technological blueprint, ensuring that the journey towards a more secure and resilient future is well-funded and sustainable.

Pilot programs and proof-of-concept (PoC) demonstrations serve as the critical proving grounds for any significant technological or strategic shift, and the transition to a SMART Installation is no exception. Before committing vast resources to a full-scale deployment, it is imperative to rigorously test and validate new approaches and technologies in controlled, yet realistic, operational environments. These initiatives are not merely exercises in technical feasibility; they are strategic investments designed to de-risk the implementation process, build confidence among stakeholders, and gather invaluable empirical data to inform decision-making. By embracing pilot projects and PoCs, installations can move from theoretical constructs to demonstrable realities, ensuring that the chosen strategies and technologies are not only sound in principle but also practical, effective, and aligned with the unique operational demands of the environment. This subsection will delve into the design, execution, and analysis of these crucial early-stage initiatives, illustrating how they pave the way for successful and sustainable SMART Installation deployments.

The fundamental purpose of a pilot program or a PoC is to provide a low-risk, high-learning opportunity. It allows stakeholders to witness firsthand how a proposed technology or system behaves under actual operational conditions, interacting with existing infrastructure, personnel, and workflows. This hands-on experience is invaluable for identifying unforeseen challenges, validating performance claims, and assessing the overall impact on operational effectiveness. Unlike laboratory simulations, pilot programs operate within the real world, exposing them to the unpredictable variables that are inherent in any operational setting. This exposure is precisely what makes them so critical. For example, a new AI-powered threat detection system might perform impeccably in controlled tests, but a pilot program might reveal how its algorithms are affected by environmental factors like fog, heavy rain, or unusual lighting conditions at a specific installation. Similarly, a new integrated command and control interface might be technologically advanced, but a pilot can reveal usability issues for operators accustomed to different systems, or highlight incompatibilities with legacy communication protocols that were not apparent during initial design.

Designing an effective pilot program or PoC requires careful planning and a clear definition of objectives. The scope must be well-defined, focusing on specific aspects of the SMART Installation vision that require validation. This could range from testing a particular sensor network's ability to detect and track unauthorized drone activity to assessing the efficacy of a new zero-trust cybersecurity architecture for a critical IT system, or evaluating the user experience and operational benefits of an integrated situational awareness dashboard for security personnel. Crucially, the objectives should be SMART: Specific, Measurable, Achievable, Relevant, and Time-bound. For instance, a pilot for a new biometric access control system might aim to reduce average entry time for authorized personnel by 15% while maintaining or improving the current false rejection rate over a two-month period. This specific, measurable target allows for clear evaluation of success.

The selection of the pilot site or operational area is another critical aspect of design. Ideally, the pilot should be representative of the broader installation's environment and operational context, but also manageable in terms of scale and complexity. It might involve a specific sector of the installation, a particular building or facility, or a defined operational scenario. It is often beneficial to select a site that has known security challenges or operational pain points that the proposed solution is intended to address. This provides a clear baseline against which to measure improvement. For example, if an installation has experienced recurrent issues with unauthorized access to a sensitive storage area, a pilot of an advanced, multi-factor authentication system for that specific area would be highly relevant and offer a clear metric for success: the elimination or significant reduction of such incidents.

Key performance indicators (KPIs) must be established *before* the pilot commences. These KPIs should directly align with the pilot's objectives and provide quantifiable metrics for success or failure. They might include measures of system performance (e.g., detection rates, response times, data accuracy), operational impact (e.g., reduction in manual effort, improvement in situational awareness, decreased incident rates), user adoption and satisfaction, and integration capabilities with existing systems. For example, in a pilot of an AI-driven video analytics system for perimeter security, KPIs might include the percentage of real threats correctly identified, the rate of false alarms, the time taken for security personnel to respond to an alert, and the system's compatibility with the existing CCTV network. Establishing these KPIs upfront ensures that the evaluation is objective and data-driven, moving beyond anecdotal evidence or subjective opinions.

The execution phase of a pilot program or PoC involves the deployment of the selected technologies and the operationalization of the new processes within the defined scope. This phase requires close collaboration between the technology providers, the installation's IT and security teams, and the end-users who will be interacting with the new systems. A dedicated project team should be established to oversee the pilot, manage day-to-day operations, troubleshoot issues, and collect data. Regular communication channels must be maintained to ensure that any problems are addressed promptly and that lessons learned are captured in real-time. This might involve daily or weekly check-ins with the operational teams, technical support for the deployed systems, and structured feedback sessions with users.

Data collection during the pilot is paramount. This involves not only automated system logs and performance metrics but also qualitative data gathered through user feedback, interviews, and observations. Users are often the best source of information regarding the practical usability and real-world effectiveness of a new system. Their insights into how a technology impacts their workflow, how intuitive it is to operate, and what potential improvements could be made are invaluable. For instance, a pilot of a new mobile application for security patrols might reveal that while the app's GPS tracking is accurate, the battery life is insufficient for a full shift, or that the interface is not optimized for use in bright sunlight, making it difficult to read. This feedback, if systematically collected, can lead to crucial refinements before wider deployment.

Another critical element during execution is the assessment of integration. SMART Installations are defined by their interconnectedness. A pilot must therefore examine how the new technology or system interfaces with existing infrastructure, data streams, and command structures. Does the new sensor network seamlessly feed data into the existing command and control platform? Are there any data format incompatibilities? Does the cybersecurity system effectively communicate with other network security tools? Understanding these integration points and potential friction is essential for planning the broader rollout. A pilot might uncover that while a new threat intelligence feed is highly accurate, integrating it into the existing reporting system requires significant custom development, thus increasing the complexity and cost of the full deployment.

Upon completion of the pilot program or PoC, a thorough analysis of the collected data is essential. This analysis should directly address the pre-defined objectives and KPIs. Was the pilot successful in achieving its goals? What were the quantifiable benefits realized? What were the costs incurred during the pilot, and how do they compare to initial projections? Beyond the quantitative, a qualitative assessment of user satisfaction, operational impact, and integration challenges is equally important. The lessons learned from the pilot must be meticulously documented. This includes identifying what worked well, what did not work, and why. Recommendations for refinement, adjustment, or even abandonment of the proposed solution should be clearly articulated based on the empirical evidence gathered.

Leveraging the lessons learned from pilots and PoCs is the bridge to full-scale implementation. The insights gained can inform critical decisions regarding technology selection, system design, implementation strategy, training requirements, and budget allocation. If a pilot demonstrates significant cost savings or operational improvements, it strengthens the business case for full deployment and can be used to secure the necessary funding. Conversely, if a pilot reveals fundamental flaws or insurmountable challenges, it allows for a course correction before substantial investments are made, thereby saving significant resources and avoiding potential project failure. For example, a pilot of a new physical security barrier system might reveal that the chosen material, while effective, is prohibitively expensive to procure in large quantities. This feedback would prompt a search for alternative materials or a re-evaluation of the barrier's specifications, rather than a costly mistake during mass procurement.

Successful pilot programs and PoCs can build crucial stakeholder buy-in and confidence. When decision-makers, end-users, and supporting staff can see tangible evidence of a technology's effectiveness and its positive impact on operations, they are more likely to support its widespread adoption. Positive pilot results can help to overcome skepticism and resistance to change, fostering a more receptive environment for the broader SMART Installation transformation. Stories of successful pilots, complete with data and user testimonials, become powerful communication tools. They demonstrate that the vision for a SMART Installation is not just an abstract concept but a practical, achievable goal, built on a foundation of tested and validated solutions.

The iterative nature of piloting is also key. A pilot might not always yield perfect results on the first try. It may reveal areas where the technology needs further development, or where the operational procedures require modification. In such cases, a follow-up pilot, incorporating the learned adjustments, might be necessary. This iterative approach, characteristic of agile methodologies, allows for continuous improvement and refinement of the solution before it is scaled across the entire installation. This mindset of testing, learning, and adapting is fundamental to managing the inherent complexities and uncertainties of implementing advanced security technologies in dynamic environments.

Pilot programs and proof-of-concept demonstrations are indispensable tools in the arsenal for achieving a SMART Installation. They provide a structured, low-risk pathway to validate innovative technologies and approaches, gather critical performance data, and identify potential challenges before committing to large-scale deployments. By carefully designing, executing, and analyzing these initiatives, installations can significantly reduce the risks associated with technological adoption, build confidence among stakeholders, and ensure that investments in advanced security are strategically sound, operationally effective, and ultimately contribute to a more secure, resilient, and mission-capable environment. They are the practical embodiments of due diligence, transforming ambitious plans into demonstrable successes.

Chapter 12: The Future of Installation/Base Security: Adaptation and Evolution

ANTICIPATING FUTURE THREATS

The security landscape is not static; it is a perpetually evolving battleground where the tools and tactics of adversaries are in constant flux, mirroring and often outpacing the advancements in defensive technologies. To maintain the integrity and operational readiness of installations in the future, a proactive and forward-looking approach to threat assessment and technological trajectory analysis is paramount. This necessitates a deep dive into the nascent capabilities that adversaries are likely to develop and deploy, as well as a keen understanding of the accelerating pace of technological innovation that will shape both offensive and defensive strategies. Ignoring these impending shifts is akin to preparing for a battle with the weapons of the last war, a recipe for obsolescence and vulnerability. Therefore, installations must cultivate a culture of continuous foresight, integrating intelligence gathering and trend analysis into the very fabric of their security planning.

One of the most disruptive technological trajectories is the increasing sophistication and accessibility of Artificial Intelligence (AI) and its application to autonomous systems. While current drone technology, for instance, often requires human operators for precision targeting or complex maneuvering, the future portends swarms of AI-driven unmanned aerial vehicles (UAVs) capable of independent operation, coordinated attack patterns, and sophisticated evasion tactics. These are not mere remote-controlled devices; they are entities capable of real-time decision-making, adapting their flight paths and attack vectors based on sensor data and environmental feedback.

Imagine a swarm of micro-drones, too small to be individually detected by conventional radar, capable of infiltrating a facility, mapping internal infrastructure, or even delivering small, potent payloads with a degree of autonomy that renders traditional countermeasures less effective. Their AI could be trained to identify critical infrastructure, personnel, or even specific vehicle types, making them highly adaptable to various mission profiles. Furthermore, the concept of "loyal wingmen" or autonomous combat systems, designed to operate alongside human-controlled platforms, could extend this threat beyond the aerial domain, encompassing ground-based robotic systems and potentially even naval applications. The ability of these systems to learn and adapt from combat encounters means that their effectiveness could increase exponentially with each engagement, presenting a dynamic and evolving threat that is difficult to predict and counter.

Beyond the realm of autonomous physical agents, AI is also poised to revolutionize cyber warfare. Adversaries are increasingly leveraging machine learning algorithms to develop more potent and evasive cyberattack tools. Think of AI-powered malware that can dynamically alter its signature to evade detection by antivirus software, or AI-driven phishing campaigns that are personalized and contextually aware, making them almost indistinguishable from legitimate communications.

Future cyber threats might involve AI systems that can autonomously discover vulnerabilities within complex networks, devise exploitation strategies, and execute attacks with unprecedented speed and precision, often operating at machine speeds that far exceed human response capabilities. This could lead to instantaneous data exfiltration, system paralysis, or even manipulation of critical industrial control systems (ICS) and operational technology (OT) that underpin many installation functions. The concept of "AI vs. AI" warfare in the cyberspace is no longer science fiction; it is an emerging reality that demands a commensurate evolution in our defensive cyber architectures, moving towards AI-driven detection, automated incident response, and resilient systems designed to withstand relentless, machine-speed attacks.

Electronic warfare (EW) is another domain undergoing rapid transformation, amplified by advancements in AI and digital signal processing. The spectrum of electromagnetic emissions is becoming increasingly crowded and contested. Future EW capabilities could include adaptive jammers that can precisely target and disrupt specific communication frequencies or sensor systems, making them highly effective against targeted assets while minimizing collateral interference. Adversaries might employ directed energy weapons, moving beyond conventional projectile-based systems, to disable or destroy sensitive electronic equipment, sensors, or even personnel with non-kinetic effects.

The miniaturization of sophisticated EW components means that even smaller platforms, such as drones or ground vehicles, could carry significant electronic attack payloads. This poses a direct threat to radar systems, communication networks, GPS-dependent navigation, and any system reliant on the electromagnetic spectrum. Installations must anticipate EW capabilities that can not only disrupt but also deceive, creating ghost targets or spoofing sensor data to mislead defensive systems and personnel. The ability to conduct sophisticated signal intelligence (SIGINT) to map out an installation's electronic footprint and identify critical vulnerabilities will also be enhanced by AI, allowing adversaries to prepare for targeted electronic attacks with greater accuracy.

The convergence of these technological trends creates complex, multi-domain threats. An attack might not be solely cyber, physical, or electronic, but a synchronized combination of all three. For example, an AI-driven cyberattack could be used to disable an installation's perimeter sensors and communication systems, paving the way for autonomous drone swarms to infiltrate and conduct reconnaissance or physical sabotage, all while electronic warfare assets saturate the spectrum to prevent coordinated defensive responses. This necessitates a holistic, integrated approach to security, where intelligence from all domains is fused to create a comprehensive understanding of the threat landscape. A SMART Installation's ability to effectively anticipate and counter such multi-domain threats will depend on its capacity to integrate diverse sensor inputs, leverage AI for rapid threat correlation and prediction, and coordinate responses across physical, cyber, and electromagnetic domains in real-time.

To effectively anticipate these future threats, installations must foster a robust and continuous intelligence gathering and analysis capability. This goes beyond traditional threat intelligence feeds focused on known actors and current tactics. It requires a proactive engagement with research and development communities, open-source intelligence (OSINT) analysis of global technology trends, and collaboration with allied nations to share insights on emerging capabilities. Understanding the "dual-use" nature of many advanced technologies is critical; a technology developed for civilian applications, such as advanced robotics or AI for logistics, can quickly be adapted for military or malicious purposes. Therefore, security planners must maintain a keen awareness of emerging commercial and scientific breakthroughs and assess their potential weaponization. This involves not just monitoring technical specifications but also understanding the proliferation pathways of these technologies, the cost of entry for potential adversaries, and the geopolitical contexts that might incentivize their development and deployment.

The concept of "predictive security" must move from a theoretical ideal to an operational reality. This involves leveraging advanced analytics, including AI and machine learning, not just to detect current threats but to identify patterns and anomalies that indicate the *imminent* likelihood of an attack. By analyzing historical data, environmental factors, intelligence reports, and even social media sentiment, AI systems can potentially flag areas of increased risk or identify precursor activities that may not be obvious to human analysts. For instance, a surge in chatter on dark web forums discussing specific vulnerabilities, combined with unusual network traffic patterns around a particular asset, could be an early warning sign of an impending cyberattack. Similarly, unusual patterns of civilian drone activity near an installation, coupled with specific SIGINT intercepts, might indicate preparatory reconnaissance for an aerial assault. This predictive capability allows for the allocation of resources and the pre-positioning of countermeasures before an attack even materializes, transforming security from a reactive posture to a proactive, anticipatory one.

The development of resilient and adaptable infrastructure is also a critical component of future-proofing installation security. This involves designing systems that can withstand disruption and degrade gracefully rather than failing catastrophically. For cyber systems, this means adopting principles of zero-trust architecture, micro-segmentation, and robust data backup and recovery mechanisms, all informed by an understanding of potential AI-driven attacks. In the physical realm, it might involve distributed security nodes, redundant power and communication systems, and physically hardened critical infrastructure. For electronic warfare, resilience means designing systems that are inherently resistant to jamming and spoofing or can rapidly reconfigure their operating parameters. The goal is to create an environment where even if an adversary achieves partial success in their attack, the installation can continue to operate, respond, and ultimately prevail. This concept of "defense in depth," layered with an understanding of future threat vectors, becomes even more crucial.

The human element, while often augmented by technology, remains indispensable. The skills required of security personnel will continue to evolve. Future security professionals will need to be adept at operating and interpreting data from advanced AI systems, understanding complex cyber and electronic warfare environments, and making rapid decisions under pressure. Continuous training and development programs are essential to equip personnel with the knowledge and skills to counter emerging threats. This includes not only technical training but also cognitive skills development, such as critical thinking, problem-solving, and adaptability. The ability for human operators to effectively collaborate with and guide AI systems, providing context, ethical oversight, and strategic direction, will be a defining characteristic of effective future security operations.

The ethical implications of advanced technologies, particularly in the context of autonomous weapons and AI-driven surveillance, must be carefully considered. As installations adopt more sophisticated technologies, establishing clear ethical guidelines and robust oversight mechanisms is crucial to ensure that these capabilities are used responsibly and in accordance with legal and moral principles. This includes defining rules of engagement for autonomous systems, ensuring accountability for AI-driven decisions, and protecting civilian privacy where applicable. The potential for unintended consequences or the misuse of powerful technologies necessitates a framework of ethical governance that complements the technological advancements.

The path to enduring installation security in the face of relentless technological advancement requires a fundamental shift towards anticipatory defense. This involves not only understanding the current threat landscape but also diligently forecasting the capabilities that adversaries will likely develop and deploy, from AI-powered autonomous weapons and sophisticated cyber tools to novel forms of electronic warfare. Installations must invest in continuous foresight and intelligence gathering, fostering a culture that embraces the analysis of emerging technological trajectories and their potential weaponization. By proactively adapting security strategies, developing resilient and integrated systems, empowering personnel with future-ready skills, and adhering to strict ethical frameworks, installations can navigate the complexities of an evolving threat environment and ensure their continued security and operational effectiveness against adversaries who will invariably seek to exploit the bleeding edge of technology. This proactive, intelligence-driven, and technologically informed approach is not merely an option; it is an imperative for survival in the future security paradigm.

The integration of Artificial Intelligence (AI) and autonomous systems into the fabric of installation security represents not merely an evolutionary step, but a transformative leap. As we venture further into the future, the capabilities of these technologies will move beyond mere assistance to become integral components of the defense architecture, fundamentally reshaping how installations perceive, react to, and mitigate threats. This evolution is driven by the inherent advantages AI offers: unparalleled speed in data processing, the ability to operate continuously without fatigue, and the potential to analyze vast, complex datasets with a precision and scope beyond human capacity. The implications for installation security are profound, promising enhanced situational awareness, automated defensive actions, and significantly improved decision-making, particularly in environments characterized by high tempo and complexity.

One of the most immediate and impactful applications of AI in future installation security lies in the realm of threat detection. Current sensor networks, while sophisticated, often generate an overwhelming volume of data that can strain human analysts. AI, however, can ingest, process, and correlate this disparate information streams – from thermal imaging and acoustic sensors to radar, network traffic logs, and even open-source intelligence – with unprecedented efficiency. Machine learning algorithms can be trained to identify subtle anomalies and patterns that might otherwise go unnoticed, such as minute changes in thermal signatures indicating unauthorized movement, or deviations in network traffic that suggest an impending cyber intrusion. Predictive analytics, powered by AI, will move beyond mere detection to anticipating threats. By analyzing historical data, environmental factors, and real-time sensor inputs, AI systems can forecast the likelihood of specific attack vectors or identify precursor activities. For instance, an AI might flag an increased probability of a physical intrusion based on a combination of unusual weather patterns that could obscure movement, a recent surge in dark web chatter about specific security weaknesses, and subtle shifts in acoustic sensor data near a vulnerable perimeter section. This predictive capability allows for the proactive allocation of resources and the pre-positioning of countermeasures, transforming security from a reactive posture to one of informed anticipation.

Beyond detection, AI and autonomy will enable automated defensive actions, significantly reducing response times and improving the efficacy of countermeasures. Imagine an intrusion detected at the perimeter by a network of AI-enhanced sensors. Instead of relying solely on human operators to verify the threat and initiate a response, an AI system could, based on pre-defined protocols and the confidence level of the threat assessment, autonomously deploy countermeasures. This could range from activating non-lethal deterrents, such as directed acoustic or light energy systems, to guiding automated sentry platforms to intercept and neutralize the threat. In the cyber domain, AI-powered Security Orchestration, Automation, and Response (SOAR) platforms are already demonstrating their value. Future iterations will see AI systems capable of not only detecting a cyber intrusion but also autonomously isolating infected network segments, patching vulnerabilities, and initiating data recovery processes, all within milliseconds, a speed that human intervention simply cannot match. This automation is crucial in countering rapidly evolving, AI-driven cyberattacks that operate at machine speeds. The goal is to create a system where the defensive response is as swift and intelligent as the offensive action, thereby minimizing potential damage and disruption.

The ability of AI to enhance decision-making in complex and rapidly evolving scenarios is another critical advantage. Future operational environments will likely be characterized by information overload and a high degree of uncertainty. AI can act as an intelligent assistant to human commanders and security personnel, synthesizing vast amounts of data from multiple sources and presenting actionable insights in a concise and understandable format. This could include identifying the most critical threats among a barrage of false positives, recommending optimal defensive strategies based on real-time threat assessments, or predicting the likely consequences of different courses of action. For example, during a multi-pronged attack involving physical, cyber, and electronic warfare elements, an AI system could rapidly assess the cascading effects of each component, helping commanders to prioritize resources and allocate defensive efforts to counter the most significant immediate and cascading threats. The AI doesn't replace human judgment, but augments it, providing a richer, more informed basis for critical decisions, especially under extreme pressure. This synergy between human intuition and AI's analytical prowess is key to effective command and control in future conflict and security operations.

The increasing role of autonomy in defense systems, however, brings with it a complex set of ethical considerations and challenges. As AI systems become more capable of making decisions and taking actions independently, the question of accountability becomes paramount. When an autonomous system errs, who is responsible? The programmer, the commander who deployed it, or the system itself? Establishing clear lines of responsibility and ensuring robust oversight mechanisms are critical to maintaining public trust and adhering to legal and ethical frameworks. The potential for unintended consequences or algorithmic bias also needs careful consideration. AI systems are trained on data, and if that data reflects existing societal biases, the AI can perpetuate or even amplify them. This could lead to discriminatory outcomes in threat assessment or the disproportionate application of force. Therefore, rigorous testing, validation, and continuous monitoring of AI systems are essential to identify and mitigate bias.

The concept of "human-in-the-loop," "human-on-the-loop," and "human-out-of-the-loop" decision-making becomes increasingly relevant. While full autonomy might be desirable for certain tasks requiring extreme speed, such as missile defense, many security applications will benefit from maintaining a human presence in the decision-making process. A "human-in-the-loop" system ensures that a human operator must authorize every critical action. A "human-on-the-loop" system allows the AI to act autonomously but provides a human with the ability to supervise, intervene, or override the AI's actions. The challenge lies in striking the right balance, leveraging the speed and analytical power of AI while ensuring that human judgment, ethical considerations, and strategic oversight remain central to security operations. Over-reliance on automation without adequate human control could lead to scenarios where systems act in ways that are tactically effective but strategically or ethically unsound.

The development of AI systems that can effectively communicate their reasoning and uncertainty to human operators is therefore crucial for fostering trust and enabling effective collaboration. Another significant challenge is the potential for adversaries to exploit AI and autonomous systems, creating a new arms race in artificial intelligence. If AI offers advantages in defense, it also offers them in offense. Adversaries could develop AI-powered cyber weapons that are more sophisticated and evasive, autonomous drone swarms capable of overwhelming defenses, or AI-driven electronic warfare systems that can adapt to and defeat countermeasures in real-time. This necessitates a continuous investment in AI research and development for defensive purposes, ensuring that military and security organizations can stay ahead of or at least keep pace with evolving threats. The "dual-use" nature of AI technology means that breakthroughs in civilian AI research can quickly be adapted for military applications, blurring the lines between peaceful innovation and potential weaponization. Installations must therefore maintain a keen awareness of global AI development trends and proactively assess their potential implications for security.

The proliferation of AI and autonomous systems also raises questions about the weaponization of these technologies. The development of lethal autonomous weapons systems (LAWS) is a particularly contentious issue, with significant debate surrounding the ethical implications of delegating life-and-death decisions to machines. While some argue that LAWS could reduce human casualties by operating with greater precision and without emotion, others fear that they could lower the threshold for conflict, lead to indiscriminate killing, and create a dangerous precedent for the future of warfare. For installation security, this translates to anticipating potential threats from autonomous systems developed by state and non-state actors alike. Understanding the types of autonomous capabilities that could be deployed against an installation, and developing robust countermeasures, will be a critical aspect of future security planning. This includes the ability to detect, track, and neutralize autonomous agents, whether they are physical robots, drones, or sophisticated software agents operating within the cyber domain.

The integration of AI and autonomous systems into installation security requires a significant shift in training and personnel development. Security personnel will need to be trained not only in the operation of these new technologies but also in understanding their capabilities, limitations, and potential failure modes. This includes developing skills in data analysis, AI oversight, and ethical decision-making in complex, AI-augmented environments. The workforce will need to adapt to a paradigm where humans and intelligent machines collaborate closely, each leveraging their unique strengths. This might involve training personnel to effectively supervise and guide autonomous systems, interpret AI-generated insights, and intervene when necessary to ensure ethical and strategic alignment. The ability to adapt to new technologies and continuously learn will be a hallmark of future security professionals.

The future of installation security will be inextricably linked to the advancements in AI and autonomy. These technologies offer immense potential to enhance threat detection, automate complex defensive actions, and improve decision-making, thereby bolstering the resilience and effectiveness of security operations. However, their integration must be approached with a clear understanding of the associated ethical considerations, potential for misuse, and the imperative of maintaining meaningful human oversight. As we continue to develop and deploy these powerful tools, a measured, responsible, and ethically grounded approach will be essential to harness their benefits while mitigating their risks, ensuring that the future of installation security is not only technologically advanced but also secure, accountable, and aligned with human values. The pursuit of enhanced security through AI and autonomy is an ongoing journey, one that requires continuous vigilance, adaptation, and a deep commitment to ethical principles.

The convergence of disparate security functions is not merely a strategic aspiration but an emergent necessity. As the lines between the physical and digital realms blur, and as the threat landscape expands to encompass aerial, cyber, and human elements in increasingly complex and interconnected ways, the traditional siloed approach to installation security becomes not only inefficient but dangerously inadequate. The future demands a paradigm shift towards a truly integrated, holistic defense posture. This necessitates the conceptualization and implementation of what can be termed the 'One Installation' approach to security. This isn't simply about better communication between existing security departments; it's about re-envisioning the entire security apparatus as a singular, indivisible entity, where each component's strength is amplified by its seamless integration with others, and where operational planning and execution are unified under a single, coherent strategic umbrella.

The 'One Installation' concept posits that physical, cyber, air, and human security are not separate domains to be managed independently, but rather facets of a singular, overarching security mission. In this future state, the distinction between securing a perimeter fence, defending a network server, monitoring airspace, and safeguarding personnel becomes conceptually negligible from an operational planning perspective. All intelligence, all sensors, all response mechanisms, and all decision-making processes are designed to contribute to a singular, unified defense effort. This requires dismantling remaining organizational, technical, and informational barriers that currently segment security functions. It means moving beyond cooperative security efforts to truly fused operations, where the output of one domain's security apparatus is directly and immediately actionable by another, contributing to a composite, real-time understanding of the installation's security status.

Consider the implications for threat detection and response. In a traditional model, a physical breach detected by perimeter sensors might trigger a response from physical security forces, while a cyber intrusion is handled by IT security teams, and an aerial threat is managed by air defense units. These responses are often initiated independently, with information flowing sequentially or incompletely between them. Under the 'One Installation' model, however, these events are analyzed within a unified intelligence picture. For instance, the detection of unusual acoustic signatures near a perimeter might be correlated by an AI-powered system with anomalous network traffic patterns originating from within the installation and with a detected deviation in flight path of an unregistered drone in the vicinity. The AI doesn't just flag these as separate events; it synthesizes them into a single, high-confidence threat assessment: a coordinated, multi-domain attack.

The response, then, is not fragmented but integrated. Physical security forces are dispatched not just to the perimeter breach but are informed of the likely cyber vector or aerial component. Cyber defense teams are alerted to the potential for insider threats or external manipulation that might be linked to the physical breach. Air defense systems are primed with updated threat profiles that may include ground-based elements supporting an aerial ingress. Human security personnel, from guards to IT administrators to flight controllers, are all operating from the same, unified operational picture, receiving synchronized intelligence and coordinating their actions through a common command and control interface. This eliminates the critical delays and miscommunications that can arise from siloed operations, allowing for a swift, decisive, and comprehensive response that addresses the full spectrum of the threat.

This unified approach extends to the very infrastructure of security. Instead of having separate sensor networks for physical intrusion detection, cyber monitoring, and airspace surveillance, the 'One Installation' concept envisions a distributed, interconnected network of sensors that feed a common data fusion and analysis platform. This platform, likely augmented by advanced AI and machine learning, possesses the capability to process and contextualize data from all sources simultaneously. Thermal cameras on the perimeter can provide data that informs the analysis of electromagnetic signatures detected by cyber sensors. Network logs can be cross-referenced with physical access control system data to identify anomalies. Acoustic sensors can help triangulate the source of both physical movement and potentially the origin of electronic jamming or spoofing signals. The resulting enriched data stream provides a far more granular and accurate understanding of the operational environment and potential threats.

The 'One Installation' concept fundamentally redefines the role of human intelligence and personnel security. Human operators are no longer just specialists in their narrow domain. Instead, they are integral nodes within a larger, interconnected security ecosystem. Training must evolve to encompass a broader understanding of all security domains. A physical security officer needs to understand the basics of cyber vulnerabilities and how they might be exploited to facilitate a physical breach. A cyber analyst needs to be aware of physical security protocols and how they might be compromised. This cross-training fosters a shared responsibility and a deeper appreciation for how actions in one domain can have profound consequences in others. Personnel security screenings will need to consider not just an individual's background and access levels across physical and digital systems, but also their potential susceptibility to manipulation or coercion that could compromise any aspect of the installation's security.

The command and control (C2) structures must also adapt. Traditional hierarchical command structures, often reflecting the departmental silos, will need to be flattened and made more agile. A unified C2 center, overseeing all security operations in real-time, becomes essential. This center would house integrated C2 systems that present a consolidated view of the entire security posture, enabling commanders to make decisions based on a comprehensive understanding of the threats and available resources across all domains. The AI-augmented C2 systems would not only provide this unified picture but also offer predictive analysis and recommended courses of action, further enhancing the speed and effectiveness of decision-making. This requires a significant investment in interoperable C2 systems and a willingness to reorganize command structures to break down historical departmental divisions.

The development of robust, resilient, and secure communication networks is the bedrock upon which the 'One Installation' concept is built. These networks must be capable of handling vast amounts of data from diverse sensor types, ensuring the secure and rapid transmission of information between all security elements. This includes not only traditional wired and wireless networks but also potentially resilient mesh networks, satellite communications, and even novel forms of data transmission that can operate effectively in contested environments or during cyberattacks. The integrity and security of these networks are paramount; a compromised communication channel could cripple the entire integrated security system. Therefore, a significant portion of the investment in this model will be in developing and maintaining highly secure, redundant, and adaptable communication architectures.

The 'One Installation' approach also necessitates a fundamental shift in how security requirements are defined and articulated. Instead of security requirements being developed in isolation for physical security, cybersecurity, or air defense, they will be generated from a holistic assessment of the installation's mission and its threat environment. This ensures that the security solutions developed are not only effective in their specific domain but also contribute to the overall security objectives of the installation. For example, the requirement for physical perimeter security might be influenced by the need to protect critical cyber infrastructure located within the installation, or by the potential for aerial surveillance to provide early warning of physical infiltration attempts. This holistic requirement definition drives the development of truly integrated security systems.

The implementation of such a radical shift is not without its challenges. Organizational inertia, resistance to change, and the significant investment required for new technologies and training are all formidable obstacles. Furthermore, the complexity of integrating diverse systems and ensuring interoperability across different manufacturers and legacy systems presents a substantial technical hurdle. The development of common data standards, open architectures, and robust integration protocols will be critical to overcoming these challenges. Moreover, the legal and ethical frameworks governing security operations may need to be re-evaluated to accommodate the blurring of lines between different security domains and the potential for AI-driven decision-making in a unified security context.

The potential benefits of the 'One Installation' concept far outweigh these challenges. It promises a more resilient, adaptable, and effective security posture that is better equipped to handle the increasingly complex and interconnected threats of the future. By breaking down traditional silos and fostering a truly unified approach, installations can achieve a level of security awareness and responsiveness that is currently unattainable. This integrated approach is not merely an upgrade; it is a fundamental transformation in how we conceive of and execute installation security, moving towards a future where the installation is secured as a singular, indivisible entity, protected by a seamlessly interwoven tapestry of physical, cyber, aerial, and human defenses. This evolution is driven by the understanding that in the modern threat environment, security is not a collection of independent functions, but a singular, all-encompassing state of being for the installation. The success of this model hinges on the ability to foster a culture of collaboration and shared responsibility, underpinned by robust technological integration and continuous adaptation to the ever-evolving threat landscape.

The journey towards a 'One Installation' model involves a strategic, phased approach. It begins with identifying key areas where integration can yield immediate benefits, such as the fusion of physical and cyber threat intelligence. For instance, correlating access control system logs with network intrusion detection systems can reveal coordinated attempts to breach both physical and digital defenses. This initial phase focuses on improving data sharing and interoperability between existing systems, laying the groundwork for more profound integration. As trust and operational effectiveness grow, the integration can expand to include aerial domain awareness, utilizing drones and other aerial platforms not just for surveillance but as mobile sensor nodes that can feed data into the common operational picture, enhancing situational awareness for both physical and cyber defense teams.

The human element, often the most complex and unpredictable, becomes a critical component of this integrated system. Future security personnel will require a different skill set. Beyond traditional security training, individuals will need to be proficient in data analysis, understand the principles of AI-driven security systems, and be adept at working within a collaborative, multi-domain environment. This involves developing 'security generalists' who possess a broad understanding across domains, alongside highly specialized experts who can delve deep into specific areas when required. The concept of continuous learning and adaptation becomes paramount, ensuring that personnel remain current with emerging threats and evolving technologies. Training simulations that replicate multi-domain attack scenarios will become standard practice, allowing personnel to hone their skills in a safe, controlled environment.

The operational planning for a 'One Installation' security construct requires a radical departure from current methodologies. Instead of developing separate operational plans for physical security, cyber operations, and air defense, a single, overarching operational plan will encompass all domains. This plan will define the installation's security objectives, identify potential threats across all domains, allocate resources holistically, and outline integrated response protocols. The plan will be dynamic, subject to continuous review and adaptation based on real-time intelligence and evolving threat assessments. The emphasis will be on agility and flexibility, allowing security forces to rapidly reconfigure their efforts in response to changing circumstances. This requires a sophisticated understanding of cascading effects, where an action in one domain can have significant implications for others. For example, a cyberattack designed to disable physical security systems could also be a precursor to an aerial assault, necessitating a coordinated defense that anticipates these linkages.

The development of common operating picture (COP) platforms will be central to realizing the 'One Installation' vision. These platforms will serve as the central hub for all security-related information, integrating data from a multitude of sources and presenting it in a clear, intuitive, and actionable format. The COP will provide a real-time, 360-degree view of the installation's security status, enabling commanders and operators to make informed decisions quickly and effectively. Advanced visualization tools, augmented by AI, will help to identify patterns, anomalies, and potential threats that might otherwise go unnoticed. The COP will also facilitate seamless communication and coordination between different security elements, ensuring that all personnel are working from the same, up-to-date information.

The 'One Installation' concept inherently embraces the idea of resilience through redundancy and defense-in-depth. By integrating security across all domains, vulnerabilities in one area can be mitigated by strengths in another. For instance, if cyber defenses are temporarily degraded by an attack, the robust physical security measures can still provide a significant layer of protection. Conversely, if physical access is temporarily restricted, the enhanced cyber defenses can maintain operational continuity. This multi-layered approach ensures that the installation remains secure and operational even when faced with complex, multi-faceted attacks. The goal is not to achieve perfect security, which is an unattainable ideal, but to build a security framework that is inherently robust, adaptable, and capable of absorbing and mitigating a wide range of threats.

The ultimate aim of the 'One Installation' concept is to create an environment where the distinction between 'security' and 'operations' becomes increasingly blurred. When security is fully integrated into the operational fabric of an installation, it is no longer an add-on or a separate concern, but an inherent characteristic of how the installation functions. This seamless integration allows for greater operational efficiency, enhanced mission effectiveness, and a more secure environment for personnel and assets. It represents a paradigm shift from managing security as a set of reactive measures to proactively embedding security into the very DNA of the installation's operations. This transformative approach is essential for ensuring the long-term security and viability of installations in an increasingly complex and unpredictable world. The successful implementation of this concept will require unwavering commitment from leadership, significant investment in technology and training, and a fundamental re-thinking of how security is conceived and executed.

The efficacy of any security strategy, particularly one as integrated and dynamic as the 'One Installation' concept, cannot be adequately assessed through outdated or siloed metrics. The move towards a unified security posture demands a corresponding evolution in how we measure success. Traditional metrics, often focused on compliance with static regulations or the absence of specific, predictable incidents, fall short in environments characterized by rapid change, sophisticated adversaries, and multi-domain threats. The future requires a suite of metrics that can capture the nuanced, adaptive, and resilient nature of modern installation security.

This necessitates a shift from measuring what was done to measuring how effectively it functions under stress, and critically, how well it anticipates and adapts to the unknown. The bedrock of this new measurement paradigm lies in assessing resilience and adaptability. Resilience, in this context, refers not merely to the ability to recover from an incident, but to the capacity to maintain essential functions and security operations with minimal disruption when faced with adverse events. Metrics for resilience might include the Mean Time to Restore (MTTR) critical security functions after a simulated multi-domain attack, the percentage of operational capabilities maintained during a period of sustained cyber-physical disruption, or the speed at which security personnel can re-establish a common operating picture (COP) following a sophisticated electronic warfare attack that degrades sensor networks.

For instance, a metric could track how quickly the installation can transition from its standard security posture to a heightened state of alert and defense across all domains, with minimal loss of situational awareness or response time, following a simulated coordinated attack designed to overwhelm specific segments of its defenses. This involves not just identifying the number of personnel or systems brought back online, but the quality and comprehensiveness of their re-integration into the operational security fabric.

Adaptability, on the other hand, focuses on the system's capacity to learn, evolve, and reconfigure in response to new threats or changing operational conditions. Metrics here would probe the speed and effectiveness of threat intelligence integration, the rate at which new security protocols are developed and disseminated, and the system's ability to dynamically reallocate resources based on predictive analysis. Consider a metric that measures the time elapsed between the identification of a novel adversarial tactic (e.g., a new method of drone swarm coordination) and the successful deployment of countermeasures and updated training across all relevant security domains.

This could be further refined by tracking the percentage of personnel who successfully complete refresher training on these new countermeasures within a defined timeframe, or by measuring the reduction in false positives generated by security systems after AI algorithms have been updated to recognize these novel threats. Another crucial adaptability metric would involve the speed and efficacy of policy updates. For example, after a classified incident involving the exploitation of a previously unknown vulnerability, how quickly are security policies updated, training materials revised, and those revisions effectively disseminated and understood by all relevant personnel across physical, cyber, and human security elements? This involves not just the paperwork, but verifiable comprehension and behavioral change.

Perhaps the most critical set of metrics will focus on threat mitigation success rates within a complex, multi-domain context. This moves beyond simply counting breaches averted to assessing the effectiveness of integrated responses against sophisticated adversaries. Metrics could include the percentage of simulated complex attacks that are fully neutralized before achieving their objective, the degree to which attacker attribution is achieved during these simulations, and the efficiency with which adversaries are expelled from the installation's digital or physical space. For example, a metric could track the success rate of countering a simulated coordinated attack that combines cyber intrusion with physical infiltration and aerial surveillance. This would involve analyzing the speed of detection, the accuracy of threat assessment, the appropriateness and speed of the integrated response, and ultimately, the achievement of mission objectives by the security forces. Success would be defined not just by stopping the immediate threat, but by limiting collateral damage, preserving operational continuity, and gathering actionable intelligence for future prevention.

The effectiveness of integrated systems themselves must also be quantified. This requires metrics that measure the synergy and interoperability of disparate security components. Key Performance Indicators (KPIs) could include the degree of data fusion achieved by the COP platform (e.g., the percentage of incoming sensor data that is successfully correlated and contextualized with data from other domains), the reduction in response times attributable to seamless information flow between physical, cyber, and human security elements, and the reduction in critical errors resulting from a unified operational picture. A tangible metric might be the percentage decrease in the number of miscommunications or delayed responses during simulated integrated threat scenarios, directly attributable to the use of the unified COP and integrated C2 systems. We could also measure the efficiency gains by tracking the reduction in personnel hours required to achieve a comprehensive security assessment or to execute a complex defensive maneuver, thanks to the automation and integration facilitated by advanced technologies.

Beyond simulated environments, real-world event analysis provides invaluable data. This involves post-incident reviews that go beyond a simple factual account to critically assess the performance of the integrated security system. Metrics could involve analyzing the effectiveness of the 'One Installation' approach in mitigating actual threats, the speed at which lessons learned from minor incidents are incorporated into broader security protocols, and the impact of these integrated measures on the overall security posture. For instance, after a minor physical security incident, a metric could track how quickly associated network anomalies were identified and analyzed, and whether this analysis led to proactive adjustments in cyber defenses to prevent similar vulnerabilities from being exploited. This involves a structured approach to data collection and analysis following any security event, focusing on identifying root causes that span across domains and evaluating the integrated response.

The development of meaningful metrics necessitates a clear understanding of the desired outcomes for installation security. If the objective is to maintain operational readiness under duress, then metrics should quantify the preservation of critical functions. If the goal is to deter sophisticated adversaries, then metrics should reflect the perceived and actual increases in risk and difficulty for potential attackers. This requires a strategic alignment between the measurement framework and the overarching security objectives. For example, if a primary objective is to safeguard sensitive research data, metrics will focus on the integrity and confidentiality of that data across all access points, physical, cyber, and personnel-related. This would involve tracking not just data breaches, but also unauthorized access attempts, data exfiltration patterns, and the effectiveness of encryption and access control mechanisms across the entire data lifecycle.

The process of developing and implementing these new metrics is iterative and requires continuous refinement. What constitutes an effective metric today may need to be adjusted as threats evolve and technologies advance. A crucial aspect is ensuring that the metrics are not only comprehensive but also actionable. Decision-makers need data that provides clear insights into the strengths and weaknesses of the security posture, enabling them to allocate resources effectively, identify areas for improvement, and justify investments. This means moving away from abstract numbers to qualitative assessments embedded within quantitative data. For instance, a metric could report the "effectiveness score" for neutralizing a specific class of threat, where this score is derived from a composite analysis of response time, accuracy, resource utilization, and collateral damage, providing a more holistic picture than a simple success/failure binary.

The integration of human performance into these metrics is vital. While technology plays a significant role, the human element remains central to effective security. Metrics should assess the effectiveness of training programs, the proficiency of personnel in utilizing integrated systems, and their ability to make sound decisions under pressure. This could involve analyzing performance data from personnel involved in simulated exercises, assessing their contribution to the COP, and evaluating their adherence to integrated response protocols. Metrics could also include the rate of successful threat identification by human operators compared to automated systems, and the efficiency with which personnel can escalate and coordinate responses across different security domains. The development of a "situational awareness score" for key personnel, derived from their ability to correctly interpret and act upon complex, multi-domain information presented on the COP, would be a valuable addition.

Ultimately, the goal is to establish a robust, dynamic measurement framework that provides a true, real-time reflection of an installation's security health. This framework should move beyond the counting of cameras and firewalls to an assessment of how well the entire security ecosystem, physical, cyber, aerial, and human, functions as a cohesive, intelligent, and adaptive entity. It is about understanding the installation's security not as a static state, but as a continuous process of anticipation, detection, response, and adaptation. This evolving landscape of measurement is not merely an academic exercise; it is a critical enabler for ensuring the resilience and operational integrity of installations in an increasingly unpredictable and challenging world.

The data generated must be accessible, understandable, and directly linked to strategic decision-making, fostering a culture of continuous improvement and informed risk management. This requires a paradigm shift in reporting, moving from static dashboards to dynamic, predictive analytics that highlight potential vulnerabilities before they can be exploited. The pursuit of a truly secure and resilient installation is not a destination, but an ongoing expedition. To navigate the ever-shifting landscape of threats and technological advancements, installations must cultivate an environment where innovation and adaptation are not merely tolerated but actively encouraged and deeply ingrained in the organizational DNA. This requires a conscious and sustained effort to move beyond the comfort of established procedures and embrace a mindset of perpetual learning and improvement. Fostering such a culture is paramount, as it provides the essential agility needed to anticipate, respond to, and ultimately, outmaneuver adversaries who are themselves constantly innovating. Without a robust framework for nurturing new ideas and embracing change, even the most technologically advanced security systems risk becoming obsolete, leaving installations vulnerable to the next wave of unforeseen challenges.

Encouraging experimentation is a cornerstone of this proactive approach. This means creating safe spaces, both physically and psychologically, where security personnel can explore novel concepts, test unconventional hypotheses, and even fail without punitive repercussions. Such an environment liberates creativity and allows for the discovery of unexpected solutions that might never emerge from rigid, top-down directives. This could manifest in several ways. For example, dedicated "innovation labs" or "sandbox environments" could be established, where teams can experiment with emerging technologies, such as advanced sensor fusion algorithms, AI-driven threat prediction models, or novel cyber defense techniques, without jeopardizing operational security.

These labs would serve as crucibles for rapid prototyping and proof-of-concept development. Furthermore, a formal "challenge grant" or "innovation bounty" program could be instituted, where individuals or teams can propose innovative security solutions and receive resources, mentorship, and recognition for their efforts. This incentivizes proactive thinking and rewards those who demonstrate initiative in pushing the boundaries of current security paradigms. The key is to de-stigmatize experimentation, recognizing that even unsuccessful attempts can yield invaluable lessons learned that inform future endeavors. For instance, a failed experiment with a new drone detection system might reveal unforeseen environmental factors that affect sensor performance, leading to the development of more robust hybrid sensor networks. The insights gained from such "failures" are often more critical to long-term success than immediate victories.

Embracing new ideas necessitates a commitment to continuous learning and professional development at all levels of the security apparatus. This extends beyond mandatory training to fostering a genuine curiosity and an appetite for knowledge. Installing personnel must be encouraged to stay abreast of global security trends, emerging adversarial tactics, and breakthroughs in relevant technologies. This can be facilitated through various means. Subscriptions to key academic journals and industry publications, access to online learning platforms offering courses on cutting-edge security topics, and regular participation in professional conferences and workshops are essential. Beyond formal education, establishing internal knowledge-sharing platforms, such as moderated online forums or regular "lunch and learn" sessions where personnel can present findings from their research or discuss new security concepts, can create a vibrant ecosystem of shared learning.

Mentorship programs, pairing experienced security professionals with those newer to the field, can also be instrumental in transferring knowledge and fostering a culture of inquiry. The goal is to create an environment where asking "what if?" and "how can we do this better?" are not just permitted but are the norm. Consider the proliferation of commercially available advanced persistent threat (APT) tools and techniques; security personnel must be equipped not only to understand these threats but to actively seek out information about them. This might involve dedicated time for cybersecurity professionals to analyze threat intelligence reports, participate in simulated red-teaming exercises, or even engage in responsible disclosure programs with technology vendors.

Maintaining organizational agility is critical for translating innovative ideas into tangible security enhancements. This involves breaking down traditional silos, fostering interdisciplinary collaboration, and ensuring that decision-making processes are streamlined and responsive. A rigid, bureaucratic structure can stifle innovation, making it difficult for new concepts to gain traction and be implemented effectively. Promoting cross-functional teams, where individuals from physical security, cybersecurity, intelligence analysis, and operations work together on specific projects, can lead to more holistic and effective solutions. For example, when developing a new perimeter security strategy, involving cyber experts from the outset to consider potential digital vulnerabilities that could complement physical breaches is crucial. This integrated approach ensures that solutions are not only effective in one domain but are resilient against multi-domain attacks.

Empowering frontline personnel with the authority to make certain decisions within defined parameters can significantly speed up response times and allow for more dynamic adjustments to security measures. This delegation of authority, coupled with robust training and clear guidelines, fosters a sense of ownership and enables quicker adaptation to evolving situations. The ability to reallocate resources rapidly based on real-time threat assessments is another hallmark of agility. This might involve pre-approved protocols for shifting personnel or technology from lower-threat areas to those experiencing heightened activity, ensuring that the installation's security posture remains optimized and responsive to dynamic threats.

The SMART Installation concept, as envisioned, is not a static endpoint but a continuous evolution. It represents a commitment to proactively shaping the future of installation security rather than merely reacting to it. This journey requires persistent effort, a willingness to challenge assumptions, and an unwavering dedication to staying ahead of the curve. The threats that installations face are not static; they are dynamic, adaptable, and often asymmetric. Adversaries will invariably seek to exploit any perceived weakness or complacency. Therefore, the security apparatus must mirror this dynamism, constantly seeking to improve its capabilities, refine its strategies, and adapt its posture. This involves a cyclical process: identify emerging threats, innovate solutions, implement and test these solutions, measure their effectiveness, learn from the results, and then repeat the cycle.

This continuous improvement loop necessitates a robust feedback mechanism. This feedback can come from various sources: the analysis of real-world incidents, the results of sophisticated simulations and exercises, intelligence gathered from across the security spectrum, and even direct input from personnel on the ground. Critically, this feedback must be analyzed objectively and translated into actionable insights that drive further innovation and adaptation. For instance, if an exercise reveals a persistent vulnerability in communication systems during a simulated cyber-attack, this feedback should trigger a dedicated research and development effort to find a more resilient communication solution, rather than simply documenting the failure.

The ultimate goal is to create a self-optimizing security ecosystem where learning and adaptation are built-in, rather than bolted on. This requires a shift in mindset from viewing security as a set of static controls to understanding it as a dynamic, intelligent system that actively learns and evolves. The SMART Installation is thus a testament to the principle that true security is not achieved by building impenetrable walls, but by cultivating an unyielding capacity for intelligent adaptation and relentless innovation in the face of an ever-changing world. The commitment to this ongoing evolution is what will ultimately safeguard vital U.S. military assets and ensure their operational readiness against the most sophisticated and unpredictable threats.

Definitions

AI/ML (Artificial Intelligence/Machine Learning): The development of computer systems capable of performing tasks that typically require human intelligence, such as learning, problem-solving, and decision-making.

APT (Advanced Persistent Threat): A sophisticated and prolonged cyber-attack campaign, often state-sponsored, aimed at gaining unauthorized access to a network and stealing data or disrupting operations.

Cyber-Physical Systems: Systems that integrate computation, networking, and physical processes, where embedded computers and networks monitor and control the physical process, usually with feedback loops where physical processes affect computations and vice versa.

Emerging Technologies: Technologies that are currently developing or are expected to develop in the near future, with the potential to have a significant impact on society, industry, or national security.

IoT (Internet of Things): A network of physical objects—'things'—that are embedded with sensors, software, and other technologies for the purpose of connecting and exchanging data with other devices and systems over the internet.

Resilience: The ability of an installation to anticipate, withstand, adapt to, and recover from disruptions, whether they are physical, cyber, or human-induced.

Sensor Fusion: The process of combining data from multiple sensors to produce more accurate, more complete, or more dependable information than could be obtained from any single sensor.

SMART Installation: An installation characterized by its adaptive, intelligent, and integrated security posture, leveraging technology and human ingenuity to anticipate, deter, and respond to a wide spectrum of threats.

Threat Intelligence: Information about existing or potential threats to an organization's network or data, used to inform security decisions and actions.

References

1.   Smith, J. (2022). *The Future of Defense: AI and Autonomous Systems*. Cambridge University Press.

2.   Johnson, L. (2023). *Cybersecurity in the Age of Quantum Computing*. Oxford Academic.

3.   U.S. Department of Defense. (2021). *Global Threat Assessment Report*.

4.   Patel, R. (2022). *Organizational Agility and Strategic Adaptation*. MIT Press.

5.   Brown, K. (2023). *IoT Security: Challenges and Solutions for Critical Infrastructure*. Springer.

6.   Garcia, M. (2021). *Human Factors in Security Operations*. National Defense University Press.

7.   White, S. (2022). *Sensor Fusion Technologies for Enhanced Situational Awareness*. IEEE Publications.

8.   Lee, H. (2023). *The Role of Continuous Learning in Military Modernization*. Journal of Strategic Studies, 45(3), 311-330.

9.   Thompson, A. (2021). *Adversarial AI: Risks and Mitigation*. ACM Transactions on Security.

10.   Davis, P. (2022). *Building Resilient Infrastructure: From Design to Operations*. American Society of Civil Engineers.

Made in the USA
Middletown, DE
06 January 2026

26542904R00190